John B. McMillan

The Virgin Backpacker

You Are Never Too Old

Signed First Edition

No. 350

Of 400

BrightSpark

www.brightsparkpublishing.co.uk
www.bargainbooksonline.co.uk
www.bargainprintonline.co.uk
www.scotlandswritersoftomorrow.co.uk
www.getitpersonalised.co.uk

THE VIRGIN BACKPACKER

You Are Never Too Old

John B McMillan

This Book is published by BrightSpark Publishing, 2011.

First Edition.
© Copyright 2011.

978-1-908295-00-2

The Author, namely John B. McMillan, asserts the moral rights
to be identified as the author of this book.

All rights reserved.
No part of this publication may be reproduced, transmitted, lent out,
photocopied, resold, recorded, hired out, copied or otherwise circulated
by any means graphic, electronic or mechanical, without the publisher's
prior and written consent.
To do so is punishable by law.

All characters are real, but may be under nom de plumes.

Designed, typeset, printed, and bound completely in-house
By BrightSpark,

www.brightsparkpublishing.co.uk
Office: 01343 208001
Editorial: 07967 178224

DEDICATION

For Michael, Katie, Callum and Catriona,
who regard the antics of their unconventional
grandfather with some bemusement.

www.JohnBMcMillan.co.uk

Introduction

'Youth would be an ideal state if it came later in life.'
Lord Asquith, 1923

The sound of ice grinding against the hull of the ship penetrated the drowsiness of an ebbing tide of sleep. I checked my watch: 6am – time for another snooze before breakfast. But before drifting back into the arms of Morpheus, I reached up and drew the curtain aside from the porthole: ice, everywhere. Large, white ice floes growled alongside as the ship thrust her way through a soup of brash-ice, glacial debris like the aftermath of a gigantic explosion, which covered the surface of the sea between ship and shore. It was an inhospitable coastline: no beaches, no landing places. Black mountains rose steeply from the ocean. Along their ridges, deep snow had been sculpted into delicately patterned cornices by the wind. Glaciers, like giant textured brushstrokes, painted the valleys between the snow-capped peaks.

I lay back, snug in the warmth of my blankets and felt a glow, like an inward smile. Here at last. Funny how so many long-held dreams had come to pass, I reflected: exploring the sun-kissed islands of the South Pacific, the enigma that is Easter Island, diving on the Great Barrier Reef, trekking in the Andes, and now the ultimate destination – Antarctica. It has often been said to me, "How lucky you are. You have the perfect lifestyle." Luck? Maybe. Maybe not.

It's strange how the most seemingly innocuous events can become the significant waypoints of life. My mind drifted back several years to a Saturday morning when, intending to spend some time in the garden, I was taken aback when Katie, my wife, asked me to come shopping with her. This was not something we enjoyed sharing. For me, shopping is the very antithesis of enjoyment.

Seeing the look on my face, she pleaded with me. "Please. You can go to the bookshop while I do my bit. I just want you to do the driving and for company. We'll have lunch somewhere."

Something in her voice compelled me to resist the temptation to argue. I couldn't refuse, though it did puzzle me a bit.

Browsing in the bookshop, my attention was attracted by a title:

'Undertaken With Love – The Story of a DIY Funeral.' I bought the book. It described one woman's effort to have her husband disposed of as he had wished: no undertakers, just a few close friends and family, and his ashes to be dug into the garden. His unconventional wishes caused difficulties for his wife who had to overcome many obstacles and a lack of cooperation from the undertaking profession when it came to procuring a coffin. I found it absorbing. Later that night, I put my book down and turned thoughtfully to Katie.

"Maybe it's about time we should make plans for our funerals. The boys should know in case we both go at the same time. Have you any thoughts about how you would like to be disposed of when your time comes?"

She came out with a straight answer. "Well, I don't see the sense in having an expensive funeral. I don't want any money wasted on flowers. You've got tools and a shed to work in, so you can make me a box, put me in the back of the Volvo and the boys can help you carry me. There's no need to hire a hearse when there's a car perfectly capable of doing the job sitting at the door, and I don't want any miserable looking strangers in black coats messing me about."

She was right of course. The Volvo estate car could accommodate a coffin quite easily. I laughed. "That'll certainly get folk talking."

"It won't bother me. But I'm telling you now I don't want money wasted on an expensive funeral. I would rather see the money go to a good cause – like the Hospice."

"I've no argument against that."

"Fine, you can get busy anytime you like and get the coffins made while you're still fit, and let the boys know what we want done."

This very pragmatic approach to funeral arrangements by an unpretentious lady came as no surprise to me. I had been married to her for almost thirty years, courted her for three years before that and, as a dutiful husband who always did as he was told, I saw no reason to change the habits of a lifetime. It never struck me as odd that she should expect the Volvo still to be around when she died. Well, they do last forever, don't they.

Considering that we disagreed on just about everything else in life, it was a bit of a relief. Well, that's not quite accurate. The notable exceptions were the really important things, like bringing up children, care of our dogs, and the sanctity of our marriage. Apart from these three we had disagreed on just about everything else. It was nice to find a fourth thing we could agree upon.

There's nothing original about the idea of a DIY funeral. You only need to go back a few generations to find that, in many rural areas at least, it was the norm rather than the exception. In many societies in other parts of the world it would be unthinkable to hand over the preparations for the disposal of the dead to anyone outside the family.

I laughed at the thought of a pair of coffins lying about the house.

"Still, I suppose we could use them for storing the bedding until we need them." On Monday morning I was back at work and forgot the matter.

I didn't know it then, but my wife was dying of cancer.

It was back in 1964 that I had vowed to care for Katie 'In sickness and in health, till death do us part.' This had never been a difficult promise to carry out, for she had consistently enjoyed good health. Apart from the two pregnancies, she had only consulted a doctor once in the thirty-three years I had known her. The true meaning of our marriage vows was finally realised in April 1994, almost a year after our coffin conversation, when she was diagnosed as suffering from an incurable cancer of the bladder. I cared for her as 'the big C' painfully and messily destroyed her body. We knew the cancer would win the physical battle, but we were determined it would never defeat our spirits. We laughed a lot in these last few months.

Four months later she was dead.

I respected her wishes. I made her a coffin, and we had a DIY funeral. The reaction of friends and family was interesting with comments ranging from, "Oh, no! Don't you know you can get counselling?" to "That is inspiring. I wish more people had the courage to do that." The two boys and myself – yes, just the three of us – carried her from the church to the Volvo. A single red rose from our garden was all that adorned her coffin. The funeral costs amounted to only £94, but along with generous donations from mourners who packed the church, we donated the cost of a commercial funeral to the Highland Hospice and Macmillan Cancer Relief.

My wife had never been keen on travel, and I had envisaged life in retirement as a chain of endless days pottering in the garden. But now, the large garden where we had spent so much time had become a burden. It was laden with memories of our life together, and part of me seemed to have died with Katie. It is difficult to describe the void left behind by death. We had long since ceased to be two separate people – we had become a couple, and one half of that had died.

My response to stress had always been to keep busy so that I wouldn't have time to dwell on things. Always active in the community, I found I was now so busy that I had no time left for myself. No time to do what I wanted to do, rather than what was expected of me – no time to grieve, even. I was suffering from exhaustion and bouts of depression. I felt directionless, like a ship without a compass, lost in a fog; my self-esteem plunged.

I had to get out of this rut. I remembered her words to me as she lay dying: "Make the most of every day." Both my sons were married, so I only had myself to look after. I retired at the age of 60 and moved to a cottage on the west coast, severing my ties with the community I had served as head of the secondary school for fifteen years. It was time to start a new life – to re-discover youth.

My love of sailing among the islands of Scotland's west coast would continue to satisfy my lust for adventure in summer, but I wanted to exchange the damp chill of the Scottish winter for something exotic. Package holidays and cruises do not excite me. I wanted to travel independently, explore far-off places, become acquainted with the people and their cultures. I did some sums. I could go a long way on what I could save on heating, lighting, telephone, food and car expenses. Sleeping in budget accommodation, youth hostels and the like, I could travel for months on end. Mixing with young people from different parts of the world, I would never be lonely. I bought a rucksack and a cheap Round The World air ticket. Casting off the shackles of life as a retired headmaster, I set off to seek adventures. I was a virgin backpacker. Life would never be the same after that.

Many of the young people I met had told me they were travelling, 'to find myself.' I was a bit sceptical of that notion at first. Now I'm beginning to wonder. My aim in travelling had been to observe and experience other cultures, but travel has the power of revelation, and I had also been compelled to see myself through the eyes of others. My naivety and innocence so often defined me as a virgin backpacker, with a trail of blunders and confusion littering my pathways around the world. Yet it has proved to be an amusing, cathartic and rejuvenating experience.

Retirement is not an end: it is the beginning of a new way of life, rich in opportunity. I was to find that Asquith was only partly right: youth is an ideal state – but it *can* come later in life, because you are never too old.

Chapter 1
Spoilt For Choice

"Twoeggsovereasywithhashandadoublelattenosugarwithtoasteddryeandl owfatnoncholesterolvegetableoilspreadonthesideandnopreserves!"

I gazed in stunned amazement as my host, Marilyn, spat out her order for breakfast, the words rattling out like a machine gun. And I thought we spoke the same language! Even more amazingly, the waitress understood all this gobbledygook and noted the order without a hint of hesitation. I had to have 'eggs over easy' explained to me. That's how ignorant I was. I didn't want to reveal my ignorance further by asking for a translation of all the rest. I just stayed ignorant.

The American way of life is quite beyond my comprehension. Their kitchens must be the most expensively equipped parts of their homes, and yet rarely get used for making much more than a cup of coffee. When pangs of hunger strike, they're more likely to jump in the car and head for the local diner rather than stroll into the kitchen and rustle up an omelette. Marilyn had insisted that I savour this aspect of American culture and took me out for breakfast.

Out for breakfast? In Scotland, I sup my porridge at home; still half asleep, hair tousled and eyes half-closed. But here I was, seated hungrily in what looked remarkably like a railway dining car, a fugitive from the despondent gloom of an imminent Scottish winter. I was on my way to Tahiti to spend a few months exploring the islands of the South Pacific, but London to Tahiti is a long haul (it's even longer from my home in Lochcarron, Scotland), so I had included a stopover in the USA for a few days to visit Marilyn and Alex, a couple of school friends I hadn't seen for thirty-six years. This would also allow me to see the fabled glories of New England in the Fall and observe the behaviour of *Homo Sapiens Americanis* in his native habitat. It was an interesting diversion.

I studied the menu with little understanding and looked around in amazement at the enormous plates heaped with food being consumed by the other patrons. It's little wonder they have an outsize obesity problem. The waitress looked at me expectantly.

I recognised the word 'oatmeal' in the menu and made a guess that this meant porridge and asked for some with a cup of tea. Very Scottish.

Nice and simple, I thought. Huh! Nothing is that simple. In the USA you gotta have choices!

"What kinda tea d'ya like?" spat out the waitress through her chewing gum, with the characteristic staccato accent of the north-eastern cities of the USA. "Indian, Chinese, green, iced, herbal, camomile, lavender, raspberry...?"

"Have ye no' got just an ordinary cup of tea? You know, the kind you make with a tea bag?" I pleaded, establishing that I was indeed a low form of life.

"You mean regular tea?" she asked incredulously, her surprised attitude suggesting that asking for regular tea must be most irregular.

"Is that the kind that comes hot, with a dark brown colour and you put milk and sugar in it?" I asked uncertainly.

"Yeah. Like English breakfast tea?" That sounded more promising.

"Aye, that'll do fine." I was relieved to be getting somewhere at last.

"D'ya like milk?" she fired back rapidly. "Full cream, half cream, semi-skimmed, skimmed, soya milk, coconut milk, goat's milk, yak's milk, camel's milk..."

"Cow's milk, full cream," I interrupted before she named every animal with a mammary gland that had escaped the flood and booked a berth on Noah's Ark. I was getting the hang of this game now, I thought. Maybe I could beat her at her own game and added, "From a Jersey cow, fed only on grass, not silage, and drawn by the hand of an eighteen year-old virgin, with golden hair tied in pigtails, from the rear, left teat on the udder of the fourth cow on the north side of the milking parlour, pasteurised, homogenised and chilled to exactly a temperature of four degrees Celsius – please."

It costs nothing to be polite after all and my mother had always insisted on good manners. I sat back smugly. My smugness quickly evaporated under another barrage of choices.

"D'ya like sugar? White, brown, demerara, honey, syrup or saccharin."

"White, please."

"D'ya want toast?"

"Yes, please."

"Whitewholemealorrye?"

"Pardon?"

She repeated, but I was still none the wiser. I gaped pleadingly at Marilyn, who translated slowly: "White bread, wholemeal bread or rye bread." By now I was not only exasperated, I was feeling decidedly stupid as well.

"Wholemeal," I muttered.

"Butter, margarine, low fat, unsaturated, easy spread, low cholesterol vegetable oil..."

"Butter," I spat out.

"Is that regular butter or peanut butter?"

"Regular!" My voice raised a decibel or two.

"D'ya like marmalade, jam, honey, marmite, vegemite..."

"Marmalade!" I roared at her.

"Orange, lemon or lime?" I groaned. I knew she had me beaten.

"Orange," I replied meekly, "And can I please have my breakfast now? I'm hungry." That seemed to appeal to her softer side.

"Sure. Where d'ya come from? Y'aint from around these parts. I can tell." Did it show that much? Maybe she had a brain after all. I decided to play the question game.

"Where do you think I come from?"

"Canadian?" I shook my head.

"English?"

"Try again."

"Irish?"

"You're getting closer."

"Hey, I got it. You're Scottish, right?"

"Aye, how did you guess?" I muttered wearily.

"You sound just like Sean Connery," she replied brightly.

"Do you like Sean Connery?"

"Do I *like* Sean Connery?" Her eyes rolled heavenwards and then glazed over. She was on a flight path to orgasm. I titillated her further.

"Would you like to serve Sean Connery breakfast?"

"Would I like to serve Sean Connery breakfast?" Was this woman programmed only to ask questions? She savoured the thought for a moment, fantasising over a pre-breakfast romp with Mr Connery, "Ooooh yeeeaaaah!" She had her orgasm at last.

"Well, in that case would you mind serving *me* breakfast before you feel another orgasm coming on or you'll have a death due to starvation on your conscience." That broke her fantasy. She became the professional waitress again.

"Anything else ya'd like?"

I flickered my eyebrows mischievously at her. "Mmmm. I wouldn't mind some of what you'd like to give Sean Connery."

Her eyes flashed and she almost blushed. Then she smiled at Marilyn, flicked her eyes towards me and said, "He's kinda cute, aint he? I love that Scotch accent."

Then at last she marched off to get my porridge, happily fantasising about her pre-breakfast romp with Mr Connery and what sexy negligee she would wear. I have no doubt she would have a choice: Black, red, white, pink...?

Chapter 2
Meaningless Statistics

Having finished breakfast, we went off to look at the trees. Mistakenly, I expected to be able to go wandering happily through woods carpeted with fallen leaves and glowing with autumn tints. If you go further inland into the mountain areas you can do just that, but there aren't many opportunities in the hundred-mile strip between Hartford and Boston. There is the occasional designated park with well-defined tracks to wander along, but mostly it's a seemingly infinite, leafy suburbia interspersed periodically at intervals of exactly fifteen minutes driving time with almost identical civic centres comprising shopping malls surrounded by acres of tarmac with parking lots, petrol stations, used car lots, and the ubiquitous McDonald's burger joints. You can go to sleep in the passenger seat of a car and wake up an hour later and you would swear that you were in the same place.

Standing out in stark contrast to all this and the brilliant red and yellow hues of the surrounding trees are white-painted New England style churches from the 19th or early 20th century with elegant, slender spires. That I liked. Picturesque. It was a pity about the architectural heritage of the late twentieth century.

Autumn colour attracts thousands of tourists to New England. The daily weather bulletins on radio and TV even tell you what percentage of the leaves have changed colour in each district so you can pick the best bits to see. "Oak County leads the field today with 88% colour just ahead of Ash County with 85%," chirps the announcer excitedly with a dazzling smile. They always sound sickeningly excited; and I hate them for their perfectly manicured teeth.

That made me think. How do you estimate how many of the billions of leaves on all the millions of trees have changed colour? Do they have teams of people going out every day to count the red, yellow and green leaves? How do they stay awake? No, I suppose they must use satellite pictures; but fancy going to all that trouble just to count leaves.

It's the American way. They just gotta have statistics. Watch any game of American football: a great misnomer if ever there was one, for the only time ball and foot make contact is when they stop the game to allow a player to try to kick it over the goals – maybe only two or three times per match. Most of the time, the ball is incidental to the main activity which appears to be a mass orgy of cuddling while one man holds the ball, ponders for a few seconds and then throws it away. Then they all stop while the teams change players to give others a chance to come out for a hug and they get into a huddle and share secrets with each other, maybe sorting out who fancies whom.

The poor commentator has so little action to report that he has to fill in more time than is actually played by reeling out lists of statistics in a highly charged voice: "Weeeell, the Minnesota Muskrats made an advance of 3.4 yards with that play, giving runningback Joe Blogowski a seasonal average of 2.8. Great performance from a guy who has just returned from injury after being sidelined for two weeks with a scratch on his little finger. But he is one tough cookie, 6 feet 4 inches and 250 lbs of solid bone and pure-bred, mid-west beefsteak with an IQ of 15!" Or something like that.

By which time the players have told all their secrets and are itching to cuddle one another other again. After about three seconds of intense hugging and gasping, the referee stops the game before it all becomes too intimate and lets the commentator get excited over another list of figures. What it all means is entirely beyond me, but what else is there to say in a game that stops more often than it goes.

The term 9/11 is another example of the American predilection for enumeration. I first heard this used not long after the event when an American I met in New Zealand told me that so few of his fellow citizens would travel by air 'after nine eleven'. Why shouldn't anyone want to fly after eleven minutes past nine when they would be quite happy to fly at ten minutes past nine? As I pondered this peculiar behaviour, it eventually became clear from what followed that he was referring to September 11th rather than 9.11am. The fact that it was spoken rather than written put me on the wrong track – it's a reasonable excuse! So now I know. Travel is a great educator.

It reminded me of those cryptic radio messages sent by cops in the movies which end with someone saying 'Ten-four,' as if he knew what he was talking about. Seeing some cops standing around Boston with nothing much on their minds I decided to ask about 'Ten-four'. After all, I had been hearing this in films since the 1950s and still never knew what it meant.

The answer was vague. "It's just a sorta code for 'I have received your message and understood it and there is nothing more for me to say'. It's a kinda shorthand way of saying things."

"Okay. But why is it 'Ten-four'. rather than 'Nine-seven'? What is the significance of these numbers?" They all looked blank, shrugged shoulders. "Why not just use the internationally recognised VHF radio practice of saying 'Roger. Out'?" No one could answer that either.

Mind you, I have a VHF radio operator's licence, but I can't explain why 'Roger' is used in preference to 'Henry' or 'Nigel' or – let's not be sexist – even 'Agnes' for that matter.

They're addicted to codes. I had the same problem when I heard someone on a TV chat show say, with considerable gravitas, "Y'know, Oprah, having kids is twenty-four seven". Now, you don't get a degree in mathematics for nothing, and I soon deciphered that this meant a parental commitment to child-raising of twenty-four hours per day, seven days per week. Been there, done that and had two grown-up sons to prove it, so I know. I nodded sagely and muttered, "Ten-four." I was learning the language at last.

With a rapidly developing inferiority complex, it was with some relief that my brief stopover in the complex and bewildering society of the USA came to an end. Bound for the South Pacific, I was travelling light. That was fine until my last day in Boston when the first snow fell. Drawing bemused looks from passers-by, I made my way to the airport in shorts and T-shirt, my bare feet turning blue in soggy sandals. Stoically, I showed no sign of pain as the snowflakes stung my feet. I am Scottish after all, brought up with bare legs and kilt, to suffer pain in silence and never 'greet' (weep). I looked at them with disdain, all wrapped up in their coats and hats and boots, and strode manfully on.

After a long haul via Washington and Los Angeles, I arrived at Tahiti. The pilot informed us that the local time was 2.40am and the outside temperature was a cosy 26 degrees Celsius, with 87% humidity. More numbers! They are all at it. But that made my frozen feet happy. They could thaw out at last.

Chapter 3
Locked Out On Tahiti

Tahiti, island of love, a tropical paradise where visitors are welcomed affectionately and covered with flowers; an island populated by women described as among the most beautiful to be found anywhere in the world.

That was the image created by the first Europeans to visit these shores. Captain Samuel Wallis, an Englishman, arrived off Tahiti in 1767 in his ship *Dolphin*. This place had everything: delicious fruit, fowl and fish, a temperate climate, and beautiful, bare-legged and bare-breasted women with flowers in their hair who lined the beach and tempted the sailors 'with every lewd action they could think of'. Two years later when Captain Cook arrived, he confirmed that Wallis had not exaggerated. The English were captivated by the women who bathed three times a day, shaved under their arms, bedecked their hair with flowers, and anointed themselves with scented coconut oil. Unsurprisingly, their aroma was judged preferable 'to the odoriferous perfume of toes and armpits so frequent in Europe'.

With my imagination fuelled by such images, I was looking forward to my first visit to what was undoubtedly the most famous of the South Sea Islands. As I crossed the tarmac apron to the arrivals' hall, the sound of South Sea Island music drifted out in the warm night air, conjuring up images of delectable girls swaying sensuously in grass skirts, smiling a warm welcome as they draped garlands of flowers over me.

But my dream bubble was burst as inside I met three overweight men, who were dressed in skirts, playing ukuleles and singing songs!

Well, it was a welcome of sorts.

A fleet of luxurious buses waited outside the airport, their air-conditioning systems growling a cool welcome from the steamy humidity of the night. In front of the first bus stood a smiling woman of voluminous proportions, draping visitors with garlands of flowers. This looked a little more like the legendary Polynesian welcome I expected, albeit an inflated version, and I asked her if the bus was going into town.

"Which hotel?" smiled the woman, lifting a garland of flowers from the clutch she held in anticipation of draping it around my neck. I explained I was looking for a backpacker's hostel, not a hotel. The smile evaporated. The halo of flowers retreated from above my head and re-joined those in her hand. "We don't do backpackers. These buses are only for hotel guests," she muttered, with the kind of look reserved for the sole of your shoes after having stepped on something left behind by a dog.

"Is any other transport going into town, then?" I asked as politely as I could muster.

"*You...*" The way she emphasised the word made me feel like the dollop left on the aforementioned shoe! "...will have to wait until dawn, and then you can take le truck." A similarly voluminous American couple waddled over with a trailer piled high with luggage. They were the sort of people she was looking for. Ignoring me completely, she greeted them warmly and showered them with flowers. I never wanted any of her flowers anyway. Guys don't wear flowers where I come from. I turned away.

"And you can stick your flowers up your big fat a..." I didn't say it – I'm far too much of a gentleman to say such a thing (but not enough of one to not think it!).

I retreated to the airport lounge to wait till dawn, like the cheapskate vagrant I was. Dawn was at least two hours away. But Melanie was only two metres away. She smiled at me without any hint of disdain whatsoever, and said: "Hi! Care to join me?"

She was an attractive American girl who had been sitting in front of me in the plane. A flight attendant with United Airlines, she was on vacation. I spent a couple of very pleasant hours in her company, until her flight to Bora Bora was called at 5.00 am, whisking her away.

C'est la vie!

By now it was light, so I wandered out to the road. Within seconds, le truck appeared. Le truck is literally that – a truck with the cargo deck fitted out with wooden benches for passengers. They are open-sided, with a canvas canopy on top to offer some protection from the sun and tropical rain. They travel continuously round the island from dawn till late at night and stop anywhere on request. They are cheap, the transport of the poor people – like me!

The short trip into Papeete was a pleasant experience in spite of the hard wooden seats. It was refreshing to feel the wind blowing in my face as le truck sped along the coast road and the dark island faces of the other passengers bobbed around like puppets as we jolted along. It stopped periodically to load crates of watermelons, mangoes, bananas and other produce destined for the local market. I got off in the centre of town and paid the driver his 300 francs. It was worth every cent, a taste of island life, much better indeed than sitting in an air-conditioned bus with a horde of rich American tourists.

Not that I have anything against rich American tourists. They're a friendly bunch mostly and they'll talk to anyone and everyone – and that is the problem. Many of them seem to imagine that everyone within shouting distance will suffer some kind of deprivation if unable to hear what they are saying, regardless of how personal it may be. One guy, without any inhibitions whatsoever, very kindly walked about the airport departure lounge in LA to make sure everyone could hear what he was saying in a loud voice on his mobile phone: "Yeah, I miss you too, honey. Heaps. Sure honey, I love you too. Of course I'll show you how much when I get home, baby. Yeah, you bet I will, ha ha ha... Yeaaaah..." (I could sense a build up to a climax here as he panted into the phone) "Yeah, we'll make earthquakes, baby!" We don't talk like that in Scotland.

But now I was on my own, at 5.30 am, in a strange town where the locals mainly spoke French or Polynesian – and I could speak neither. The Lonely Planet Guide had four hostels listed in Papeete, but no street map. I wandered through the back streets trying to locate them; three had gone out of business, and I was left with no alternative but to book into the only one remaining. It was described as 'basic'.

With some misgivings I paid my fee for a night's accommodation and was shown to a dormitory by a surly half-Chinese woman with a face like a prune. "Bed, toilet, kitchen," was all she said, flicking a finger in the direction of each. I wasn't impressed – more depressed. Concrete floors, concrete walls, all covered in the same dark, jungle-green paint. The dormitory slept seven: three double-decker bunks were crammed into an area measuring three metres square, while the seventh mattress was on top of the partitioned area at one end. Underneath that bed were a lavatory and a cold water shower.

The kitchen looked okay until I examined the cupboards. Most were locked. The ones that weren't had a few saucepans, some plates and a few cups, but no knives, forks or spoons. Evidently you could cook food, but you had to eat it with your fingers. So that's what 'basic' meant. I put my pack on my bed and went shopping for some food.

It was easy getting to the shops. It wasn't so easy getting back. Papeete is a confusing town. The streets are laid out in a maze of irregular triangular patterns. The absence of right-angled turns is completely disorientating, and the unwary traveller may wander around for ages imagining that he is going somewhere but ends up getting nowhere. I have never been so lost in my life. The hostel was only ten minutes walk from the waterfront, yet every time I left the place I had the greatest difficulty in finding my way back.

By the time I did get back to have my lunch, I found the hostel locked up with no sign of any life around. What kind of place was this, locking me out at the first opportunity? A kindly passer-by noticed my predicament and informed me that mine host lived a few yards down the street, so I knocked on her door.

After a few moments, her bad-tempered face appeared at the door and snarled, "What do you want?"

I politely pointed out that she had taken money from me in return for the use of the hostel, and I would like to avail myself of its facilities. She opened up with ill grace and retreated to her house muttering something incomprehensible. I wasn't getting on too well with the ladies of Tahiti. What did Wallis and Cook have that I didn't?

Inside, I had lunch with Alex, a young civil engineer from Switzerland, who unknowingly had been imprisoned all morning while he had been reading Lord of The Rings in Spanish. Fluent in English, French, German and Spanish, he had now read the book in all four languages. He was killing time, having missed his flight to New Zealand the night before. We talked all afternoon and went out to dine together that evening on the waterfront.

The waterfront is the place to be in the evening. At 6.00 pm a host of mobile restaurants arrives, and tables are set out around them. It is fascinating to wander round looking at the different styles of cuisine available: Polynesian, French, Italian, Chinese, Thai, Japanese, Indian. It is amazingly good value. It is also an ideal people-watching place, eating in the pleasantly warm open air under the floodlights with all the bustle of activity around and the trees along the esplanade all bedecked with lights.

Papeete's extensive natural harbour is a source of constant interest at all times of day, with vessels of all sizes – from traditional canoes to luxury cruise liners – coming and going. Along the sea front are stylish shops selling black pearls and high quality goods for the tourist market. Behind that facade it is all bustling narrow streets with cracked pavements and dubiously smelling drains, small shops, a large and colourful market selling live chickens, dead fish, meat, local fruits, cheap trinkets, brightly coloured pareus (sarongs) and an abundance of heavenly scented flowers. The Polynesians like their flowers, and they use them to decorate themselves liberally – men and women. A gardenia tucked behind the right ear means you are spoken for, behind the left ear and you are available. So I bought one and stuck it behind my left ear. Well, you never know! I had heard that age was unimportant to Polynesian women. In spite of the disenchanting encounters with the two females I had already met, I remained optimistic. There was still something about the place that I liked.

I liked it even more when a delightful teenage girl with a beautiful smile accosted me in the market. This was more like it: the flower signal works! Or so I thought. Huh, she was only trying to sell me some wares from her grandparents' stall. I procrastinated, diverting the conversation from commerce to matters that interested me: lifestyle, language and culture. We got on well, and I started teasing her a bit, and in return for the friendly banter I allowed myself to buy some of her scented coconut oil – supposedly to protect my skin from the sun, though I suspected it would merely help fry me. At least I would cook with a pleasant aroma.

The Tahiti Carnival was held the following night. Alex and I dined on the waterfront again, accompanied this time by Kiera, a hardy Danish girl who had crewed her way across the Pacific from Panama on a yacht, and Robbie, a Scot from Aberdeen. The Carnival passed by on the esplanade. To the accompaniment of traditional drum music, hundreds of participants of all ages paraded in scanty costumes in an extremely colourful and exciting presentation of traditional dance. Dance is fundamental to Polynesian culture, and the way they move their hips... well, it is little wonder that the mutineers from the Bounty weren't too upset at the prospect of having to spend the rest of their lives on the islands.

After the carnival, a stroll along the esplanade in the warm night air took us to an open-air concert where two groups of Maori singers from New Zealand bashed out a lively repertoire of popular songs while simultaneously executing some energetic choreography. It was a really good show – and even better, it was free. I watched the crowd of several hundred people. Thousands had attended the Carnival earlier.

It was now around 11.00 pm, and certain things struck me. Whole families were there, with children of all ages. There was not a single beer can in sight and no drunken or loutish behaviour. The only people I saw smoking were Europeans. Although there were fast food stalls serving snacks, there was no litter to be seen anywhere. And everyone seemed to be having a good time. It made me think. An event like that in the UK would almost certainly be characterised by drinking, noisy, loutish behaviour, and would have required an army of people to clean up litter afterwards.

Alex was leaving for New Zealand in the early hours of the morning, so we sat up late talking. Anticipating job interviews on his eventual return, he asked me for advice. Having participated in so many interviews, both as employer and applicant, I felt I had something I could share with him, and fell into the role of educator again. On leaving, he told me he was glad he had missed his flight two days earlier as he had gained so much from our conversation and wanted to keep in contact by email. That gave me a wee glow. I felt valued, and the thirty-five year age difference had proved to be no barrier to friendship.

The name Tahiti conjures up notions of a tropical paradise, but it fails to match the image. Unlike the popular perception of Pacific islands – you know, the ones in the brochures with the swaying palms and the beautiful white sand – Tahiti has black sand, pulverised volcanic rock, and you simply cannot feel luxurious lying on what looks like coal dust. As Tahiti has the international airport, it is best regarded as a gateway to the other islands and next day I took the fast ferry to Moorea, only about an hour's journey by fast ferry from Tahiti, and one of the most beautiful islands in the Pacific.

Chapter 4
Kissing Stingrays

Moorea was the location for the 1958 Hollywood musical *South Pacific*. Its mountains, the jagged remnants of former turbulent volcanic activity, are dramatic, mystical, surreal. It is not difficult to imagine the spirits of the Polynesian gods inhabiting the lofty, virtually inaccessible, mist-capped peaks which soar almost vertically out of the jungle.

A bus took me round to the west side of the island to my hostel. The receptionist, a beautiful Polynesian girl, spoke good English, but dashed my hopes of feeling more welcomed here with her most disconcerting attitude which spoke of inner thoughts like, 'Oh no, not more tourists. Why can't they leave me in peace to do nothing all day?' It wasn't anything personal. Everyone I spoke to got the same impression.

It was a pleasant place to stay, though. The accommodation was laid out in blocks of twin rooms forming three sides of a grassy quadrangle. The open side fronted a glorious beach liberally garnished with bikini-clad bodies, and some in only half a bikini. Divesting myself of any residual Calvinistic tendencies, I took a walk along the beach to take in the scenery. The lagoon was deliciously warm, and it was a joy to lie in its soothing water after my stroll and watch the sun set, its soft golden light burnishing the bare breasts of the shapely girls who promenaded along the beach without a trace of self-consciousness.

I somehow wasn't feeling homesick at all.

The next morning I hired a bicycle, and set off to cycle leisurely round the island. Much of the road was shaded with fragrantly scented trees, and the breeze generated by cycling had a pleasantly cooling effect. It is an island of contrasts: luxurious hotels and tourist resorts with beautifully landscaped gardens, and what can only be described as hovels where many of the indigenous population lived. Their needs are simple: a roof to provide shelter from rain and sun, a mattress on the floor to sleep on, and not much else in the way of furniture.

Food is abundant. Coconuts, mangoes, paw paws (papayas), limes, bananas and pineapples grow in profusion. The lagoon is teeming with fish. Flocks of chickens run wild in the bush, and there are also roaming pigs and an occasional goat. Survival is no hardship here. The sea is always warm and the children spend hours playing in the lagoon. On Sundays, families sit out in the shade or on the beach and sing to the accompaniment of ukuleles. They appeared to be very content. Who wouldn't in this place?

So was I as I sat on the beach under the shade of some trees having a lunchtime snack. Out beyond the reef, surfers carved white signatures on the faces of the huge, looming waves that threatened to engulf them before erupting white on the coral with a boom like a distant explosion. A few feet away on the sand, dozens of small hermit crabs bustled about at the water's edge, foraging for scraps in the lapping wavelets that gently washed the beach, the dying remnants of the mighty rollers that rose dark blue, turned green and crested white away out on the protecting reef.

These islands are nearly all blessed with a surrounding coral reef, enclosing a beautiful sheltered lagoon, a haven for small fish where they are safe from large marine predators. It also provides an anchorage for the small boats and outrigger canoes from which the local fishermen cast their nets to catch the fish. Either way, the fish get eaten. Most of the lagoons are shallow and littered with coral growths offering shelter and food for the many vividly coloured species of fish. This makes for excellent snorkelling.

I enjoyed my six-hour trip round the island, but I was appalled to see the lack of care of their dogs. Herds of mongrels roamed un-neutered around the houses, all living on scraps. They were the most under-nourished, mangy animals I have ever seen, and they howl ferociously if anyone walks along the road after dark.

Back at the hostel, sitting outside in the evening writing my diary, I was disturbed by a high-pitched voice: "Hello, I'm Chris. I heard your Scottish accent earlier. Not many English speakers here so I thought you might like some company."

Chris, who was in his early forties I'd guess, looked like something I had seen many years before in a Monty Python sketch. He had all the qualifications. A bachelor living with his mum, he peered at the world through thick spectacles with a permanent look of amazement. He wore a floppy hat, baggy shorts and sandals with socks pulled half way up to his knees. He also wore a video camera. If anything moved, he recorded it. I made a mental note not to pick my nose.

We didn't have a conversation. He only did monologue. He wasn't interested in me, only my ears. I tried to speak, but each interjection was ignored as he rambled on interminably. He told me he had dined in a pleasant restaurant the night before where they served excellent traditional Polynesian food, and very cheap too. Tonight he was thinking of trying a place where they served Chinese food. That settled it. Having excused myself to freshen up, I sneaked round to the Polynesian restaurant. I hadn't been seated long before Chris wandered in and with a look of triumph, sat himself down at my table, and congratulated himself. Ever been had?

"I thought you might try this place, so I decided to come here so you wouldn't have to eat alone. My mum says it's much better to have company at dinner..." And so the monologue continued. At least I didn't have to make an effort. As long as my ears were there he just droned happily on.

His incessant soliloquy encouraged me to have an early night.

I breakfasted with a lovely couple from Ireland, Ann and Dan, whom I had met the night before when I sneaked into the hostel kitchen for a nightcap after I had escaped from Chris. They invited me to join them on a lagoon cruise. We were welcomed at the booking office by our smiling skipper. Yes, the boat would be leaving soon and we would be able to swim with the fishes and feed them and have a picnic lunch on a small island. Ann asked him when the boat would return. The Polynesians have a sense of humour.

"About 1.30." Then his eyes narrowed. He looked meaningfully at a picture of a great white shark on the wall and added ominously, "Maybe!" His face creased in a dazzling smile. "No, don't worry, that is only one of our sardines. Just go down to the beach and you will see the boat. Its name is... *Titanic*." More laughter.

The boat was a modern version of the traditional island canoe, long and narrow with an outrigger on one side and powered by a 50 HP Yamaha outboard. Our skipper kept the banter up throughout the cruise and ran a happy ship. At our first stop to feed and swim with the fish, he cast some scraps into the water; within seconds, the water was boiling as a shoal of small fish in a mad frenzy gorged themselves on the food.

"What kind of fish are they?" asked one of the passengers as we prepared to enter the water with our snorkelling masks.

"Piranhas," was the nonchalant reply. Then, with a big grin he added, "but don't worry – they are vegetarian piranhas."

After a spell of snorkelling with sharks – not great whites, but small, black-tipped reef sharks, maybe a metre and a half long and quite amicable – we moved on to another spot. Here, the water was only about a metre in depth. The skipper threw some food on the water and again, within seconds, dark shadows swept through the shallow water. About twenty large stingrays were milling around us. Casting doubts aside, we jumped in beside them. They rubbed against us, much like a cat does, and even shoved their faces up out of the water for a kiss on the nose. Amazing. They actually looked really pleased to see us.

"Of course they are pleased to see you. They know you paid 2000 francs to come and see them. That's why they want to kiss you," quipped our host.

On arriving at the beach for our picnic lunch, I waded ashore carrying a bundle of pineapples. As I grabbed the bunch, a large spider darted from the leaves, and fell onto the water. It skated with lightning speed across the surface and disappeared between my legs. I looked behind me, hoping to see it heading for the shore, but there was no sign of it. The thought that it may just have climbed up the leg of my shorts occurred to me, but I remembered that there were no deadly spiders reputed to exist on these islands. I couldn't feel anything between my legs so I waded ashore with the fruit, wondering.

Suddenly, I felt a rapid tickling sensation up my back and over my left shoulder and just caught a glimpse of a black flash as it shot up my cheek and under the wide-brimmed hat I wore to protect me from the sun. Feeling slightly uneasy, I asked Dan to have a look under the brim. Ann gasped and retreated a few paces, her hands held up over her mouth in horror.

"Oh my God, there's a huge spider hiding under the brim of your hat!" I remained calm. Dan took his baseball cap and rapidly flicked the spider onto the sand where it scuttled away into the bush.

"Oh John, how could you be so cool?" asked Ann, overcome with admiration. "I would have died."

"Och, it was only a spider," I replied nonchalantly – I then sat down before my legs gave way.

Lunch was a superb fruit and coconut salad with fresh pineapples, grapefruit, limes and melons, all prepared under the shade of the palms of a small island with a pristine beach. Our skipper demonstrated how to husk a coconut, a useful skill in these islands where the coconut liberally supplies both food and water. *Titanic* did not sink that day, and even if it had we would have been able to walk ashore, so shallow was the lagoon. Nor was anyone eaten by sharks or stung to death by spiders.

I spent another day on and in the water – kayaking on the lagoon and swimming in its brilliant blue waters. In the evening, I attended a traditional dance show. Against the background of an ancient marae –

or temple site – the local 'warriors' presented an awesome display of the ancient art of fire-dancing, accompanied by the elegant hip-swaying of the girls. Chris had insisted on accompanying me again. He had booked for a performance a few nights earlier, but claimed the transport that was to pick him up had failed to come for him. I had the distinct feeling that no matter what he tried to do, it would end in some kind of failure. At least he was quiet this time, preoccupied with recording the dancing on his video camera. It ran out of battery power half-way through the show.

I took the ferry back to Tahiti with the intention of taking the cargo boat *Vaenu* from Papeete to Bora Bora, an overnight trip of about nineteen hours. The woman in the shipping office could speak no English. I tried very hard with my limited French, but all I got was a deadpan look. I persisted. Eventually, her hands moved in imitation of large waves and she said, "Pas de bateau aujourd hui." My school French could understand that. There would be no boat today because of rough weather. It didn't seem that rough to me, but the boat had to call in at several islands and enter lagoons through narrow, shallow entrances, so it was maybe better to be prudent as there was a big swell running.

I groaned at the thought of spending another night in Papeete at Chez Madame Sour Face, but the only other option was a hotel and they don't come cheap in Tahiti. Being a tight-fisted Scot, I plodded wearily back in the hot afternoon sun and booked in for another night. Her demeanour hadn't improved in the time I had been away. However, I was welcomed back by Roy, a Canadian writer who had rented an upstairs single room and was working on a book. I had met him only briefly last time there and we went out to dine together on the waterfront that evening. I enjoyed his conversation. He was having more success with the local ladies than I was and had arranged to meet one of them later, so I returned to the hostel alone at 8.00 pm.

It was locked!

I took perverse pleasure in hammering loudly on Madame Sour Face's door once more, and greeting her with a cheery smile and a jolly 'bonsoir'. My pleasant greeting was received with more muttered curses and my darker self silently suggested that she could go and indulge in an act of self-copulation. It was only next morning, when talking to Roy, that I learned you could have a key if you paid a deposit of 500 francs. Why didn't she tell me about that? Still, it gave me some pleasure in knowing that she had been disturbed yet again due to her own senseless lack of communication. However, the pleasure of being on this exotic island was palling. I was looking forward to getting away again.

Chapter 5
Lonely on Bora Bora

It was a relief to climb aboard the *Vaenu* at last – even though the vessel was, to put it kindly, rather geriatric in appearance. Various dents in the hull, some holes in the toe rail where the rust had eaten its way right through, and a prominent inward bend in the passenger guardrail, did not inspire confidence in the ship or the crew. Nor did the cleanliness of the ship. After leaning against the guardrail, I tested it first with a few hefty pushes and pulls, I came away with a black, greasy stain on my shirt. *Vaenu* was simply a dirty old cargo boat, and passengers were an encumbrance to be barely tolerated rather than cared for.

A leaflet offering details of the voyage proclaimed that passengers could eat in the ship's restaurant whether or not they bought food from the ship's galley. With this in mind, I had decided to keep my pack light and had not brought any food with me, other than an orange and a tin of peanuts for snacking on. I would buy dinner on board. On a voyage lasting nineteen hours they must provide food. I took my seat at a table, but there was neither sight nor smell of any food. After waiting a few minutes, watching others eating snacks they had brought with them, I went searching for the exceptionally dour, enormous woman who masqueraded as a stewardess and was told bluntly, "No food."

"But this leaflet says..."

"No food!" she grunted, glowering at me aggressively. I backed off. I am not usually a timid sort, but this big woman made Mike Tyson look like a pansy. Now I understood why someone had defaced the underside of the bunk above mine by writing 'Big Fat Cow'. Where were all these fabled lovely, eager to please, Polynesian girls of the tourist brochures?

Dinner that night consisted of half an orange and some peanuts. I kept the rest for breakfast, as the ship didn't dock in Bora Bora till 11.00 am. It wasn't very filling, but I exercised mind over stomach. I had been brought up on wartime rations after all.

Despite the deprivation, I enjoyed my cruise. As well as cabin passengers, the ship also took deck passengers, mainly islanders, who simply sleep on mats on the afterdeck, protected from the weather by a canopy stretched overhead. I had tried to book as a deck passenger, but was told there was no room left. This meant I had to pay three times as much for a cabin – but the hot shower was very welcome.

I shared the twin cabin with a French banker from Paris. A football enthusiast, he wanted to improve his English, and I was trying hard with my French so we got on very well. He asked me what I thought of the people here and I replied diplomatically that there seemed to be something lacking in their concept of service, but perhaps it was because of my difficulty with the language. He shook his head. "I find that too. They are not very sympathetic," he claimed.

He was travelling with his sister, Marie, and her husband, and we all met on deck in the evening to watch the sun setting gloriously behind the jagged mountains of Moorea. A mile off on the port side, the elegant, modern American sailing ship *Wind Song* cast a beautiful picture with her sails silhouetted against the dying light of the sun. It was all very... South Pacific.

My French friends were considerate, and helped me in my efforts to speak their language. I had forgotten so much that at one point I struggled to say, 'I think.'

Marie came to my aid: "Je pense." Then she added, by way of example, "Je pense, dunc je suis."

My eyes lit up. "René Descartes. Philosopher and Mathematician. I think therefore I am, or as he wrote it in Latin, 'cogito, ergo sum.'" I just can't prevent my classical education from surfacing from time to time.

"Ah, il'y connait!' she replied, beaming. "Nous avons un connaisseur de philosophie."

I bowed my head modestly in acknowledgement of the compliment she had paid to my knowledge of philosophy, but to pre-empt her delving any further and exposing its limited extent, I added, "Oui, mais seulement un peu. J'étais un professeur de mathématique, mais je suis retraité et maintenant je suis en vacance perpetuélles."

For those of you who know less French than I do, that is supposed to mean something like, 'Yes, but only a little. I was a teacher of mathematics, but I am retired and now I am on a continual holiday.' However inappropriate the idiom may have been, they seemed to get the gist of what I was saying and that closed the subject before it got too embarrassing.

I had a very clear recollection of exactly when I had first learned about Descartes' famous phrase. I could see the picture so clearly. It was away back in 1957 at Irvine Royal Academy and it was my French teacher, Howard Matthews to whom I am indebted for this information and those significant words. Little did I think then that it would impress a pretty French girl on a dirty old cargo boat in the South Pacific almost fifty years later. But that's education for you.

There wasn't much to do – actually there wasn't anything to do, so we all retired early. I do enjoy sleeping on ships. The steady rhythm of the engines and the gentle roll of the long Pacific swell had a powerfully soporific effect, and I was soon asleep. In the early hours I was aroused first by the absence of any roll, which indicated that we were in the sheltered water of a lagoon, and shortly after that a change in the beat of the engines signalled the approach to the harbour. It was the first of the island stops. Then came the rattle of the derrick as the cargo was unloaded. The engines picked up a few revs and we were on our way again. These were the sounds that punctuated my sleep and indicated our passage through the night as we stopped at three other islands.

Having eaten the remaining half orange and peanuts for breakfast, I went out on deck. There in the distance lay Bora Bora, from where two canoes of Polynesian sailors had set out on a long voyage to establish a settlement on Hawaii 1500 years ago. It was another dramatic, mountainous island with a superb lagoon and glorious white beaches: one of the gems of the Pacific. It is a small island, about twenty miles in circumference. The arrival of American forces during the war had a significant impact on its economy, lifestyle and its population growth, and it is now a popular holiday destination catering mainly for American and Japanese tourists.

I was welcomed at the harbour by a cheery woman in a minibus who took me to my hostel and told me I was the first Scot she had ever met. She even seemed pleased about it. The hostel was more of a holiday village with self-contained bungalows, chalets and one spacious dormitory block which slept eight.

I shared the dormitory with a couple of notable sculptors from Easter Island. The descendants of the men who had created the enigmatic moai on Easter Island, they were masters of their art, and had been awarded a commission to create sculptures for a millionaire's island home on one of the small islands fringing the lagoon. The pictures they had of their work were impressive, both in the sheer scale of some of the pieces and the imaginative blend of tradition with contemporary influences. I was impressed – and to be frank, there isn't all that much in the art world that does that to me. I had fun practising my French with them and earned the compliment, "Hey, my Eçossais friend, tu parle Francais très bien!" Très bien, maybe, but I wished I could speak a bit more of it.

Bora Bora boasts an exceptional lagoon so I booked a cruise. As well as snorkelling with the sharks and rays again, this allowed me to view the entire island from the sea as the boat motored all the way round within the shelter of the reef. We hadn't gone far before an ominous looking black cloud obliterated the sun, and a ferocious squall blew in from the sea. The skipper issued oilskins to us all and we sat huddled together with our backs to it. Thankfully, it passed over in a few minutes, just as we beached the boat on one of the small islands where an excellent barbecue lunch with fish and chicken and all the usual local vegetables and fruits was provided.

Polynesians have a long tradition of tattooing, and someone asked the skipper about the significance of these. He explained that they were once indictors of a person's status in society. A chief would have a certain pattern, his sons something else. You could tell who the boatbuilder was; a married woman could be identified from a single girl and so on.

"But now it doesn't mean anything," he said disdainfully. "When the Methodist missionaries came to the islands they destroyed our culture. Our music and dancing were 'sinful', and our women had to cover their bodies and wear European clothes." He rolled his eyes heavenwards and shook his head scornfully. "When the white man came here, he spoiled everything."

The hostel staff were friendly here. Each morning, as I sat outside eating my breakfast, the girls from the office called out with a big smile, "Bonjour, John. Comment ca va?" Now that intrigued me, because I was the only one they greeted by name. The others just got a 'Bonjour'. They were also chatty each time I returned from my adventures, asking what I had been doing and how I was enjoying my stay. I complimented Nir, the manager, on the friendly service of his staff. He was an Israeli who spoke fluent English.

"Ah John, you are just getting back what you give to them. The others come here, just do their business and that's it. But you come with a friendly smile and always talk with them. You try to speak their language and they appreciate that. And you are the first person from Scotland we have ever had here. To them, you are exotic with your fair hair and fair skin... and your accent – that's something special."

That accent again? Exotic? Hmm. I'd never thought of myself as exotic, but I could get used to the idea. "So maybe there's hope for me yet to impress a vahine manea (beautiful woman)?" I had picked up some important Polynesian words too.

He laughed. "I would say, if you stick around here, John, your chances of getting yourself a nice Polynesian girl are very good."

The general standard of accommodation of the islanders here was higher than in Moorea. Most people are employed in tourism. The island is rich in plush beach resorts patronised by the rich and famous: film stars, astronauts, US presidents and playboy princes. It is also a favourite place for honeymooners. At times, I felt like an interloper on Noah's Ark. Everywhere, couples strolled hand in hand. I was alone. What they had, I had lost, and it hurt still. I plunged into the sea and swam vigorously across the bay to drown the anger and grief which welled up inside me.

After the swim, I walked along the beach to dry off in the afternoon sun. I stopped to look at a boat drawn up on the sand and immediately was hailed by a man sitting nearby with his wife. "Hey, you want to buy?"

I declined, explaining I already had a boat. They seemed interested in me, introduced themselves as George and Marie, and started asking questions. With their French with a little English and my English with a little French, we soon became friends and they invited me to join them and have a beer.

Later they asked me to stay and have dinner with them and took me across the road to their home to meet Granny. Marie said something in Polynesian I didn't understand. Granny's mouth opened in a toothless laugh and she nodded her head in agreement. George explained. " My wife tell her mother you very *exotique*. She like your fair hair and skin and her mother think you very nice too," he told me. " But, hey John, remember, she *my* wife!" And then he roared with laughter. That was more like the Polynesian welcome I had expected. Nir's words came back to me. I was getting used to being an exotic creature.

After five days there I decided to move on, cutting my time in French Polynesia from three to two weeks. When I announced my departure to Nir he said, "John, we'll all miss you." He didn't have to say anything, but the fact that he did made it all the more appreciated. I actually felt quite sorry about going, but it was an expensive place for a backpacker and there weren't many around.

I took my flight back to Tahiti and connected with a flight over to Rarotonga in the Cook Islands at 3.40 am. The flights between the different island groups always seem to be in the middle of the night, but it was better than spending another night being locked out at Chez Madame Sour Face. And whatever French Polynesia lacked, the Cook Islands had in abundance.

Chapter 6
Cook Islands Welcome

It was 5.20 am and dawn was just breaking when the Air New Zealand Boeing 767 whispered over the reefs and touched down gently at Rarotonga. In the terminal building the immigration officer looked at my passport, his eyebrows raised with interest.

"Scotland? Mmm. You have come a long way. Welcome to the Cook Islands. How is your rugby team doing these days?" They are keen on their rugby here, but he was asking the wrong guy. I'm strictly a soccer man myself. He smiled a real smile and passed the passport back. "Have a good holiday in the Cook Islands." And it all sounded and looked absolutely genuine.

I passed through the gate and moved towards a lady holding up a card with Tiare Village printed on it. Wearing a garland of flowers on her head and a figure-hugging slit skirt which revealed a shapely thigh, she moved forward with a smile. "John? Kia orana. I am Mata. The minibus is over there. I have one other passenger to collect." She planted a fragrant Tiare Maori (gardenia, the national flower) behind my ear, and brushed my cheek with a welcoming kiss – and hey, I was only a backpacker! How very different from my arrival in Tahiti.

The other passenger was Kenny from Liverpool, a short-legged, stocky character, an inveterate traveller crouched under the biggest backpack I have ever seen. Viewed from behind, he was a rucksack with feet. Here was another comedy character, an incessant talker whose speciality in the art of conversation was repetition. "This is a great place, this is. A great place, a real 'ome from 'ome. Yeah, a real 'ome from 'ome. I was 'ere three years ago. Best place in the world, this is. Best place in the world. A real 'ome from 'ome, it is. I was 'ere three years ago and couldn't wait to come back. I never felt so much at 'ome anywhere. A real 'ome from 'ome it is. It's a great place this is, a great place." There was certainly no chance of missing anything he said and he never stopped.

Mata made a mistake and placed me in a single room in a chalet instead of the dormitory, and suggested we should both try to catch up on sleep. I didn't feel like arguing at that time in the morning and it gave me some respite from Kenny's incessant chatter. We formally checked in at 10.00 am, which is when the hostel realised their mistake – they transferred me out of the chalet and into the dorm. That was okay, because that was where I wanted to be anyway. It was two dollars a night cheaper, and I sleep much better knowing that I am saving money at the same time. Then a guy called Dave-in-the-bus (he lived in an old bus in the grounds) drove us into town to show us shops, bank, pubs, where to hire motorbikes... every place, in fact, that we needed to know about. How different from Tahiti. I was beginning to believe Kenny. It was a great place. A real 'ome from 'ome.

Small motorbikes are the most popular form of transport on the island. If you don't already have a motorcycle licence, you have to take a driving test to get your Cook Islands Driver's Licence.

This is not something to worry about. You report to the Police Station and an officer indicates the route for the test. Drive round the block, four left turns until you have arrive back at the police station. If you manage not to get lost (and some people do!) and haven't killed anyone on the way, you pass.

I passed, feeling quite confident in my ability to make left turns, but wondering how I would fare if I had to turn right. However, my mathematical background enabled me to solve that problem. The road is circular, running right round the island, so you can just carry on until you are back where you started without the need to turn right at all. It takes about an hour, but what does that matter? Here they live by island time. Punctuality is a concept they have yet to embrace.

That evening, Dave offered to drive us to a local restaurant to see a show of traditional Cook Island dancing and music. A few more people had arrived during the day and we all went out together, a pattern that was repeated throughout my stay there. The dancing was a delight. Beautiful girls with garlands of scented flowers crowning their heads, long hair flowing majestically down their backs, a pair of coconut shells to cover the forward superstructure, and low-slung grass or cotton skirts barely clinging to their hips – *this* was the south sea islands as I had imagined them to be. Arms and hands carved pictures of poetic grace, symbolic of the traditional fable of each dance while hips and thighs swayed seductively in a delectable combination of elegance and eroticism to the throbbing excitement of the drum music. I was enchanted. Oh, and by the way, the men looked pretty good too. Their powerfully energetic warrior dances with aggressive arm and leg movements had a similar effect on the female members of the audience.

Some visitors pour scorn on these cultural displays as just trash for the tourists, but it keeps their traditions in dance and music alive. It gives the young people a healthy activity in the evenings. It is physically demanding and they practice long hours to achieve high standards. They attend international cultural festivals, not only in the Pacific region but in Europe and the USA too. The dancers displayed a clear enjoyment of their art, and I found it was impossible not to be moved by it all.

Once again the sense of humour of the islands' people was in evidence as the compere introduced each dance. The finale was always an invitation for audience participation, each dancer selecting a partner from the audience.

"Let me remind our visitors, you are not allowed to refuse an invitation in the Cook Islands. Shaking your head sideways means 'yes' in the Cook Islands. Nodding your head up and down means 'yes' in the rest of the world. No matter what you do, we take it as 'yes'. We don't understand 'no' here. Maybe that's why I have twelve children."

The visitors selected to dance were invited to introduce themselves and offer their dancing partners a traditional embrace and kiss on the cheek, but with one exception.

"Okay, Mike from New Zealand, say hello to Krystina, but Mike, wait. No kissing for you. That's my daughter." When the girl ignored this and planted a kiss on the young man's cheek, to which he responded warmly with a hug and a peck on her cheek, the MC roared, "Hey, Mike! I told you no kissing. Get your hands off!" He then turned, made a gesture towards the band, all big fellows: "Mike, meet the brothers." After a pause for laughter: "You got a credit card, Mike? Okay. 20,000 dollars and she's yours."

Then the drums beat their intoxicating rhythm, the dancers wiggled and swayed, their hapless partners tried their best, and the rest of us laughed. It was all good fun.

Afterwards, I had the opportunity to congratulate some of the dance team who joined in the open dancing that followed. On hearing I was from Scotland, Krystina's eyes lit up and she told me she had danced at the Edinburgh Festival the previous year, one of a dance team from the Cook Islands who had performed before an audience of 10,000 people on the Castle Esplanade as part of the Military Tattoo. Now, you don't get invitations to the largest festival of the arts in the world if you are just performing 'tourist trash', and that year the Cook Islands dancers took Edinburgh by storm with their scintillating performances.

"It was an awesome experience," said Krystina. "You come from a very beautiful country."

A charming girl with absolutely no pretensions, self-assured and socially mature, I would have loved to talk more with her, but the music was too loud and I left her to dance with her friends. However, we were soon to meet again.

The friendliness of the islands seemed to rub off on its visitors who were equally affable. Tiare Village is by far the most sociable hostel I have stayed in anywhere in the world. It had a family atmosphere with most of the guests mixing well, socialising around the swimming pool and grouping together for outings, day and night. The following evening I was relaxing on the deck when Kenny called out. "Come on, grandad, we're going out for a drink!" I hesitated.

"Yeah, come on John, you're coming too," urged Lorna – she was harder to resist. Beautiful, blonde, very shapely and wearing... well, I don't really remember, except that it was not very much at all. She took my arm and hauled me (but I didn't offer too much resistance) on to the pillion of Kenny's bike, and off we went.

I had mixed feelings about a night out with youngsters in their early twenties. Still, I could slip into the background and have a quiet drink or two and let them whoop it up a bit. Especially when they took me to a karaoke bar.

Now, let's face it, karaoke is positively the lowest possible form of 'entertainment' There was no way in the world that I would ever consider becoming involved. No way. Not me!

Anyway, a couple of drinks later – combined with Lorna's seductive charm – and, lo and behold, there I was at the mic, crooning the old Elvis Presley song 'Love Me Tender'. I gave it my best shot and got so carried away doing the Elvis impression that I lost track of the words. But like a real pro, and without a break in rhythm, I made up a few of my own till I could pick up the thread again. I finished to rapturous applause – well, it sounded rapturous to me.

The female announcer growled lustily into the microphone, " What a performance! Oh, John, marry me!" That brought even more rapturous applause, and quite a few laughs, from the audience, who then showered me with congratulatory remarks as I made my way back to our table.

Lorna got out of her seat and gave me a lingering hug. "John, you're a star!" Her eyes glowing with admiration (or was it just the effect of the vodka?), she then asked me what I had done for a living before I retired. This is the question I dread.

"I was the head of a secondary school," I muttered.

"Bloody 'ell!" she exclaimed in disbelief in her broad Lancashire accent. Stereotypes. Headmasters are not expected to behave like that.

Punanga Nui, the open-air market where local fruits, vegetables and crafts are sold, is a great place to meet people on Saturday mornings. It is almost obligatory to be there, and that day there was an added attraction – the opening ceremony of the annual flower festival, The Tiare Pageant, with the initial appearance of the contenders for the title of Miss Tiare. Six local teenagers presented themselves as contestants for the title, and eventual crowning as Queen of the Pageant after a week of performances of singing, dancing, dress, public speaking and interviews.

The girls, all beautifully dressed in colourful pareus, paraded along a catwalk and briefly introduced themselves. Number six was Krystina, whose performance as a dancer and whose maturity, poise and friendliness had created such an impression a few days ago. I was amazed. She was only fifteen years old.

She impressed me again with her self-assurance and public speaking ability. Afterwards, as all the girls lined up for photographs, I had an opportunity to congratulate her once more. I had forgotten to take my camera, but Mii, her mother, invited me to join them on the beach that afternoon for a photo shoot. I did not require any persuasion and, as well as the pleasure of taking photographs of a really beautiful girl in a dream setting by the lagoon, I had the chance to talk with her once more. I have met many youngsters in my career in teaching, but very few of her age impressed me as much as this girl did. It came as no surprise that a week later she was crowned Miss Tiare. Four years later she was crowned Miss Cook Islands and went on to win the Miss South Pacific title as well. Mii and Krystina, were my first ever Cook Islands friends. I had no idea at the time, but they were the daughter and grand-daughter of a queen who, on a subsequent visit, would invite me to be her guest on Mitiaro, one of the small outer islands.

Attending a church service, if for no other reason than to listen to the magnificent singing, is one of the outstanding memories of a visit to the Cook Islands. Traditional hymns are sung in the Maori language with obvious and infectious pleasure, often unaccompanied by music, but so rhythmic and resonant with male and female voices singing different parts. The order of service is similar to that of the Church of Scotland, so I felt quite at home. A nice touch, typical of the friendliness of the islanders, was the projection of the words of many of the hymns on to a screen so the visitor could participate in the singing in Maori.

Dress for church is formal: modest yet striking, compared to the sombre shades of dress in Scotland's kirks. It is not uncommon to see men wearing white, yellow, green or bright blue as well as dark coloured suits. The women usually wear white dresses with hats, each individually crafted, woven from dried pandanus leaves and decorated with bright flowers. This presents an aspect of purity and humility, yet is characteristic of their celebration of the natural resources of their islands, particularly the flowers.

After the church services, the visitors are invited into the church hall for a buffet lunch. Several church members join in this occasion, so typical of the friendliness that abounds here. In a welcoming address by an elder of the church, the visitors are told of the turbulent cannibalistic past of the islands before Christianity came – when 'having visitors for lunch' meant that they would be on the menu! This hospitality is now an expression of the islanders' desire to adhere to the Christian principle of brotherly love. The food is prepared each week by a group of 'mamas', and there is always plenty of it. It was here that I met a lady who has become one of my great friends: Aunty Nancy, who insisted on taking care of me and kept filling my plate with more delicacies, a trait characteristic of the Cook Islanders.

As we were enjoying the food, Aunty Nancy's niece introduced herself. Ina was a former college of education lecturer in New Zealand. Now widowed with a grown up family, she had returned home to finish her career teaching on her home island. She offered a lift back to the hostel to anyone without transport. I had my motorbike, but some of the others went with her, and by the time I arrived back she was already sitting on the deck eating fruit with the others. We sat there all afternoon talking with her, after which she invited us all for a barbecue at her home a few days later.

Seventeen backpackers drove out in a convoy of motorbikes taking something for the barbecue, but even so she had an enormous spread laid out for us. She had also invited her relatives and neighbours to what turned out to be an international gathering of people of all ages. For many of the younger backpackers this was an eye-opening experience. They responded magnificently, helping to clear up and wash the dishes, and they all thanked her profusely on leaving. Before I left, Ina cajoled me into staying a little longer.

"John, please sit down and have a cup of tea with me. I just want to sit and talk for a few minutes to wind down. It has been such a lovely evening. It was just like having my family with me again. All these young people remind me of my own daughters, and they were so charming." I felt like a headmaster again, getting a favourable report on my pupils' behaviour.

On my second Sunday at church, Aunty Nancy invited to join in the evening service as well, and again there was a feast to follow. After the dinner, a form of Bible study was conducted, and I stayed on to witness that. Being conducted in the Maori language I had no idea what was being said, but Nancy explained in broad terms what it was all about. Challenged by the minister to discuss the message of psalm 121, several men in the audience stood up and spoke with such conviction, oratorical skill and humour that the language difficulties seemed irrelevant. Without knowing a word that was said I still found it inspiring.

Interspersed with these discourses, groups of women erupted with apparent spontaneity into rousing songs, the powerful rhythm inspiring other, usually elderly, women to take to the floor and dance, their expansive hips swaying sensuously to the music, drawing smiles of amusement from the audience and the two ministers. It was all so contrary to the stern Calvinistic attitudes portrayed so often in Scotland, where such behaviour would be unthinkable. These people obviously enjoyed their religion. I recalled a few words spoken in English during the first sermon I heard on Rarotonga, "If you're happy and you know it, then you really ought to show it." They certainly did.

There was no doubt, this place lived up to the claims I had read on the website before I left Scotland: '*The people of the Cook Islands are well-known for friendliness, openness and a gentle, easy-going spirit and will happily introduce themselves with their local greeting "kia orana" (may you live on)*'.

One writer described Rarotonga as '*a dream island of white sands, clear Pacific waters, a reef teeming with fish, lush green forests and seemingly limitless flowers and fresh fruits, but its greatest asset, though, is its people - who can only be experienced to be believed*'.

I couldn't agree more.

Chapter 7
Around Rarotonga

Is there any nation on earth more endowed with eccentrics than the English? I can understand grown men wanting to play with model railways, but to own your own railway with a full-sized steam locomotive on a small tropical island in the South Pacific almost beggars belief. Yet this is exactly what I discovered on Rarotonga: a puffing, hissing, smoke-belching, steam locomotive resplendent in green livery, standing at a station on a railway line in the owner's back yard!

English-born lawyer Tim Arnold met a Cook Island girl in New Zealand, married her and settled on the family land on Rarotonga where he now practices his profession. That's the weekday job. His weekends for over ten years had been spent renovating a magnificent fifty year-old steam locomotive in his backyard and building the railway line and station so he could play with his toy when it was ready to run. Bought in Poland, it had been shipped to Auckland and then on to an inter-island freighter to Avarua, the only harbour on Rarotonga. Craned off the ship, it had travelled the last few miles to his back yard by road transport. Now it stood hissing impatiently on the track. It didn't have far to travel with only 150 metres of track between the buffers!

However, that was enough to enable me to realise a boyhood ambition to become a train driver. I had grown up in the age of steam and had gazed in awestruck wonder at those mechanical monsters belching out clouds of sulphurous smoke, their wheels, connecting rods and pistons all smelling of steam and hot oil. They were simply wonderful. In my youth, every small boy's desire was to be a train driver: here I was, standing on the footplate for the first time in my life.

I asked Tim hesitatingly if he would let me drive, and to my delight he agreed. His 12 year-old son acted as fireman and heaped more wood into the firebox to raise steam while Tim explained each of the controls to me. I released the brake, eased the regulator down a little and I was moving. With pistons hissing and connecting rods thrusting those massive steel wheels around, I was rolling this green monster down the Rock Island Line. It was exhilarating, belching out clouds of smoke and steam, thundering down all 150 metres of track at a maximum speed of maybe close to 10 miles per hour. I brought her grinding to a stop, then reversed back along the line and into the station without mishap. Fair enough, the round trip was only 300 metres, we never got beyond a geriatric jogging speed, but a dream had been realised – I WAS Casey Jones! And that's what counts.

It seemed totally incongruous that I had left Britain where the first steam locomotive was built and had travelled halfway round the world to a small tropical island without any railway system to realise my ambition, but the absurdity of it all tickled me. Who but an Englishman would be mad enough to dream up such an idea?

My younger son, for several years a professional diver with a fish farm company, had tried for years to get me to take up diving. My elder son had also taken a recreational diver's course. I suppose I had always been too busy with work and sailing to allow myself to become involved, but my appetite had been whetted by snorkelling and now seemed the perfect time to do something about it at last. The cost was reasonable, the water warm, so where better to do it? The final push came from Matt, an American who'd just completed the Open Water Diver's Course and whose feedback fired me with enthusiasm. To be honest, it irked me that the boys could do something their old man had never mastered. If successful, I could go on to dive on The Great Barrier Reef – that would give me something to brag about when I got back home.

There were only three of us on the course. The other two were a likeable American couple from Phoenix, Arizona, an odd sort of place to be a diver, I thought, away out there surrounded by desert. The woman was deafening. She didn't talk, she broadcast – to the world! – and she punctuated every sentence with a great belly laugh.

"Why do you guys want to learn to dive?" asked our instructor.

"I just looove the ocean. HA HA HA HA!" she bellowed.

Her husband, by contrast, was so quiet he must have graduated with honours from the American School of Slow Talking. In a hesitant, nasal, western drawl, his words were laboriously prised out, "Waaaal I... ah... sorta... enjoy... like... ah... swimming... in the ah... pool... in our... ah... back yaaaard."

"Yeah, we got like a pool in our backyard, in Phoenix, Arizona. HA HA HA HA," the woman roared again. For her, laughter was the essential punctuation mark, the full stop at the end of every sentence. Mind you, it was a good thing she always spoke for husband or we'd never have got through the course on time.

In our underwater practical tests we had to descend to eighteen metres to perform some exercises: disconnecting the air supply, signalling for the use of our buddy's emergency regulator, making controlled breathing ascents, etc. The poor guy went down to that depth without equalising the pressure in his ears by holding his nose and blowing in the recommended manner. He suffered unbearable pain and panicked. Releasing air into his buoyancy jacket, he shot straight up again, not a clever thing to do as any air in your body expands rapidly as the water pressure decreases. By the time he reached the surface, blood was erupting from his nose. He gave up at that point and clambered into the boat before the smell of blood got to the sharks. It was a graphic reminder of the need for care, calmness and control of ascent. Discipline is essential in this activity, but the rewards are great. His wife carried on with the course and laughed her way through all the exercises, even underwater!

Outside the reef a shelf of coral with large pinnacles and canyons lies encrusted on top of the underlying volcanic rock. The shelf gradually increases to a depth of around thirty metres at the edge of the wall where the shadowy sides of the ancient volcano fall steeply away to the ocean floor, some 4000 metres (13,000 feet) below in the inky darkness. Looking over the edge was like looking into space: gloomy, mysterious, infinite. I had enjoyed an acquaintance with the sea for so long from the surface, sailing, kayaking, swimming; but diving was something altogether more intimate. Exploring this submarine wonderland was so unlike anything that could ever be imagined. I was enthralled.

The Cultural Village, a group of traditional huts furnished with displays and artefacts, offers short lectures and demonstrations designed to inform the tourist. It was a good place to learn more about the islands. Greeted by a smiling girl at the reception desk, I was informed that I had to book ahead as only guided tours were allowed, and, with a feast of traditional food included, they had to know exact numbers for catering. We spent a few minutes in pleasant conversation as she probed to find out more about me, all done with a charming innocence without any sense of intrusion. When I left she expressed the hope that I would return. The following week, I did.

On my arrival at the reception desk again she looked up, her lips parted in a huge smile and she said, "Oh, it is John from Scotland. I'm so pleased you have come back." Well, so was I. It gives me a wee glow to meet people who seem pleased to see me. You don't get much of that as a headmaster.

She guided me to a hut filled with historical artefacts to await the first lecture. There we learned about the migratory patterns of the ancient

Polynesians, the conflicting theories about how people first came to these islands and the story of the development of their society to the present day. In other huts we learned about fishing methods, food and cooking, herbal medicines, jewellery, tattoos... And all the various uses made of the amazing coconut tree. That versatile tree meets almost every need of the islander, from food and drink to construction materials. Its leaves are used for weaving mats and hats and making clothing. The so-called grass skirts are actually made of shredded bark. Pau, the traditional wooden drums, are hollowed out from the trunk (we were taught how to play them). A very informative morning, laced with humour, was rounded off with an excellent lunch of roast chicken and fish, accompanied by local vegetables, pineapple, melon and limes, all served on a 'plate' of woven fresh green leaves.

Then the entertainment began, music, singing and dancing with the obligatory participation of the visitors at the end. The girl at reception, now performing as one of dancers, took my hand in hers and led me on to the floor. When the drums beat their intoxicating rhythm, I gave it all I had, legs going like bellows and arms stretched out as I had seen the warriors do. She beamed and waggled her hips seductively, then moved in close between my outstretched arms, turning slowly as she danced, her body tantalisingly close to mine. Her dark eyes, smouldering with passion, held me entranced as they looked into mine through lustily lowered eyelids. This was getting a bit too hot – and it wasn't just the exercise. I had to call on a lifetime of stern Calvinistic discipline to keep my primitive urges under control. Then the music stopped and I was relieved of the burden of self-denial at last. She turned to face me again, smiled and clasped me in a lingering embrace, kissing me gently on the cheek.

"That was great," she murmured in my ear.

"Aye, the earth moved for me too," I murmured in hers.

She withdrew and smiled at me once more, then left the floor with the others and it was all over.

I drove back to the hostel and plunged into the pool to cool down.

Chapter 8
The Art of Diplomacy

"C'mon, John, we're all going out tonight," cried one of the girls.

"No way!" I had just settled down with my book. Night clubbing is not really my sort of thing, but my protests fell on deaf ears.

"Oh, c'mon, you know you'll love it."

Two of the girls mounted a pincer attack, grabbed me by the arms and hauled me out of my chair. Well, the laying on of hands worked miraculously, transforming me from pensioner to playboy and so, resignedly, I went along with them. As usual.

I like dancing. When I grew up in the west of Scotland if you didn't dance you were destined to remain single: the dance hall was where everyone met their future partners. That night, inspired by the primitive beat of the music and the seductive sway of female hips, my creativity found expression on the dance floor and I incorporated some traditional Cook Island dance movements into my repertoire.

A big, brooding Cook Islander stared at me intently. I ignored him. He still stared. I still ignored him. Cool as a cucumber, I carried on dancing. And still he stared. My eye took a few quick snapshots. It wasn't comfortable viewing. With these shoulders he would have to turn sideways to get through a doorway, his chin grew out of his chest and his ears seemed to rest on his shoulders. The guy had no neck; probably had his head hammered into his chest over the years in the front row of a rugby scrum. Long, heavily muscled arms dangled to somewhere just above his knees, just waiting for something to grasp and crush. I was sure I had seen this guy somewhere before. In the movies. Then it came to me – King Kong. He was built like a gorilla, but he had the intensity of a cat stalking its prey, his eyes focused on my every movement.

I stayed cool. Like hell I did! Maybe he was deeply offended. Maybe he was going to defend his island's traditions from irreverent assault by this pale-skinned northerner. Maybe he was going to crush me with those enormous arms. There were no 'maybes' about his ability to do so because they were as thick as my thighs. No, that's not strictly accurate – they were thicker!

The music stopped. The three girls from the hostel who had dragged me on to the floor to dance with them and got me into this predicament departed to the ladies room – as women do, all three of them together – leaving me alone to face King Kong. In all versions of the film, the hero always shoved the girl out first to divert the monster gorilla's attention while he bravely hid in the bushes. There was no hiding place for me. He lumbered slowly, menacingly, towards me.

I took a deep breath. My mind slipped into top gear. This called for guile, subtlety, the application of intellect. I was a mathematician, a problem solver. Now I had a problem to solve – urgently. Being of relatively slight stature all my life (I had been reared on wartime rations, after all!) I couldn't hope to compete with him physically. I picked up my drink and took a casual sip, playing it real cool, concealing my intention to throw the rest in his face as an initial shock tactic before I delivered my first strike. Even the mightiest warrior can be incapacitated by a well-aimed kick between the legs, and if the family jewels were in proportion to the rest of his physique, I could hardly miss. Then I would run like hell!

He held out his hand and smiled warmly. "Hi, I'd like to congratulate you on your dancing. What is your name?"

"Oh," I almost trembled with relief. "I'm John." I pumped his hand enthusiastically.

"Good to meet you, John. I am Terry."

"Terry? You have an English name?"

"Oh, no. We spell it T-e-r-e. My full name is Teremoana Nui O Kiva. It means 'Voyager on the great blue ocean'. My ancestors were great sailors. Where do you come from, John?"

"Scotland. And my ancestors were sailors too." We had something in common. Tradition and ancestry is important in the Cook Islands.

"Scotland? You have come a long way. You are a great traveller, too. I've been watching you, John. You are a cool dancer. I was very impressed."

"Oh, thank you." I bowed my head slightly in modest acceptance of the compliment. Maybe he wasn't going to kill me after all.

"We are very friendly people here in the Cook Islands, John. We like to share what we have with our visitors."

"Och aye, we're a bit like that in Scotland. Hospitality is an important part of our culture too." Recognition of common traits must help international relations, I thought.

"That's good. We are the same kind of people. So tell me John, what is your secret?"

The glass I was raising to my lips stopped short; my mouth hung open in paralysed anticipation. I looked blank. My eyes flicked sideways towards him.

"What secret?"

"Oh, come on John, we're friends now. Friends share things. I've got to know your secret, man."

I didn't want to offend him now that we were friends and gave a self-deprecating laugh. "Look, I'm maybe a wee bit thick, but I really don't know what you are talking about. Can you spell it out for me?"

"John, I've been watching you. You came here with three lovely blonde girls, you've been dancing with them all night – not one, but all three of them! – and they are showing no interest in anyone else but you. Now, let's be honest John, how can an old guy like you attract three beautiful blondes? I need to know your secret, man. Let's share the good things in life!"

I roared with laughter. "Well, there really is no secret. I just came with these girls from the hostel. They look on me as a sort of father figure, I suppose. Most of the young guys here just seem to want to stand and drink, but I like dancing so they asked me to dance with them. That's all there is to it."

He shook his head, unconvinced. "No John, I think you're hiding something. You must have something special to have three gorgeous girls hovering around you all night."

At that point, the girls returned. "Hi, girls, let me introduce you to Tere. He'd like to meet you." After a few introductory remarks I suggested, "Why don't we all move to the dance floor and cut some groovy shapes?" See, I learn fast – I'd picked up some cool talk on my travels. As we followed the girls to the dance floor, Tere pumped my hand warmly.

"John, you're one cool guy!"

I heaved a sigh of relief. I was still alive. I had made another friend. And my ego had received another boost. I was cool!

A few nights later, a crowd of us from the hostel attended one of the Island Night shows. It was our farewell party for Jason, a Canadian fire fighter who'd been with us for a week. After the show, we were all leaving the car park on our motorbikes when I noticed a couple from our group, Jim and Anna, seated on their bike, having an altercation with a large local hulk who looked rather menacing. My heart sank. Everyone had been so sociable up till now and we could do without this to spoil things. I got off my bike and walked over. After all, Jim was only 21 and maybe not as experienced in the arts of diplomacy as I was. The few words I heard were enough to convince me that the situation called for some urgent action.

Just then, my attention was distracted by a voice in the shadows. "Hi John, it's good to see you again." It was Tere, holding out his hand in friendship. I hadn't recognised him in the darkness. I grasped it warmly and we exchanged a few pleasantries.

"Do you know what this is all about?" I asked.

"Oh, my friend has had too much to drink and didn't like the way the boy was looking at him." Jim hadn't liked the way the hulk was looking at Anna – but to be fair, she was configured in a way that couldn't avoid attracting attention. They were at the staring-each-other-out stage and growling like tomcats.

"Right," I said. "Let's help them both avoid getting into trouble. Can you hold him back and I'll get the boy out of here."

"Yeah, sure." The gorilla arms encircled his friend and I turned to Jim who was still sitting on the bike ignoring Anna's plea to leave.

"Get the bike into gear and get out of here – now!" I snarled at Jim and started pushing the bike away.

Jason had also seen what was happening. He roared up on his bike and grabbed the handlebar on the other side, towing him away. "Yeah, come on Jim. Drive!" Getting him rolling did it, and he sped away.

Tere released his friend. "Well done John, you're a good man." Then he turned to his grumbling, belligerent mate and said, "Hey, lighten up. This is my friend John, from Scotland. He's a cool guy."

I held out my hand and smiled warmly. "Glad to meet you." Okay, I wasn't particularly, but I was still operating in diplomatic mode, so a wee white lie was allowed.

The hulk glowered at me for a moment, then slowly held out his hand. Through lowered eyebrows he peered at me drunkenly and registered some surprise, "You're an old guy! What are you doing here?"

I laughed lightly and punched him playfully on the arm. "Somebody has to keep you young guys out of trouble."

His head swivelled slowly and drunkenly to look at Tere, then back at me as I walked over to my bike before my luck ran out. He raised his hand, gave me a 'thumbs up' sign and called out, "Cool".

The others had gone on to a beach party, but I'd had enough for one night. Diplomacy is a tough business and I was only an old guy after all.

But a cool one!

Chapter 9
Pain in Paradise

From an altitude of 5000 feet, I could see Aitutaki ahead, the largest of a ring of islands encircling a pale greenish-blue lagoon. Taking a wide sweep round the north end of the island, I dipped the starboard wing, levelled off again and dead ahead lay the white airstrip of crushed coral. Easing her down, down, down, gliding over the multicoloured coral reefs below, over the end of the runway, levelling off, I reduced throttle and we gently touched down. A quick burst of reverse thrust on the propellers to slow her down, taxi over to the terminal, brakes on, flick the switches to shut down both engines. "Alpha–Romeo-One-Seven to Rarotonga Control. Arrival Aitutaki 14.19 hrs. Out."

These small planes are a great way to travel between the islands. And sitting close behind the pilot, you can easily pretend you are in control. I did – I suppose it was the same small boy within me who'd had the ambition to drive a steam locomotive. And the great thing is, the pilot did everything just as I had. He was really quite good at it.

Aitutaki is a delight, the archetypal tropical island. Part of an atoll, its pristine beaches, the pale turquoise lagoon and the small islands along the reef are the stuff of dreams.

I had travelled over on the small plane with Hilde, a tall, blonde Norwegian girl who had also been staying in Tiare Village. A welcoming party consisting of one man and a wee ten year-old boy was at the airstrip to greet us and garlands of flowers were placed over our heads. The wee boy looked longingly at Hilde's blonde hair and elegant limbs and then said something in Maori which drew a big guffaw from the man. He turned to Hilde with a grin and told her, "He wants to know if you are married." Testosterone is not in short supply in the islands.

A young woman from the hostel had a minibus waiting for me and chatted all the way, telling me what to see and do during my stay.

Driving around on my hired motorcycle I was greeted everywhere with friendly waves and offers of fruit. Mangoes were dropping off the trees and the locals insisted that I take armfuls of them. They weren't trying to sell them – they were giving them away. People sat cross-legged along the roadside taking things easy, for what else is there to do.

Energetic activity is alien in such a place. As I drove past, the sight of a light-skinned, fair-haired northerner excited them sufficiently to summon the energy to raise an arm and call out, "Kia orana." I smiled and waved back. I'd come to love that warm, melodic greeting.

The beaches here are among the best to be found anywhere in the world. Wandering out of the hostel in the morning with some fruit for breakfast, I sat on white sand in the shade of the trees fringing the lagoon and sunk my teeth into a ripe mango, its juices cascading down my chin. The early morning sunlight danced with joy on the turquoise water of the lagoon. This must be as close to heaven as it gets.

One of the highlights of a visit to Aitutaki is a lagoon cruise. The usual activities, swimming, snorkelling over a giant clam garden and feeding the fish are all on offer, but exploring the uninhabited islands of the atoll was an added bonus. Here you can sense the elemental powers that create these living, growing islands and actually see the development of a landscape in progress. Unlike the rocky Scottish islands, which are slowly being eroded away, these islets are in the process of being formed. The pulverised remains of coral broken off the reef by the power of the waves has been ground into fine sand over the years, building sandbanks on top of the reef. Coconuts are washed ashore and take root, binding the sand and reducing the risk of it all being washed off or blown away in storms. Other seeds fall and take root and the vegetation thickens trapping more sand and adding humus. An island is born. This was a family of living, growing islands.

Having landed on an extensive sand bank, I strolled over to investigate just such a young plantation at the far end. On my way back to the boat, I wandered along the water's edge, head down, looking for shells and odd forms of life. I got more than I bargained for when I was startled by the sudden emergence of a beautiful young woman from the sea. Slim, elegant, with long, dark hair glistening wet in the sun, her pareu, now clinging wetly to her body, accentuated her exquisite form. Sunlight sparkled on the droplets of water that clung to her bare shoulders. It was like a dream. A mermaid. Standing knee deep in the water, she engaged in conversation with our skipper for a few minutes. When our boat headed off, she stood there waving to us, a solitary figure silhouetted against the white sand, then slowly she entered the water again until all that remained in view was the dark pinpoint of her head, like a seal. I was mesmerised.

I turned to the skipper. "Where did she come from?"

He pointed to an island half a mile away. "Over there. She is camping on that island. That's where the people of Aitutaki go for holidays. They just take a boat across the lagoon and live the simple life: swimming, fishing, eating, sleeping. They make a fire for cooking and build a kikau hut to sleep in. That's all they need." I thought about that. When you live in paradise, why go anywhere else?

We stopped for lunch on One Foot Island, another uninhabited island with superb beaches. Legend has it that once upon a time some warriors were in pursuit of a man and his son who had landed on the island. The man ordered his son to walk in front and he placed his footprints on top of his son's so that only one set of prints was showing in the sand. The boy was ordered to hide among the leaves of a palm tree while the father awaited his fate below. The warriors arrived and killed the father, but having seen the footprints of only one person on the island they departed leaving the son to survive. And so it came to be called One Foot Island. Well, it's a good yarn for the tourists.

Although uninhabited, the island has its own post office in a corner of the open-sided dining shelter where you can buy One Foot Island postcards and have them and your passport stamped with the One Foot Island icon, a footprint. It amuses the tourists and it's good for business.

While we dined on a barbecue of chicken, fish, vegetables and fruit, the skipper took out a ukulele and entertained us with songs about virtually every country represented by the visitors. He was stumped when it came to Scotland, but he knew about the Scottish rugby team and its former captain: "Hey Scottish," he called to me, " tell Gavin Hastings that Captain Perfect was asking for him. I brought him here once. Great player and a nice guy, too."

After lunch I wandered barefoot around the island strolling along the water's edge under a cloudless sky, the sun glowing warm on my back. Languid palms slept in the still afternoon air, their listless fronds casting dappled shadows over white sand. Before me lay one of the most beautiful lagoons in the world, encircled by a scattering of small islands edged with the most magnificent beaches I had ever seen. Beyond the lagoon the ocean murmured softly, caressing the reef with delicate white fingers. This was a perfect day. I floated on a tide of euphoria. How richly blessed I felt to be here, especially on such a perfect day.

The island was shaped like a teardrop and I had now reached the sharp end, but as I turned round the point, my heart wrenched. Coming towards me was a couple, idyllically strolling hand in hand. I looked behind me. Two more couples meandered along the water's edge, their arms around each other's waists. My feeling of euphoria rapidly ebbed. This wasn't *quite* perfect. One important thing was missing – that special someone to share it with.

A wave of emotion welled up within me. My heart ached. Thoughts, like clouds, now cast shadows over the day and a hot mist filled my eyes. I turned away from the shoreline and sat in the shade of some trees, gazing out over the sea, and the memories of the girl I had loved and lost came flooding back.

Travelling alone around the world was not a lonely experience. There were plenty of other loose cannons around and being single was never problematic. Just occasionally, like now, alone amongst others who dreamily wandered hand in hand, I was reminded of something precious that I'd once had: the intimate pleasure of sharing treasured moments with one special person. It was only because she had died that I was here enjoying this most heavenly day; my pleasure, bought by her suffering and death.

As I grieved, I heard her words again, 'Make the most of every day'. Even in death she nagged me; she would never tolerate my sitting around doing nothing and the tide of emotion and self-pity began to ebb. Yes, thoughts are like clouds; they may cast shadows, but they do drift away. I had this side of the island to myself once more and I sat a little longer in the sunshine, soaking up the serene beauty of the place.

It had been a perfect day - almost.

Chapter 10
Someone to Care - Someone to Share

Scottish visitors are relatively rare on Aitutaki. However, I was informed by the woman who ran the hostel that Aitutaki had a resident Scot, a woman who had married a local lad. My host insisted that I must visit her and bring her news of Scotland. I followed the directions given and found myself at the most northerly house on the island. A big, handsome Maori came to the door and grinned a warm welcome.

"Kia orana."

As soon I replied he knew from my accent where I came from and brought me in to meet his wife. She greeted me in the traditional Scottish manner: "Och, come in. You'll have a wee cup of tea." She was from Kirkintilloch, near Glasgow. I was curious to know how a girl from Kirkintilloch came to be living in this remote paradise in the Pacific. She had met her husband while travelling in New Zealand. Some years later they returned to the island and set up a safari tours business.

"Do you miss Scotland?" I asked. She laughed.

"You've seen this place. Would you miss Scotland? Family and friends, yes. I would love to see more of them, but it is so far away for them to visit. But the weather – the wind and rain and cold – no thanks. I'll stay here."

She had a point. When I left, they insisted I return again to see them on my next trip. It was just taken for granted that there would be a next trip, and a return visit was therefore obligatory. I could feel these islands working their magic on me, weaving a web from which I would find it difficult to escape. I wasn't sure I wanted to escape; a sense of belonging had already been established.

Dating from 1823, the church on Aitutaki it is the oldest building in the Cook Islands, and there I found a similar passion for singing and a welcome to rival that of Avarua Church in Rarotonga. After the service, the minister came down from the pulpit to greet all the visitors personally and insisted we stay for lunch. It was a hot day and they served up gallons of ice cream for dessert. They love ice cream and don't mind how it is served. I delighted in the sight of all the dignified ladies, elegantly dressed in their Sunday-best clothes, with plastic cups filled to overflowing with ice cream – and scooping it out with their fingers. Dignity here demands re-definition. It is something deep and personal, much more than superficial displays of temporaneous manners.

The young people began to rehearse some dances, and when I asked what was going on I was told they were practising for a youth rally to be held that evening at Vaipae, a village on the other side of the island. Again, I was invited to join them. Everything closes on Sundays so without other distractions, I drove over in the evening. People from the various churches sat in groups on benches forming an arena, but immediately I sat down on the grass, a bonnie girl in her mid-teens left her group, came over and sat down on the grass beside me.

"Hello, it's good to see you again. I'm glad you could join us," she said cheerily, having recognised me from the morning service. She was 15 years old. How many back home would have done that, I wondered. We chatted for a short time, then she re-joined her group and the show began: singing, dancing and dramatic activities laced with humour. In the finale the amassed choirs sang together, including a song with the words, "Someone to care, someone to share." I felt a lump in my throat. It encapsulated everything that my experience of these lovely islands had been about and highlighted what was absent from my life. When the show finished, I stood up to go, but my arms were seized. It was Captain Perfect, the skipper from the lagoon cruise.

"Hey, Scottish, you can't leave yet. You must eat first. Hospitality is compulsory here." I was frog-marched into the village hall and the words of the song came back to me with even more meaning: someone to care, someone to share.

Two long tables were laden with food; roast chicken, tuna, taro root, taro leaves, breadfruit, vegetables, bread, fresh fruits. Having often watched, with hungry frustration, the antics of British people at buffet dinners, slowly working their way along the tables, trying to select morsels of food using spoons and forks with dignity and gentility, taking ages to get from one end to the other, this was a refreshing change. The crowd swooped on the tables like vultures and grabbed what they fancied; no waiting politely in long queues, no false manners, no knives or forks either. You simply scooped up what you wanted with bare hands. Fingers dipped into stews and dishes of vegetables; no concern about hygiene here. And you ate with your bare hands. All the genteel manners my mother had insisted upon were discarded. The Aitutaki style suited me fine.

I took my plate of food outside and sat in the dark eating it. Several girls in their mid-teens came over and joined me, quite uninhibited in their eagerness to satisfy their curiosity. After the usual, where from and what is your name, it got more personal.

"Are you married?" I shook my head and explained my wife had died.

"How old are you?"

"Oh, far too old for you."

"Age doesn't matter," she countered, with a coquettish look to the accompaniment of giggles from her friends. I liked her quick banter and, always a sucker for a bit of flattery, I fired back.

"How old do you think I am?"

"Mmmm, maybe forty-five?"

"Oh, you sweet-talking flatterer," I mocked, but she had scored heavily on the compliments so I conceded my age. That convinced her that I was well past my use-by date and she started to shop around.

"Do you have any sons?"

"Yes, but they are both married." She was persistent.

"Do you have any grandsons?"

"Aye. I have one who is 16 years old." Her eyes flashed.

"Is he as good looking as you?" I liked this girl even more.

"Oh, much *better* looking." My modesty is overpowering at times.

"Can I have his address please?"

The conversation turned to other matters. On discovering I had been a teacher, they insisted that I visit their school next day. It would be no problem with the principal they assured. Visitors were always welcome.

And they were right. Next morning I presented myself at the principal's office and told him some of his students had invited me to visit the school. "Yes, you are very welcome to look around. Just go and introduce yourself to the teachers. I have a meeting to attend now." It was that casual. The teachers were equally casual. It was nearing the end of term and apart from a few senior students swotting for exams, the others had freedom to go out and play football, socialise, or sit talking in classrooms while the teachers got on with paperwork. I was therefore a useful diversion.

Once again the thing that struck me was the open friendliness displayed everywhere I went. The pupils were a delight, well mannered, but relatively uninhibited compared to their Scottish counterparts. They were intensely curious about me, and Scotland, a place few could identify on a map. They had a vague notion that it was somewhere in the northern hemisphere, but that was about it. Yet they all knew about the Loch Ness Monster, kilts and bagpipes!

It doesn't take long to establish a reputation on these islands. A girl approached me and said, "Hey, I know you." I laughed.

"Och, no, you're mistaken, I come from Scotland."

"Ah, but I still know you," she insisted with all the confidence of a born-again Christian with four aces up her sleeve. "You were dancing with Bibiana Paulo at the Blue Nun on Saturday night."

"Who on earth is Bibiana Paulo?" I protested.

"She's the dancer who picked you out of the audience to dance with her at the end of the show. She went all the way to the back of the room to get you, and you danced with her and she put her ei..." (a circular head-dress of flowers) "...on your head at the end of the dance because you were the best dancer among the visitors." The evidence was overwhelming. Correct in every detail.

"I can't do anything on this island and not be found out," I muttered.

"Did you enjoy yourself?" she asked.

"Who wouldn't, dancing with Bibiana?" I growled. "The way she moved, my eyes just glassed over."

"We noticed!" she retorted, with a laugh. "She's one of the best dancers on the island. That was quite a compliment she paid you. You danced really well." I acknowledged the compliment with my usual humility and changed the subject before I revealed any more fantasies. I was enjoying myself with these kids.

Speaking with the youngsters, I observed a contentment with their environment and culture. Only a few were concerned about leaving the island to find work. Most were quite happy at the prospect of living locally, marrying and having families. They all seemed to love children and most had experience of looking after babies within their families or caring for the children of friends and neighbours. You could see this in the churches, the shops, on the beaches and at the youth rally the night before. The evidence that family is important was everywhere. It reminded me of my early life, when older girls often acted as an assistant mother, helping with the younger members of the much larger families that were common over half a century ago.

At lunchtime, a few boys were kicking a football around and I joined in. The speed and agility of youth may have deserted me long ago, but the ball skills remain, and this impressed the lads. "Will you stay and be our coach?" they asked. I was touched when they expressed dismay on hearing that I was moving on next day. "But we want you to stay," they protested. "And you'll miss our cultural week when we have competitions for singing and dancing and music. You'll enjoy all that."

I instantly regretted my decision to stay only a few days on this idyllic island, but unlike the islanders, I still had not relinquished obedience to the great ruler, Time, and next day I took my scheduled flight to Atiu.

Chapter 11
Underground on Atiu

Atiu is an island of raised coral, thrust up out of the sea by cataclysmic forces a few million years ago. It feels rather strange to wander through forests where lush vegetation grows over what were once undersea coral reefs. Many years ago, to reduce the risk of death or damage from cyclones, the missionaries encouraged the population to move from the narrow coastal fringes up to the plateau in the centre of the island and this is where everyone lives today in a series of connected villages.

Dinner each evening was pre-booked at the only restaurant on the island as part of the accommodation package, but I had to find some food for breakfast and lunch. In the village store I was met with the friendly, smiling faces of women happy to serve and genuinely interested in me, and where I'd come from. It wasn't the pre-packaged, mechanically smiled, "Have a nice day," of the Americanised shop girl. These people actually talked with you, smiled at you with warm brown eyes, laughed with you, told you about places to go and things to do, and hoped you would stay as long as possible and share in their way of life.

One enormous lady, with dark brown eyes the size of golf balls and bosoms that made watermelons look like peas, stopped stacking shelves to satisfy her curiosity. She wasn't being nosey: she was just interested. In no time at all we were laughing and joking with each other and then she asked, "But why do you come all the way from Scotland to Atiu? How did you know we were here? It is so small it isn't even on the map."

"Well, I had heard of the Cook Islands so I came to Rarotonga first and then I heard of Atiu, so here I am. Why? I am looking for a..." I paused momentarily, my eyes roaming suggestively up and down her massive shape and gave a seductive flicker of my eyebrows, "vahine manea..." (a beautiful woman) "...to take home with me."

Her eyes lit, she stretched her arms out wide, and beamed. "Take me!"

"Oh yes! My prayers have been answered," and I clutched her enormous body in a warm embrace. My arms barely reached round her shoulders. It was like squeezing a beach ball. No bones, just sackfuls of soft, cuddly flesh.

Then her face fell. "Oh, I just remembered, I have a husband."

I feigned misery. "And I thought I had found the girl of my dreams," I mourned.

She roared with laughter. "You're very welcome here, Scottish man."

There are several interesting limestone caves on the island, and this is where the kopeka (a rare species of swift) inhabits its dark, subterranean world. From mud nests stuck high up on the cave walls, the tiny fledglings begin their first flight into the total darkness of the cave and, using sonar navigation by emitting high pitched sounds, they find their way out to the bright sunlight. How they adapt to the light after living all their infant lives in total darkness is another of nature's wonders.

Trekking through this dripping humid landscape was challenging. Boots are recommended as the rocks are so sharp, but I had only sandals. Nevertheless, being fleet of foot I had no trouble negotiating the razor-edged rocky paths. It was well worth the effort.

Our guides took us deep into the caves, and when we reached their innermost chambers we were ordered to put out our headlights. Standing beside me was Jane, a lively Scottish girl who'd arrived on the same flight from Aitutaki. The darkness was total, quite unlike anything I had ever experienced, and very destabilising. With nothing to serve as a reference point, I began to lose my sense of balance, or so I thought. It was a strange sensation, as though I were about to fall, as you do when you begin to faint. Well, it was a good excuse. I reached out to catch something to stop me from falling and touched soft, female flesh. I had hold of an arm.

"Oh, sorry!" I wasn't really, but it seemed the right thing to say. "Who's that?"

"It's me, Jane."

"Oh. Me, Tarzan." Laughter broke out and the lights went on to see what we were up to. Damn!

On our trek back through the bush we stopped at a tumunu. This is an illicit drinking den deep in the jungle, comprising a small hut for brewing the local bush beer and a covered area for sitting and supping. The word tumunu originally described the traditional, hollowed-out coconut stump used for brewing the beer. Alcohol was unknown on the islands until the British whalers arrived around 200 years ago. Kava, a mild relaxant, was then the traditional communal drink. Atiu had an abundant supply of oranges, so the whalers brewed a sort of orange flavoured bush beer, and once the locals had acquired a taste for alcohol, well, like every other primitive society to which it was offered, they embraced it warmly. Nowadays, the beverage is brewed in plastic barrels and uses imported hops with orange flavouring. It is drunk only in small quantities. It is very potent.

Every evening, a group of local men gather there to discuss the matters of the day, to sup some of their illegal jungle juice, and to sing and ease away the tensions of life. This is stress management, Cook Islands' style. It reminded me of the bothans on the outer islands of Scotland – remote shelters where men furtively assemble to sip and socialise, fugitives enjoying a few hours respite from the perceived cruelties of the merciless severity of a culture dominated by Calvinistic Presbyterianism.

There are several tumunu on the island, but having gained popularity with the tourists, the police turn a blind eye to their presence. Or maybe it is divine intervention. Drinking never starts without a prayer, and it struck me that there was a kind of delightful absurdity in this. There was none of this 'give unto Caesar that which is Ceasar's' stuff here. It was only man's law, made on far away Rarotonga they were breaching, not God's law. Maybe the prayers worked. Nobody misbehaved, the police stayed away and everybody had a pleasant time. It was all so civilised.

It was a serious, ritualistic business, at least at the start. Seated on palm logs in a circle, we were asked by the chairman for the day to introduce ourselves. When I mentioned Scotland, our chairman's eyes immediately lit up. "John, my great-grandfather came from Scotland. My name is Rory," he announced with pride. You don't get much more Scottish than that, and when Jane also mentioned Scotland he insisted on having a photograph taken with us, with me sitting on one knee and Jane on the other. It was no problem for him. He was a big guy.

Introductions over, we were then given the lore about the drink and its place in local culture – and warned about its potency. "Don't sit down for too long or you'll discover you have rubber legs. Get up and walk around after every two or three drinks and you should be okay."

It is a ceremonial affair. A small conical cup is filled from a barrel and passed to each person who swallows and passes the empty cup back to be re-filled. The process is repeated with the next person and so it goes on round the circle. After a few rounds the seriousness evaporated, the guitars and ukuleles came out and the singing started. Now we were having real fun, and by the time our transport returned to take us back to the hostel we were in such high spirits we couldn't care less about dinner. However, courtesy dictated that we had to say our farewells to the boys, though with much reluctance. It had been a memorable cultural experience. Even better, there was not a trace of hangover the next morning.

On the flight back to Rarotonga, I discovered I had forgotten to hand in the key for the hostel on Aitutaki. I felt bad about that. They would have to phone the hardware store in Rarotonga for a replacement and then have it flown to the island. That wouldn't be fair. I had to get it back to them. I could mail it back, but that would take time. A better solution occurred to me.

These islands reminded me in many ways of the Scottish islands where they live by a different set of rules; bureaucracy is tolerated only when it has to be. There are other ways of getting things done.

At the airport I went to the Air Rarotonga desk and asked the girl, "Could you give this key to the pilot of the next flight to Aitutaki and ask him to pass it on to the bus driver to drop it off at Papa Tom's Beach Hostel on his way round the island?"

"Certainly sir, no problem. Glad to help." Now that's what I call service. I was really beginning to feel very much at home here. Can you imagine going to the British Airways desk at Heathrow when you've discovered the hotel key from New York is still in your pocket and asking the girl to pass it on to the pilot of the next 747 heading that way to give to the shuttle bus driver etc? Mmmm, I might just try that next time I'm in Heathrow. It might provide a little entertainment playing the daft highland laddie after a long-haul flight.

On my return to Tiare Village I was asked by Poko, one of the hostel staff, if I had met her brother.

"I don't know," I replied. "I met a few people, but the only guy whose name I can remember was at Sam's Tumunu. He was called Rory."

"That's my brother," she replied. The Cook Islands really is a small community.

Chapter 12
Are You Single?

The waitress smiled and welcomed us in the traditional Cook Islands manner: "Kia orana."

"Kia orana. Pe'ea koe?" I replied. That took her by surprise. She beamed, her eyes suddenly alight with interest.

"Meitaki ma'ata. Pe'ea koe?" she replied graciously, smiling back at me. She had a lovely smile, her white, even teeth contrasting beautifully with the dark colour of skin and hair.

"Meitaki au," I murmured softly, my eyebrows simultaneously flickering upwards in an affirmative gesture. In the Cook Islands they don't just use words for communication; a variety of facial expressions, grunts and glottal stops are also part of the essential vocabulary. As you can see, I hadn't frittered my time away, and having exchanged our initial greetings, she chose to offer a compliment and switched back to English.

"You speak our language very well for a papa'a." (A white man). "Where did you learn to speak Maori?" She was nibbling the bait.

"Oh, I've been here for a few weeks," I muttered modestly.

"You're doing very well." Then she flashed an inviting look. "You should stay longer."

Well, this was all developing very nicely. Unfortunately, it was my last night on Rarotonga and ten of us from the hostel, a mixed group, singles and couples, had gone out for dinner. The waitress helped us put two tables together to accommodate the whole group and cheerfully re-set the cutlery. I stood back and observed as she worked her way round the table, bending over, presenting me with the opportunity to study her aesthetic qualities from various angles.

A typically attractive, honey-coloured Cook Island girl, she wore a floral cotton blouse and a black, tight skirt of mid-thigh length which clung sensuously to hips and thighs, accentuating their gentle curves – well, you can't help but notice these things. The fragrant, creamy-white gardenia tucked above her ear contrasted beautifully with her dark hair, swept back and bundled tightly in the style usually worn in daytime or for work. Modest, yet alluring, the subtle underplay of the hairstyle accentuated her fine Polynesian looks, a beauty perhaps enhanced with a blending of European genes to lighten the colour of her skin slightly. My imagination toyed with images of how inviting she would look when she untied her long hair and allowed it to cascade down her back in the style worn when dancing. Then it overtly denies subtlety, artfully transforming the image of humility, purity and chastity into one of unashamedly ostentatious eroticism. The females of this race are skilled in the arts of visual seduction, and with skin treated with scented coconut oils they smell so sweetly, too. Well, that fairly helped to pass the time until we were all seated.

She took out her notebook and stood closely beside me. I inhaled her sweet, subtle fragrance as she took my order. Then, tilting her head slightly, her dark brown eyes looking down inquisitively into mine, she stunned me by asking, "Are you single?"

Was I hearing right? She didn't beat about the bush, did she? I couldn't believe my luck, a delectably attractive Polynesian girl propositioning *me*? At last! I'd been told so often that age was irrelevant here, that Polynesian maidens often regard the more mature, experienced European male as an attractive proposition: exotic, kinder and more gentle, more caring and considerate, more skilled in the arts of love, with an emphasis on the quality of the experience. Yes, that's me, alright. This was my dream come true!

"Yes," I gasped. "And are you single?"

"Yes." There was just a hint of puzzlement in her voice. Of course, I hadn't read the signs. She was wearing the flower over her left ear: flower on the right ear, she's spoken for; on the left ear, she's available – remember? The way ahead was clear. This was too good a chance to miss. I didn't beat about the bush either.

"Well, since we're both single, how about getting together after you've finished work tonight?"

She regarded me with some bemusement for a moment. "I only wanted to know if you would be paying for one meal or two when I make up the bill." My face fell and roars of laughter exploded around the table. Maybe I should stick to Maori.

Afterwards, when I went over to the desk to pay the bill I engaged in some banter with her again. The manager, a pleasant, middle-aged woman, came over. "Enjoy your meal, sir?"

"Yes indeed," I assured her, "and I'd like to pay tribute to the excellent quality of the service. Our waitress was not only efficient and effective, but utterly charming and hospitable throughout." The manager beamed approvingly at the waitress. I then explained my disappointment over the language difficulty when she had been taking the order and that brought another laugh. "I've travelled all over the Pacific looking for a vahine manea, and I thought that tonight my dream had come true." Then I hung my head mournfully, "But she turned me down."

"Oh, I'm sorry, but I will be working till very late tonight," the girl explained. The manager and the girl looked at each other. Not a word was spoken, but I could see from the looks and the eyebrows flickering almost imperceptibly that some meaningful exchange had taken place. The manager looked back at me, raised her eyebrows and said, "She's not working late tomorrow night."

The girl looked sideways at me, her dark eyes raised invitingly. My heart fluttered. "Does that mean you'll be free tomorrow night?"

She smiled coquettishly. "I'll be at the Cocobar at ten o'clock."

"Great!" I whooped. Then... Disaster. "Oh no! I have to be on the plane to Fiji at ten o'clock tomorrow night."

She shrugged her shoulders and flicked a mischievous smile at me. "Maybe you should come back some other time."

"Oh, ka 'oki au!" (I will.)

She smiled at me invitingly and murmured softly, "Ka kite." (See you). There was nothing ambiguous about that.

Ach, but it was only a wee bit of banter. She couldn't possibly be interested in an old guy like me. Could she?

For those of you who like a happy ending, forget it. I returned a year later but the restaurant was under new management and I never saw the waitress again.

Chapter 13
Last Night on Rarotonga

After dinner we went to see an Island Night Show. I was delighted that it was Te Korero Maori, Krystina's dance team who were performing on my last night out on the island as they had done on my first night here. When the show finished, our dancing began. We were in a party mood, and Lorraine, an Irish–born girl from Leeds, didn't need any courage from a bottle, so we were the first couple on the floor. After a few minutes, a young American came over during a break in the music.

"Hi. I'm Roy from New York. I'd like to congratulate you. You have quite a fan club over there. There are fifteen young ladies all wishing they had boyfriends who could dance like you."

"Och well, you just tell them to come and join us." And shortly afterwards they did, shaking ass, flashing eyes and muttering words like 'Cool' and 'Groovy'. From then on the place was jumping, and by the end of the evening I had become acquainted with many more backpackers from other hostels. On leaving, a minibus from another hostel drew up beside me in the car park and hands were thrust out to grasp mine. "You're a star, John. I can't believe you were once a headmaster!" Nor could I. Life was never like this at home.

I had a few things to attend to in the morning, and after returning the hired motorbike I wandered along the street with my thoughts, just killing time. I regretted that I had been so busy dancing and I hadn't said farewell to Krystina and Mii the night before. As I gazed in a shop window I heard a voice behind me, "Doing some last-minute shopping?" I turned round and there was Mii, smiling at me.

"Och, I was just thinking about you. I didn't get a chance to say goodbye last night."

She invited me to join her for lunch and when we parted she said, "Now you must keep in touch."

"I will," I assured her.

Virtually the entire hostel was leaving that night, some heading eastwards to Los Angeles and then England, others westwards to Fiji. A host of backpackers from other hostels were on the move too, and the airport was seething. I felt more than a tinge of sadness, for here in the

Cook Islands I had found something special among a circle of friends to whom age and nationality were irrelevant. Barriers had been removed, and my future was beginning to define itself.

The social boundaries within which I had been constrained had evaporated in the greenhouse atmosphere of backpacker life on Rarotonga. Back home, my social life had comprised almost exclusively of events at which I performed in some capacity: as an after-dinner speaker, compering charity shows, chairing meetings. I only went out if I had a duty to fulfil. I avoided dances especially: they brought back too many heart-wrenching memories.

Here, the environment was different. For a start, the music was different, so it didn't evoke memories of the past, as familiar tunes do; and I wasn't always the single man among couples of my age group. Having been press-ganged into going out on that first night, I then yielded readily to the exhortations of the young backpackers. That they should want me to go out with them surprised me, and I enjoyed it, which surprised me even more. I had lived in social isolation for too long and besides, this trip was all about new experiences and exploring the international backpacker culture, which seemed just as valid as exploring the cultures of the societies I would visit. I was not only a curious observer, I was also a participant. In my own youth I had never partied so much. My age didn't seem to matter to them, so why should it matter to me?

Several of the friendships have endured, despite a gap measured not in years, but generations. Jason, the handsome Canadian fire fighter adored by all the girls but faithful to his girlfriend at home, was a mere twenty-three years old. When he left for the airport in his taxi, we followed in a motorcycle cavalcade, and when we drove off, all blowing our horns in final salute, he was almost in tears. He'd stopped off in the Cook islands for a week on his way back home after taking part in the World Fire Fighter Games in Auckland, and had been blown away by the friendliness he encountered here. In spite of almost forty years difference in our ages we hit it off right away, and his parting words to me at the airport were, "As long as I live, I'll never forget you, John."

He didn't. Back home in Scotland six months later I was aroused by a phone call from Edmonton. "Hi, Johnny Boy! I'm celebrating my 24th birthday and I just had to call you to hear that Scottish accent again."

"Oh, that's very nice. Happy birthday," I murmured. He detected the sleepiness in my voice.

"Hey, what time is it there?" The guy had no concept of time zones.

"4.30am."

"Oh, shit! Hey, I'm really sorry for wakening you up, Johnny. I never thought."

"Ach, don't be daft. I'm delighted to hear from you, you big, daft lump. Happy Birthday!"

" Hey, when are you coming over to Canada to see me, John?"

"Oh, I'll fit in a visit on one of my trips," I assured him. After our call, I fell asleep again with a smile on my face.

Matt from Colorado, a youth in his early forties, travelled the world in celebration of redundancy. Rather than feel despondent about being forced out of work, he regarded it as a heaven-sent opportunity to take a year-long trip round the world with the intention of visiting as many countries as possible, seeing everything and doing everything. Easy-going, fun loving and a great mimic, there were always laughs when he was around. His ever-cheerful, positive attitude was an inspiration. I love the company of positive thinkers. When the time came for him to move on to Fiji, he hugged me (to my extreme embarrassment, I might add – we don't overdose on that sort of thing in the north of Scotland!) and said, "John, I sure wish I'd had you as my high school principal. Keep in touch, Buddy." I did, and six months later he spent a week as my guest in Scotland during the European part of his tour.

Once again the premise that, by mixing with positive, enthusiastic people you will gain so much more from life, held true. It was his infectious enthusiasm that inspired me to take up scuba diving, opening up opportunities for exploration of the amazing world beneath the waves and developing new friendships. My graduation as a diver may have come late in life, but it was no less satisfying. Youth had not deserted me yet.

A goodbye chat with a couple of the girls before they left for the airport one evening transformed into an impromptu 'Interview Tutorial' in the hostel lounge as they waited, packed and ready to go. It developed out of a conversational remark about the nerve-wracking prospect of having to face job interviews, but once the advice started flowing the backpacks were opened again and out came the notebooks. Two more then joined in. They listened and reflected, questioned and wrote notes and frequently stopped me with remarks like: "Just say that again, John. That sounds really good. Oh, yes, I'll use that." They began to realise that though short on work experience, they had developed marketable qualities. They had proved themselves adaptable by travelling independently for a year or more, living in different societies with different cultural values in a variety of living conditions, and they were capable of establishing effective communication, sometimes in languages unknown to them before they started. They had proved themselves able to get on with people and work as a team. They had developed the organisational skills necessary to deal with the logistics of world-wide travel and the ability to cope with all sorts of unexpected difficulties.

Now, they began to see themselves differently. "Hey, I never realised that I could turn my travel experience to such advantage. This has been really illuminating. Thanks John." They embraced me warmly and left with glowing smiles. Like Alex on Tahiti, they were now empowered with a new confidence. I had been a teacher again and had revelled in the experience.

I began to develop a new self-awareness. Having felt so often that I was drifting, a piece of flotsam, part of the debris of a shipwrecked life, I was now finding a purpose in my travelling. My experience could be shared and bring some benefit to others. I began to feel as though I may still have some worth. Retirement is not human a scarp yard, but an opportunity for self-development.

Another ingredient in the recipe for change came from discussions with Mark and George (Georgina). They moved on to do volunteer work in Sri Lanka, looking after orphaned baby elephants. Having kept in touch and been inspired by their experiences in voluntary work, I became convinced that this should be a focus in future travels: staying longer in one place, making a contribution to the community. I had a lifetime's experience in education to offer. Surely I could be of some use here in the Cook Islands. I had learned that Global Volunteers, an American organisation, sent tutors to the Cook Islands to help children with learning difficulties improve their English. That interested me, and I spoke with the programme coordinator with a view to becoming involved on my next visit. I had already decided I had to come back, so I now had a real purpose in returning to the Cook Islands. I had the opportunity to put something into a community that had received me with such warmth.

But now my flight was being called. There were hands to be shaken, goodbyes to be uttered, and girls to be hugged. Ed, a wee Irishman, with all the loquacious charm for which his race is renowned, had a word for everyone. I was last in line. He looked at me for a moment, then grasped my hand and said, "John, for once, words fail me!" Then he disproved it. "You've put us all to shame. You'll never grow old."

As the Air New Zealand Boeing 767 soared into the night sky, I watched the lights of Rarotonga fall away beneath us, quickly becoming lost in the wraiths of cloud. With a heavy heart, I curled up under my blanket as the plane turned westwards towards Fiji. Under closed eyelids, a tide of images of the Cook Islands flooded my mind. Beautiful island beaches, glowing white under gently swaying palm fronds bordering serene, turquoise lagoons; and behind them mysterious, mist-capped peaks rising loftily from the jungle. Playbacks of dancing, swimming, diving, bush-trekking, socialising round the pool. Laughter, with so many of the people I had met, people I could now call friends. The unforgettably passionate singing in the churches, and the generous hospitality offered afterwards. Bibiana crowning me with her ei on Aitutaki; the kids at school, chatting so freely and pleading, "We want you to stay". The boys at the tumunu on Atiu singing and sharing their bush beer with us. Krystina, Miss Tiare, charming, beautiful and unaffected by her success, dancing gracefully in her traditional costume and Mii, her mother insisting, "You must keep in touch."

And again I heard the voices of the young people on Aitutaki singing their song: "Someone to care, someone to share." That was what I had found here among the backpackers and the people of the Cook Islands. And now I was leaving, my heart ached and a hot mist filled my eyes.

I had been enchanted by these islands. I had to return.

Chapter 14
Fitting in on Fiji

Fiji International Airport is at Nadi on the west side of the main island, Viti Levu. After spending the first night there it took a six-hour bus ride to reach Suva, the capital, a modern city with a population of about 150,000. The buses were just a step up the transport ladder from 'le truck' in French Polynesia: old, battered vehicles with no glass in the window frames (it's what they call air-conditioning here) and they have tarpaulins to roll down if it rains. The buses, which run more or less continuously round the island, all seemed to be packed almost to capacity – and they are cheap.

My hosts in Suva were Ray, an Australian in his early fifties, Head of the Department of Aeronautical Engineering at the Fiji Institute of Technology, and his partner, Wainese, an attractive Fijian girl. I had been introduced to them by email through a common friend, Cecily, an Australian girl I had taught over thirty years previously and with whom I had recently become re-united through the internet. She had written to them asking if they would offer me some hospitality and help me get around.

Viti Levu, the main island, is a large mountainous mass with over three hundred small islands scattered around it. Vanua Levu, another large mountainous island, lies to the north. On Viti Levu, sugar production is the mainstay of the island's agriculture.

Outside the main centres of population – Suva, Nadi and Lautoka – the smaller towns had more of a third world appearance. Many of the buildings and streets were dirty, littered, and lacked maintenance. Drainage was poor and smelly. At the comfort stops (a real misnomer, for the toilets were far from comfortable, defying description in most cases), fast food was available at shops and kiosks – but their grubby appearance dispelled any pangs of hunger, and who knows how long the heaps of pre-cooked food had been lying there? The shops all seemed to be run by Indians or Chinese.

The rural dwellers were usually indigenous Fijians, living in villages of simple bungalows made of timber or corrugated iron. Some still occupied thatched vernacular huts constructed of woven palm leaves tied to a simple timber frame. They had a certain ethnic charm, but little in the way of amenities. Suva was like any western city; bustling with traffic, busy wharves, fine shops, tall office blocks and elegant houses in the leafy suburbs.

The indigenous Fijians were friendly and you could count on complete strangers smiling at you in the street and addressing you cheerfully with their standard greeting, "Bula!" They were always curious to know where you had come from, if you were married and how old you were. Fiji, at the confluence of the ancient Polynesian, Micronesian and Melanesian migratory patterns, has a real mixture of races with all sorts of hybrids. On top of that, more recent migrations have brought a significant influx of Indians and Chinese as well as a fair proportion of Europeans.

In common with their other Pacific neighbours, the Fijians love their flowers. I had been invited to attend Wainese's graduation ceremony at the Fiji Institute of Technology. For eight hours the previous day, her mother had sat on the floor, intricately weaving and binding row after row of flowers into a circular garland; called a sulusulu, it is worn over the shoulders. A beautiful synthesis of colours, texture and fragrance, it celebrated not only the long tradition of appreciation of an abundantly floral environment and the exuberant gaiety of these people, but also a mother's pride in her daughter's achievements. It was a work of art. Every graduate wore one, each unique, on top of their academic gowns in a colourful ceremony blending the ancient culture of the islands with the European tradition of celebrating academic achievement.

While that was a memorable occasion, it was overshadowed by our visit to Wainese's grandmother afterwards to let her see her granddaughter in her graduation robes. Here we entered what was very much a third world environment, a cluster of corrugated iron shacks only a few minutes drive yet a whole world away from the bustling, modern, city centre of Suva.

Granny sat cross-legged on the floor of the hut, always smiling, as did all other members of the extended family who had gathered there. Children appeared, gazed in wonder and disappeared again. It was an open house. No formality, no barriers, everyone welcomed. Ray and I shared the sofa which, apart from a well-worn chair, was the only item of furniture. Everyone else sat on the floor. Bare, unclad corrugated iron sheets nailed to rough wooden supports formed the walls and roof. Windows were simply open gaps with wooden flaps to offer protection from inclement weather. A mat of woven pandanus leaves covered the floor. There was no running water or electricity.

Refreshingly, they displayed none of the affected attitudes commonly encountered in the western world where an impromptu visitor is so often greeted with, "Oh, you'll have to excuse the house." The house didn't matter; hospitality did. I was welcomed with genuine warmth and made to feel immediately at home. Everyone was simply but colourfully dressed, and despite the absence of plumbing, everything they wore was spotlessly clean. They were constantly smiling, laughing and completely at ease with their visitors. When I took photographs of Wainese and her family with my digital camera they were thrilled at being able to look at the images on its small screen. Any reserve initially displayed by the children evaporated rapidly. They hovered around me like flies eager to see each picture as it formed on the screen, then squealed with delight at the image.

Wainese's cousin Dika, an attractive girl with two bonnie young children, sat on the floor and chatted to me. Bright, intelligent and charming, her brown eyes glowed as she looked up at me. The smile never left her face, and she laughed so readily as we shared some happy banter. It was impossible not to be attracted to her.

What future might this girl have had given different circumstances, I wondered? She seemed destined to remain in these humble surroundings, would no doubt bear more children and live in poverty for the rest of her life. But poverty presents itself in many guises, of which lack of money and material comforts is but one; there is plenty of emotional poverty in our affluent western society. In spite of the lack of what we would regard as essential amenities, this girl looked clean, healthy and happy. She had two beautiful children, and the support of her extended family around her. Perhaps there was something to be envied in her life.

When the time came to leave I kneeled down and kissed Granny on the cheek much to her delight and that of her family, shook hands with the grinning uncles and cousins and kissed Dika softly on the cheek and wished her well. She smiled and hugged me. Everyone – except Granny, who remained seated on the floor – followed us out to the car, repeatedly calling out, "Bye, John. Bye, John."

When outside, a group of neighbours' children assembled and joined in the cacophony with yet more cries of farewell: "Bye, John!"; "John, John – goodbye!" All waved enthusiastically as we reversed down the rough track to turn for home.

In those few moments I felt honoured. The Queen herself couldn't have had a better welcome. This was a taste of the kind of island life I wanted. Forget the tourist resorts with all the contrived pleasures they purported to offer. I wanted to mix with Fijian people, share in their lives, experience their culture and learn from them.

That evening, Ray responded to my sentiments by organising an itinerary for me. It only took a few phone calls. In the morning I was to catch a bus to Beqa Lagoon, renowned for its soft coral, where I would do some diving and then return to spend the night with Ray and Wainese again. The day after, I would catch another bus and head north. It would drop me off at a remote bridge on the road round the island. I would be met there by a small boat and taken to a tiny island called Caqalai (pronounced Thang-al-eye), where I would stay for a few days with a Fijian family, the only regular inhabitants of the island. I would sleep in a bure (a traditional hut made of rough-hewn timber frames and woven palm leaves). There would be no running water or electricity: instead, there would be bucket showers and oil lamps for light at night. There would be beautiful beaches, shady palms, a beautiful lagoon to swim in and friendly people who would cook traditional food for me and allow me to share in their way of life.

That night I lay in bed and wondered what adventures might be in store for me here.

Chapter 15
Special Offer

"Come in. Come in," called the woman as I poked my head through the open doorway of the shop. I had just spent an exciting day diving on reefs and wrecks in Beqa lagoon. Now, with time to spare before catching the bus back to Suva, I had been attracted by the traditional carvings on display and accepted her invitation to browse. Noticing I was alone and no doubt realising that a woman was more likely to be tempted to spend money than a man she asked, "Where is your wife?"

"I don't have a wife. She died some years ago."

"Oh, you poor man! But who takes care of you?"

"I take care of myself."

"Oh no! You can't take care of yourself. A man needs a woman to look after him. Do you not have a woman to look after you at all?" I shook my head in mock sorrow.

"Oh, but that is not good. You must have a woman to take care of you. Would you like me to find a good Fijian woman for you?"

"That sounds like a good idea to me," I laughed, wondering if I was about to be introduced to her attractive young assistant. Maybe the girl read my mind, for she made some excuse in Fijian and left the shop hurriedly. The shopkeeper continued enthusiastically.

"I know just the woman for you. My aunty needs a husband."

Now this wasn't exactly what I had in mind. I'd barely been in there for sixty seconds and here she was talking of marriage – to aunty! Now I don't want to offend aunties, but somehow the word lacks a certain appeal. This was suddenly uncomfortable, but there was no stopping her.

"What do you do for a living?"

"I've retired."

"What did you do before you retired?"

"I was the head of a secondary school."

"Mmmm. That sounds perfect. You would be ideal for my aunty. She is an intelligent woman. She is a good cook, and will look after you well, take good care of you and..." she gave me a meaningful look, "... she will make you very happy." Then, in case I was too thick to realise what she was talking about (which of course I was), she moved in closer, the voice dropped a little, became quietly confidential. "Fijian woman knows how to make good sex, keep a man happy in bed. You give me your name and address and telephone number and I will get my aunty to call you and you can meet her. Then you can try her for yourself."

Well, how was that for a deal? Test-drive the aunty? I'd expected to experience cultural differences on my travels, but this was an eye-opener.

"But I'm backpacking. I'm staying with friends tonight, but I don't know where I'll be tomorrow." That should let me off the hook, I thought. I thought wrongly.

"No problem. I will give you my telephone number and you call me and I will arrange for my aunty to meet you here."

"But your aunty wouldn't want to meet an old guy like me," I protested. Funny how that phrase was sticking.

"You're not old!" she scolded. "Look at you. How old are you?"

"I'm sixty."

"No! You don't look that old. I would have guessed no more than about forty-five." She looked me up and down appreciatively and added, "Mmm. You look very fit. You got a good body." Then she leaned towards me, touched my arm reassuringly and whispered, "I would like to have you for myself, but I have a husband and it would only complicate things. But you would be perfect for my aunty. She is forty-seven."

"But no Fijian woman would want to marry a Scotsman. It is cold in Scotland. She would only be miserable."

"You don't need to take her to Scotland. You can live here. My family are quite important here. We own a lot of property. Family is very important in Fiji, and if you marry my aunty, my family will take care of you. Give you both a house to live in. It's no problem." She certainly had all the answers. I think she saw me wilt under this relentless onslaught and moved in to clinch the deal.

"You must come back this way. Call me and I will arrange for my aunty to be here to meet you, then you take her out for dinner. Buy her a nice meal and maybe one or two drinks – just one or two, Fijian woman doesn't like any drunkenness – and then you bring her back here. Take her to the beach house over there and you spend the night there with her. You take her to bed and she give you good sex, make you very happy and then you go to sleep. I make breakfast for you in the morning."

But she wasn't finished yet. She reached into a basket and lifted out a bar of soap. "Here. I give you some of this soap." She sniffed the wrapping. "Sandalwood. This is good for sex. Wash yourself all over with this first, then you smell good. We like that. Makes sex better."

Now, who ever had a blind date set up so well? She had already thrust her telephone number into my hand. I was trembling, speechless. Only two days in Fiji and I had already been offered not just a dinner date with a lady, but a beach house, special pheromone enhancing soap to guarantee good sex, complimentary breakfast thrown in, a wife, the use of a house for as long as I wanted – no need to suffer any more cold damp winters in Scotland – and an important Fijian family to look after me in my dotage. My destiny was all mapped out. What an offer! So what did I do? I looked at my watch.

"Oh, my bus will be here shortly. I must leave now," I stammered.

"Okay. But remember to come back this way. You need a good woman to look after you. No man should be living alone."

I bailed out and ran off to the bus stop. Sitting in the bus on the way back to Suva I began to see the funny side of it all. Ray and Wainese had some friends round for a barbecue that evening and they all had a good laugh at my predicament.

"Well, you never know, the aunty might be a stunner," laughed Ray. "Don't be put off by the fact that she is forty-seven and still looking for a husband. A lot of Fijian women won't put up with the way some Fijian men treat them. European men are highly regarded here, and although there is an element of the good provider in all this, they are loyal and look after their men well. Aunty could be just what you need, John. Maybe it would be worth exploring this further."

Maybe. I still had the piece of paper with the phone number on it!

Chapter 16
It's An Ill Wind

It was an instinctive reaction. Well, what do you do when three lanes of growling traffic suddenly roar angrily away from the lights while you are crossing the road in front of it?

Sprint!

Well, that was the intention, but it is not a good idea at 8.00am with a backpack on when you haven't done your warm up exercises. With a snap like a rubber band breaking I felt a massive stab of pain, as if I had been chopped in the back of my leg by an axe. Instead of describing the graceful, propulsive, forward movement of an athlete my left leg dragged sickeningly, toes down, along the tarmac. I gasped and hopped like mad for the other side. Once there, I put my foot down and nearly collapsed. I couldn't walk.

I was about to catch the bus that would take me to Wandalice Bridge, where I was to be picked up by boat and taken to Caqalai. If I went to a doctor now I would miss the bus. The boat would have had a wasted trip, and who knows what the doctor might say? They are always such spoilsports. The worst of the pain was deep inside the calf muscle and my thought was that if I had torn it, rest would almost certainly be the best thing. Forget the doctor. Might as well get on the bus. Climbing up the steps was agony. I flopped into the seat behind the driver and wondered how this would affect my subsequent travels.

Meantime, all I could do was watch the scenery roll past as the bus made its way round the island. The scenery along the coast road was vividly green, with lush forests and fertile farmland interspersed with villages and only the occasional small town. A long way from nowhere, the driver turned round and called, "Wandalice Bridge."

I stumbled off and, bearing my weight on one leg, slung my backpack on my shoulders. A dirt path led down to the water's edge. I regarded it with a lack of enthusiasm: never was a trek so painfully or painstakingly undertaken. Any stretch on the back of my leg sent an agonising pain into the depths of the calf muscle, and the ankle itself was now swollen and intensely painful. Clambering down a steep path to the riverbank while carrying a backpack was not what my leg wanted at this time.

Once down, I dropped the backpack, sat on the bank and leaned back against it. Silence. It was 10.30am – pick up time. There was no boat, no jetty, only a sluggish, muddy river with heavily wooded banks. I sat and looked at the trees. And waited. Ten minutes later, I heard the sound of an outboard motor. A boat with three men and a boy on it appeared. It was coming downriver. Wrong direction! It beached below the bridge, and the crew began unloading sacks filled with clams and carried them to the roadside. I was getting worried in case I was in the wrong place and checked with them. They confirmed that the boat from Caqalai would arrive here – eventually.

A minibus stopped up at the roadside. The shellfish and some of the crew went aboard and it left. The others walked away to who knows where. I was alone with the river and the trees and the silence once more. I could only sit and wait, in pain. In the silence. Silence may be golden, but it can also be unnerving. I listened intently. Only the odd crab scuttling about in the mud at the water's edge, the shrill cry of a kingfisher, and the rumble of an occasional vehicle on the bridge overhead. And more silence.

Here I was, a pensioner, virtually crippled, about as far from home as it's possible to be on this planet, not quite knowing where I was supposed to be going and, literally, quite unable to go anywhere. What would my mother say if she could see me now? Funny how you think of your mother at a time like that. If the boat doesn't show up, what then? This was not a time for negative thoughts. Stay positive in the face of adversity. I could always hitch a lift and beg for a bed somewhere along the road. These were friendly people.

A better idea occurred to me: I could telephone the shopkeeper at Beqa Lagoon and ask her to send Aunty out for me! Let her take care of me, feed me, wash me with sandalwood scented soap and give me good sex, then I could go to sleep. Bliss! But with a backpack to carry and only one serviceable leg, how do I find a telephone in this wilderness?

Fifty minutes had passed since I got off the bus when I heard a man-made sound: it *was* the sound of a boat's engine, wasn't it? Coming up river too! The sound appeared to change direction several times – the river wound through mangrove swamps. As it got closer I realised that it *was* a boat. After an age, it appeared. A young man in his early twenties was at the helm, and a youth in his late teens sat forward. It headed in towards me.

"John?"

"Aye, that's me," I called back with some relief.

The helmsman jumped ashore and held out his hand. "I'm Mopsje.

This is Scorese. Where are you from, John? Give me your pack. Come aboard and take a seat. We have to go to the village for a few minutes."

I settled down on a pile of lifejackets, and they disappeared along the road to the next village. The boat was about 24 feet long, was narrow in the beam, and had a fibreglass hull. Powered by a 30 HP Yamaha outboard, its shallow draught and planing hull were well suited to the local conditions. Fiji is surrounded by extensive shallow lagoons liberally sprinkled with lumps of coral lurking just below the surface. This boat could skim across the surface drawing only a few inches of water and beach anywhere.

Half and hour passed before the boys appeared again with a bag of provisions and a large plastic box of ice cream. They cast off, the engine roared into life and we turned and headed down river rapidly, bow rising, stern digging in, leaving a white, churning, V-shaped wake. Scorese tore open the lid of the box of ice cream and turned towards me.

"Do you like ice cream, John?" and offered me the box.

"What do I eat it with?" I asked.

He looked at me with some surprise. "Fingers," and made a scooping gesture. Of course! I dug two fingers in and took a genteel portion, about a teaspoonful. Mother had always insisted on good table manners, that I must not be greedy.

"Oh, take more than that," he remonstrated. He then dug in his own fingers: four of them went in like an excavator bucket and scooped out a massive lump of ice cream, which went straight into his mouth. Mopsje then bent forward and did the same. Then the box came back to me. Well, I did want to savour Fijian life after all. I dug in four fingers and scooped out a sizeable lump. I might as well get my share before this pair of gannets scoffed the lot! And so we ate. I gave up a few scoops later; their fingers were dipping into my territory and I had no way of knowing how clean they were. They carried on scooping ravenously until there was only a milky mush in the bottom, then lifted the box to their lips in turn and drank what was left. Two litres of ice cream devoured – mainly by them – in just a few minutes.

After about ten minutes winding through the mangroves, we cleared the river mouth and headed out to sea. Dotted incongruously around the lagoon, clumps of trees seemed to be growing right out of the sea, creating a rather surreal effect, like a mirage. These palms had grown from coconuts which had taken root on coral outcrops. About forty-five minutes later Mopsje pointed ahead and called out, "Caqalai." We swung round to the west side of the island and I looked at it approvingly. Covered in palms and other vegetation, it was fringed by white beaches.

We motored slowly towards the beach and a few buildings became visible among the trees. This looked promising: straw huts, thatched roofs, shady groves among the trees, and a glorious beach with a sprinkling of bikini-clad bodies sunbathing on it. Not bad at all.

The boat grounded gently on the sand and I swung my legs over the side and slipped into the water. It was deliciously warm and clear. My left foot sunk into the soft sand. I winced in pain, stumbling and grabbing the boat for support.

A local girl in her mid-twenties came running down the beach towards me. "Bula! I'm Dauni. What have you done to your foot? Oh, you can't walk. Here, put your arm over my shoulder." Then she put her arm round my waist and held me tightly. "Hold on to me and I'll take you to your bure." Well, this wasn't so bad after all!

Clinging to each other, we limped along the path through the palms to my beach house. "Unfortunately, your bure is furthest away," she apologised. There was no need for any apology. I would have been happy to walk round the entire island clinging to this girl.

She took me in and sat me on the floor. I looked around my quarters. The only furniture was a bed, flowery patterned sheets covering a mattress laid on a rough-hewn frame with a mosquito net bundled above. A mat of woven, dried pandanus leaves covered the sand floor. Walls and roof were of tightly woven palm leaves tied to coarse wooden frames. Three walls had tiny window openings: no glass, only wooden flaps. The doorway faced the beach just a few steps away, with waves gently lapping on the shore. Ray had fixed me up nicely. It was idyllic.

"Now, let me see your leg." she commanded. She began to massage my leg gently with my foot resting on the inside of her thigh and then murmured, "How does that feel?"

There was no way I could give the girl an honest answer! "Oh, that's good," I muttered thickly, wondering if she could hear my pulse beating loudly.

"You'll need a massage every day. Would you like me to come and massage you until it gets better?"

"Oh yes, please." I tried not to sound too delirious. This was unbelievable. Here I was on a tropical paradise island with an attractive girl wanting to massage me every day. I hoped the leg wouldn't get better *too* soon. She carried on stroking me softly, then looked up quizzically.

"Are you married?" It was a question I was getting used to. I explained my circumstances. "And do you have a girl friend?" Where was it leading to *this* time I wondered, shaking my head in reply. "Right.

You need someone to look after you. Would you like me to take care of you?"

"Oh, that would be great," I gasped.

"Okay. I will be your wife."

Oh, not *another* one!

"Eh, well, that's great, but I've got to go back to Scotland."

"That's okay. I would love to go to Scotland. When do we leave?"

I couldn't believe this. I'd only been in Fiji for three days and I'd had two offers of marriage already. This wiped out the memory of my failure to impress the ladies of Tahiti. But it was all a bit too hasty for me.

"Well, eh, marriage isn't something to leap into quickly. In my culture, we take some time about things like that."

"Okay. But you still need me to look after you here. You rest and I'll come back again and massage you." Then she left to prepare lunch, leaving me in a daze.

I wondered what lay in store for me in the next few days, or weeks. I had no idea how long my leg would take to heal – but I wasn't really bothered either! Things were looking very interesting.

It's an ill wind that blows nobody any good.

Chapter 17
In The Mood For Love

A sound like a foghorn announced lunch was ready. Siggi, our seventeen year-old waiter, blew through a large triton shell each time food was being served. We ate in a communal dining area, an open-sided shelter with the kitchen at one end and a small bar selling soft drinks and snacks at the other.

I hobbled along painfully with a stick to support me, but help was soon at hand. Epele, the ten year-old youngest son of the family, came towards me with a worried look and asked what was wrong with my leg. Then he gestured to put my arm over his shoulder and he would support me, and together we limped slowly along. He was a real star. I've never met a ten year-old with such charisma. When dancing, his confidence, sensuous movements and lack of inhibition had five lovely, bikini-clad English girls drooling. He simply oozed sex-appeal. I was envious. It just wasn't fair. Why couldn't nature spread it about a bit more?

The English girls were all mathematics graduates from Leeds University, so we struck up an immediate rapport. A couple of English lads, a Danish family of four, two American girls, and an Italian called Alberto with a limp from a broken ankle while playing football, were the other visitors.

The inhabitants of the island were Kanai, his wife Dubai, their six sons, one daughter and an extended family of several cousins, aunts, and the odd friend who dropped in for a few days, weeks, months or maybe even years to help out in return for food and lodging. This mobility appears to be quite normal. Hospitality is offered without question; drop in and you are treated as a member of the family. This made it confusing for visitors trying to get to know all the names and map out the relationships, for they came and left the island freely. The indigenous population of the island varied between twenty and twenty-five.

This tiny island, a leisurely stroll round the entire shoreline only took about thirty minutes, was owned by the Methodist Church. Kanai managed it for the church as a small holiday resort, offering a relaxed and relatively primitive holiday experience quite distinct from the more commercialised tourist resorts on Viti Levu.

Each afternoon, visitors had the opportunity to learn traditional crafts such as basket weaving, making mats, carving kava cups and making brooms. The natural resources for all of these came from the palm tree. It was a pleasant way to spend time sitting in the shade of the trees, learning new skills and socialising. Snorkelling in the lagoon and walking round the island were other popular pastimes, and at 4.30pm when the afternoon work was done, the family and visitors engaged in a game of volleyball – a daily ritual. Age, like gender, was irrelevant; young and not so young, male and female, all played the game with enthusiasm and skill. Yet their competitiveness was tempered by a tolerance of the relative lack of ability and experience of their guests and this facilitated the bonding process between visitors and locals. Unfortunately, I could only watch.

I was a long way away from any doctor and the severity of the pain when any pressure was put on the leg caused me great difficulty in walking. Kanai asked me to lie down while he had a look at my leg. He examined me carefully and sensitively, then gave the boys some orders.

"I have sent the boys into the bush to gather some healing leaves for you, John. We'll wrap them round your leg for a couple of days. That should help take away some of the pain. Bush medicine. We have our own remedies." I must have looked a bit sceptical for he smiled and added, "They do work."

When the boys returned, the leaves were layered round my leg, and a bandage wrapped round them to keep them in place. Two days later it was removed. The leaves had become a soggy, green mass and my leg had a greenish tint to it. Kanai asked me to take a few steps. I did. The pain had eased; the swelling was down significantly, too. I could walk – with care, but I could walk again. I was already on the mend. I was dancing every night too after that.

The boys provided musical entertainment while we dined each evening. Bill and Scorese played guitars, Mopsje played an improvised tea-chest one-string base and harmonised in vocals with Bill. Having learned I could play spoons, Siggi emerged from the kitchen each evening when I had finished eating with a pair of dessert spoons, pulled a chair up beside the band, laid the spoons on it and gave me a knowing smile. From then on, I provided percussion.

We had dancing, too. The girls from the kitchen and some of the boys invited guests to dance, and this was where Epele demonstrated his talent. No girl ever refused to dance with him. His eight year-old sister, equally charming and always dressed beautifully for the evening entertainment, simply ignored my impediment and with big, brown eyes looked into mine and asked, "John, you dance?" She was irresistible. I danced.

Most nights we joined the family for the traditional ritual of kava drinking in a vacant dormitory. Kava is made from the root of a shrub of the pepper family, cut up into small pieces, dried in the sun and then pounded into a fine powder. This is then placed in a muslin bag in the Kava bowl, a large basin-sized bowl carved from hardwood. Water is poured in and the bag is thoroughly soaked and squeezed until the water is a muddy, greyish colour. The resulting infusion is given a good stir and a communal cup made from a half coconut shell is used to serve it.

This ritualistic activity is carried out with due observance of protocol. Everyone sat cross-legged on the floor – chairs were non-existent here, apart from those in the dining room. On occasions, when the local chief came over from Motoriki, the larger neighbouring island, he had to be served first, and he had his own cup. The communal cup was filled from the bowl and the kava was then transferred into the chief's cup and placed deferentially on a mat in front of him. It was never handed to him directly. He clapped his hands once, then lifted the cup and said, "Bula." Then he drank, accompanied by three slow handclaps from the others.

Kanai, as head of the family, came next, followed by any distinguished visitors from the other islands such as the local minister who came over on Sunday nights for an evening service. Then came the guests, after which the cup circulated round the rest of the family. Unlike the bush beer drinking on Atiu, women were not excluded from this ceremony, although they were not in attendance as often as the men. They often still had work to do: washing clothes, preparing food, putting the children to bed...

Between rounds of the drink, Kanai picked up his guitar and sang. The others joined in, often with some skilful harmonies; their musical ability was amazing. I seemed to have been accorded special status, as a sort of representative of the guests, perhaps because of my seniority. Before each song, Kanai provided a few words of introduction always beginning, "John, this is a song about..." He never mentioned any others by name, or referred to us as a group, as though referring to me somehow included all the others automatically. My accompaniment of the music on spoons was always acknowledged at the end of the song with a polite, "Thank you, John."

Kava is non-alcoholic, but it is a mild narcotic. It is said to induce a sense of relaxation. Certainly, as the evening progressed the locals became more laid back, often stretching full length on the floor as though ready to fall asleep, but always the next song had them sitting up and singing again. Some claim it has a numbing effect on the lips. It did nothing for me. Maybe I was so laid back by now that I couldn't lay back any further for I never experienced any effect at all other than the taste. As well as looking like muddy water, it tasted like it too. I noticed the chief and some of the ladies always popped a sweet into their mouths to kill the taste after each cupful. Perhaps the only effect it had on me was to ensure that I rose early each morning – it appeared to have a slight laxative effect.

With no plumbing on the islands, rainwater was gathered for cooking and washing. Several toilet cubicles were spaced around the community of huts. These were flush toilets, but you had to fill a bucket from a barrel of seawater standing outside the door and pour it into the lavatory bowl. Outside my bure I used a large clamshell as a washbasin. Soaping my body all over and pouring a bucket of water over me served as a shower. It was primitive, but quite effective. Everyone appeared clean and tidy, and the clothes the family wore were always spotlessly clean.

The islanders all had the most beautiful, pearly white teeth. Curious about this, I asked Siggi if there was anything special they ate that could account for their magnificent teeth. Aware of Fiji's notorious reputation for cannibalism until the latter half of the nineteenth century he answered with a mischievous grin, "Yes. We eat people."

Each day followed a similar pattern: toilet, breakfast, sitting in the morning sun chatting with visitors or family, snorkelling or walking round the island. But not for me with my injury. I went back to my bure and lay on the bed and read. Then came lunch, more chat, afternoon activities such as learning traditional crafts, afternoon tea, volleyball, dinner, maybe some dancing and kava. In spite of the lack of amenities, we all enjoyed the rustic simplicity of life, and I never heard anyone complain – in fact, several visitors extended their stay. I had never felt so relaxed in my life. Maybe the kava did have an effect after all.

One evening we had a sunset cruise on the lagoon. Two boats filled with visitors and several of the locals, with a few crates of beer and some kava (none of the locals drank alcohol), set off to cruise around the island and watch the sun set in a blaze of glory. The boys had their guitars and sang for us. We joined in when we could, and danced. Epele, performing on the cabin roof on one boat, presented a seductive silhouette against the setting sun, his sinuous movements eliciting cheers of appreciation from the girls.

As darkness fell we beached beside a large bonfire where a barbecue had been prepared, and sat on the beach eating dinner. The music started up again and everyone got up to dance. I tried, but it was too painful in the sand and I was forced to sit it out. However, the girls were there to comfort me. Dauni offered another leg massage while two other girls, Sherry and Fanga, lay on the sand on either side of me, stroking my hands soothingly and teasing me mercilessly, much to the merriment of the boys.

"Oh, John, my darling, will you take me back to Scotland with you?"

"No, John, ignore her and take me. I will be your wife and take care of you and massage you every night."

When I left to go to bed, the girls mischievously called out, "Don't forget, John. Leave the door of your bure open tonight and we will come and massage you later." That drew excited gasps and a few saucy comments from the boys.

I hobbled through the bushes to my bure, smiling to myself. I had earned a bit of street-cred with the lads, for although I was the oldest man on the island, I had three attractive girls in their early twenties lusting after me, wanting to stroke my body. I didn't mind the pain in my leg one little bit: every cloud has its silver lining.

In expectation of the promised pleasures of massage – and whatever else! – I washed all over with the sandalwood scented soap the shopkeeper had given me to make sure I had good sex with aunty. We'll see how this works, I thought. I shaved once more, humming the tune, *I'm in the mood for love*. I remembered to leave the door of my bure open, then I lay back on the bed, fresh and fragrant with the scent of sandalwood, in anticipation of a night of pleasure and passion.

Yeah, right!

No one came.

Chapter 18
Always The Teacher

People arrived or left the island almost every day. The five English girls – beautiful, exuberant and intelligent – had been particularly good company, and I was sad to see them go. The Danish family had already gone, and the two lads and the American girls were also now leaving. In such a short time, we had become close friends, shared in so much fun and conversation, and enjoyed a unique sense of community on that tiny island. We all assembled at the beach and exchanged hugs, and the entire family gathered to sing a farewell song to their guests. It was a moving moment; tears rolled down the girls' cheeks. As the final words of the song drifted out over the lagoon, Mopsje pulled the starting cord and the boat's engine roared into life. Everyone waved, called out their final goodbyes and the boat reversed slowly away from the beach.

Dauni stood beside me, her arm draped over my shoulder. "John, wiggle your hips now," she commanded.

In my few attempts at dancing, I had been able to stand on one spot and wiggle my hips in something like the fashion of the Cook Islands girls. This had always been greeted by whoops of delight and, as she clapped out the beat, I swung into action. The ladies all whooped in rhythm, Dubai leading and calling out, "Swing those hips baby! Whoo, Whoo, Whoo!".

The sad faces of the girls on the boat turned to laughter and they called out, too. "Yeah! Swing it John!" The engine revs picked up and they roared out into the lagoon, all laughing, waving, blowing kisses... and then they were gone.

It was a quiet and somewhat sombre lunch that day with only Alberto and me left. However, three more visitors arrived that afternoon: Aaron, from Vancouver; and, from Australia, Susie and Heather, two very attractive sisters still in their teens. Susie was about to start university; Heather still had another year at school. They were pretty quiet at first, but the island worked its magic on them, and by the time they left they were enjoying the banter and engaging in conversation freely.

Aaron and I clicked immediately. A sound engineer, he had given up work for a year to visit his girlfriend, who was nursing in Sydney. His father lived in Nadi, so he was breaking the journey for a few days in Fiji. Despite the age gap, we quickly became very close friends. He was also very popular with the islanders, who all called him endearingly, "Aa-roni."

Until he arrived, if a group of us had been sitting around talking and any of the islanders passed by, they always called out, "Morning John. Morning everyone."

Dauni, of course, had to make it more interesting by calling out, "Good morning John, my darling sweetheart. Morning everyone." This inevitably raised a few eyebrows and I was left embarrassed, shrugging my shoulders, trying to laugh it off. "Just Dauni having a wee joke," I would say. And not one of them believed it.

But Aaron had some special quality, because after a day or so the greeting had turned to, "Morning John. Morning Aa-roni. Morning everyone."

Why we should be greeted as individuals intrigued me. I observed everyone more closely. There was something distinctive about Aaron; about the way he watched, listened, and learned the skills we were taught, about the way he interacted socially with the islanders. He was quiet, respectful, empathetic. He was that special kind of person about whom you could say 'he was one of us'. It was a good place for people watching – and learning.

Apart from the girls who cooked lunch, each Sunday the islanders went over to Motoriki for the church service. It proved to be an ecumenical experience with all the visitors joining in, regardless of religious persuasion; it was all part of the experience, living as the islanders lived, sharing in their daily lives. Dressed in our Sunday-best – long trousers and clean shirt – we arrived at the opposite shore, a flat muddy beach, and had to roll up our trouser legs and wade ashore. The two Aussie girls wore pareus and hoisted them up between their legs (Nice legs too! I couldn't help noticing, even though it was Sunday. It's not a sin as long as you don't show any obvious enjoyment).

As we walked up the beach, Kanai approached me. "The visitors will be welcomed to the church, John. Will you say a few words in reply?"

"Of course," I replied, then, a touch of panic setting in, added, "But what should I say?"

"Just say what is in your heart," and he moved off to organise everyone.

The church was located just a few yards from the beach, and we all filed in and sat cross-legged on the floor. I looked around. Dark smiling faces everywhere, all dressed in spotless white shirts and dresses,

children all turning round to gaze at the pale-faced visitors. But what
was I to say? I needed inspiration. I flicked open the Bible Dubai had
passed to me, and my eye alighted on the last few verses of St Mark's
gospel, chapter 3. Jesus had been preaching to the masses and, looking
around on those who sat about him, he said, "Here are my mother and
my brothers. Whoever does the will of God is my brother and sister and
mother."

Perfect!

Such had been the warmth of the welcome we had all experienced in
Caqalai, so well had we been cared for – especially me with my injury
– that these words more than adequately described my feelings about the
people who looked after us. I felt sure that the visitors from Italy,
Canada, and Australia would concur. I was comfortable speaking to the
congregation: it was like addressing a school assembly again, and I
could see by the reaction on the faces that my words had some effect.
Eyes glowed, mouths smiled, and some heads nodded in a silent show
of acknowledgement.

When I sat down again, Susie stroked my arm gently and whispered
softly, "That was really nice, John." Heather nodded her agreement.
Aaron, seated behind me, leaned forward and whispered, "Excellent,
John. Thank you." Alberto smiled and winked. I, for my part, heaved a
sigh of relief!

When the service was over, all remained seated as the minister came
forward and led us to the door. He placed me first then all the others in
line and everyone leaving the church shook hands warmly with us as
they emerged. When the church had finally emptied, the minister came
to me and said, "You spoke very well. What do you do in Scotland?"

I explained my former status as a headmaster, and he smiled. "Ah, I
was wondering if you had been a minister. The quotation from St
Mark's gospel was so well chosen."

"Aye, it seemed appropriate," I agreed, but I reckoned it must have
been divine intervention that opened the Bible at exactly the right page.

Another boatload of visitors arrived next morning. David and Kirsten
were from New Zealand. He had just finished working on the film
soundtrack of the second of the Lord Of The Rings trilogy. An excellent
guitarist, he too joined the band, and we had some great jam sessions
with his expertise enhancing the musical fare significantly. One
afternoon, when relatives from a neighbouring island had arrived, we
played to a large audience: a circle of dark, smiling faces with dazzling
white teeth showing their appreciation.

The spoons amused the adults and fascinated the kids. With three young volunteers arranged in a row opposite me, the boys sang an old song I remembered from my childhood – *You are My Sunshine* – which was having a bit of a revival in the islands at the time. I played the spoons on the kids' knees! They loved it.

Kirsten was studying English at Wellington University. Being incapacitated, I enjoyed many hours in her company, discussing books and writing. Mark, a 37 year-old mathematics graduate from the USA, I recognised at once. He had been on Moorea when I was there. Although he had a PhD, he had forsaken academia for world travel and had taught English as a foreign language in Germany and China. He was an interesting character with a wealth of experience to share. Caqalai was proving to be a good place to be with an injured leg, my inability to engage in any physical pursuits enabling me to exploit fully the opportunities for absorbing discussion.

Markus, a handsome Swedish professional golfer working the Australian and New Zealand circuit, was taking a break with his girlfriend Anna, a lovely, blonde banker from Stockholm. Kurt from Switzerland and Eva, his East German girlfriend, had met as students at Heidelberg University. They all spoke English fluently. They proved to be not only charming company, they were thoughtful, and impressed me greatly, but it was Eva who excited my admiration most.

Having grown up in East Germany, Russian was the only foreign language she had studied at school. She had learned her first words of English only twelve weeks previously at the English Language School in Auckland, yet now she was speaking the language with an astonishing vocabulary and familiarity with idiom. The very embodiment of determination, she had totally immersed herself in the language; she spoke only English, even with Kurt, refused even to think in German, and she now read only books written in English. She was the perfect student, stopping me to ask for an explanation of any unfamiliar word, phrase or colloquialism I may have used, repeating it and examining other words or phrases of similar meaning so she had some context within which to place it. I could only gaze in rapt admiration. This girl was every teacher's dream.

It made me feel shame at the little German I could speak after nearly six years in that country, even though it had been thirty years previously. I could never sustain a conversation for any length of time or to any depth in German, yet all four of these Europeans were able to engage me for hours in serious, analytical discussions on a wide range of issues. My current lifestyle was regarded with some envy; they thought it close to perfection, apart from my single status. Even they thought I should have a soulmate. I still had mixed feelings about that. Each mealtime was like leading a tutorial with a group of bright students thirsting for knowledge, probing the mind of their tutor and his experience of the world, devouring, digesting and debating his words and thoughts. I enjoyed that immensely, as I had always revelled in tutorials, the sharing of ideas and experience leading to better understanding and mutual respect.

On the day Kurt and Eva were leaving the island, the boat had been delayed, and I had gone back to my bure to escape the blistering heat of the sun and fallen asleep. I awoke an hour or so later, annoyed with myself, realising that by now they had probably gone and I hadn't been there to see them off. I went outside to wash my face in the clamshell.

"John! John!" I turned round and there was Eva running through the palms towards me, her arms outstretched, Kurt following in her wake.

"I've been looking everywhere for you, John. The boat is waiting, but I couldn't leave without saying goodbye to you." She threw her arms round me and gave me a lingering hug, murmuring in my ear, "John, you have taught me so much and shared so much of your experience with me and it has been wonderful to meet you. I hope you will find the happiness you deserve and someone special to share it with."

I was quite taken aback, humbled. "It has been a delight to meet you too, Eva. You are an amazing student, an example to us all. And you're no' a bad lad either, Kurt," I growled and shook his hand warmly.

"We'll never forget you, John," he said warmly.

Eva wiped away a tear and murmured softly, "Goodbye John." And they both ran back to the boat.

I sat on the beach for a while with the sadness that followed their departure, looking out over the lagoon's tranquil water shimmering in the mid-day sun. What magic this island had conjured up. What interesting people it had brought into my life, people with whom I had shared so much illuminating discussion. In these simple surroundings I was still learning. And they, too, had shown me that I was still a teacher, capable of inspiring and enabling young people.

Teaching is more than an occupation. It is truly a vocation, inescapably a way of life. The mantle of the teacher is more than a garment to be worn as the occasion demands: like a skin, it may grow, develop according to the environment, but it can never be shed.

Chapter 19
Cupid At Work On Caqalai

Sherry gave me lessons in the Fijian language. She was well spoken, possessed a degree in hospitality management, and was very intelligent, a fact that shone through her beautiful, captivating eyes. A friend of Dauni's, she was spending a few weeks on the island to help out and offer staff training. A modern, independent sort of girl with a good education and high-level interpersonal skills, she didn't seem to me to be the kind who would be content to settle for the traditional way of life, so I asked if, being in the tourism industry, she had any notions for travel herself.

"Oh, yes, I would like to travel the world, to see other places and meet people from different countries and cultures."

"Well, if you ever consider coming to Scotland, I can promise you a good welcome," I assured her, thinking I was doing my bit for Scottish tourism. She looked on it differently.

"I would love to come to Scotland," she muttered longingly. " I could take care of you and be your wife." Why did everyone want to be my wife? Why couldn't they just satiate their carnal desires with me and set me free again?

"Och, you girls should stop teasing me," I chided softly.

"We're not teasing," she murmured quietly. I looked at her. Her face told me she meant it.

"But I have so much more travelling to do. I'm restless, and I don't know when I'll ever settle down. And I'm so much older than you."

"Age doesn't matter," she countered. "And you need a woman to look after you." Did I really look so helpless?

"Mmm, maybe... but maybe not just yet."

That afternoon, some relatives came over from a neighbouring island, and Dubai insisted that I come and sit with them in the shade of the trees. The only guest to receive such an invitation, I felt privileged as she introduced me to her relatives and friends. They regarded me politely, but with much curiosity, and expressed their delight that I had travelled half way round the world to visit this little island. Inevitably, the questions became more personal; my single status had become an unavoidable topic of conversation by now. They simply found it incomprehensible that I could exist without having a woman to look after me.

"Do you have no one to take care of you?" asked one of the men incredulously.

"No."

"Oh, you need a wife. That woman over there is available. She would make a good wife for you. She is a teacher, too. Why don't you marry her?" That brought a chorus of approval from the others. The woman in question, a very pleasant looking middle-aged lady, smiled at me modestly through lowered eyelids.

I bowed my head slightly in acknowledgement of the honour that I should be accorded such esteem as to be deemed so desirable as to be offered yet another proposal of marriage – my fourth no less! I had started counting them by this time, my humility having been rapidly overwhelmed by the unavoidable recognition that the Fijians were such good judges of character as to regard me as a significant prize. But humility fought back and regained supremacy. This was a time to exercise the arts of old-fashioned, gentlemanly diplomacy.

"I am sure that such a charming lady must have a queue of far more attractive suitors to chose from. Perhaps an old man like me would only prove to be a bit of a disappointment."

"How old are you?" the man asked. That allowed the conversation to change to safer ground. I had successfully diverted the talk away from matrimony.

"How old are you?" It was always one of the first questions the kids asked every visitor. They were fascinated by age. Our ages were then often used as an appendage when they were rehearsing our names, as they often did when we sat round the table: "Aa-roni, twenty-seven; Alberto, forty-four; Anna, twenty-four; Markoos, twenty-nine; John – seexty!" The way they said it, I might have been Methuselah!

The next question was always, "When is your birthday?" As it happened, my birthday was on the following Monday, so they practised, "John, Seex-one, Seexty-one!" They laughed.

"Hey, cool off. I don't feel that old! I only feel like John one-six."

"John, one-seex? Seexteen? Ha Ha Ha!" And they all fell about laughing again. It wasn't meant to be *that* funny.

I have never been one for celebrating birthdays. It had always been just another day, not a milestone of any significance, a mere reference point in relation to the date when, released from the burden of professional responsibilities, I could live the life of a world-wide wanderer; a piece of human flotsam on the oceans of the world, carried where the tide of fortune would take me. I gave it no more thought.

The kids had other ideas. On Monday evening, as dinner drew to a close, the islanders appeared, all beautifully dressed, wearing flowers in their hair. The kitchen door opened and Siggi, with his usual dazzling, cannibal-inspired smile, came forward bearing a platter with a birthday cake and a large knife. The boys in the band struck a chord and the entire assembly broke into song with an endearing rendition of the eternal 'Happy Birthday to You'. The cake was laid before me, and on it was written: JOHN – HAPPY BIRTHDAY – SWEET 16!

I said a few words thanking them for their kindness, then the music started and we all danced. We played some silly games where we had to dance with balloons between our bodies or transfer oranges held under our chins from one to the other, and of course I had to "Swing those hips, baby!" It was all good fun. But two were missing. Sherry had a day off to visit the mainland, and Dauni was also nowhere to be seen. I wondered if I had offended her.

But I still had Fanga to dance with. Fanga managed the accounts. A tall, slim girl of Polynesian descent – the others were predominantly Melanesian – she moved with the elegant, feline grace of a panther, and when dancing demonstrated the easy flow of rhythmic sensuality accompanied by a steady, serene smile that was characteristic of her race. Apart from dancing, we spent some time talking. She was a really nice, gentle girl; quieter, more subtle than the others, but with a hint of a mischievous smile. She asked me where I had learned to dance "like that". I explained my enjoyment of Polynesian culture, especially dance, and how I had learned a little in the Cook Islands. She listened politely, then with a sideways look and a smile murmured, "You dance very well." Then quite suddenly she asked, "What kind of soap do you use?"

I was taken aback. "Why do you ask that?" I had a quick sniff at my armpits. "Is something wrong?"

She laughed. "Oh no! You smell very nice. I just wondered what kind of soap you use. It smells like sandalwood." Of course! It was the soap the shopkeeper had given me to make sure I had good sex with aunty. Maybe it was working some magic after all.

"Ah, there is a story attached to that," I muttered and told her of the shopkeeper offering me her aunty. She howled with laughter. But she didn't ask me to marry her!

The following day, Sherry returned to the island, and after lunch she and Dauni joined me. Sherry asked if I had enjoyed the party. I expressed my sorrow that she had been unable to attend, and also that Dauni had stayed away. Dauni immediately apologised explaining that with Sherry being away all day she had all the cooking to do by herself and had fallen asleep after preparing dinner.

"You fell asleep? How could you fall asleep knowing that your darling sweetheart's birthday party was due?" I asked, incredulously. "Oh, well, now I really know how little I mean to you?"

"Oh, that's unfair! Who do you think stood for hours lovingly baking that cake for you? It's no wonder I felt tired." Her protest shamed me. It was time for some old-fashioned gentlemanly diplomacy again. I bent down on one knee and kissed the back of her hand.

"Please forgive me for being so insensitive. I would like to thank you, sincerely."

She smiled graciously. "I accept your apology."

I changed to safer topics of conversation, and asked them for the name of a CD which they often played in the kitchen as they worked. It contained many of the songs sung by the boys at dinner. "I would like to buy a copy so that when I go back to Scotland I can play it to remind me of Fiji," I said.

"It would be better if you would take a Fijian wife home with you, then you wouldn't need to be reminded of Fiji," Dauni retorted. These girls don't give up easily.

"But how do I chose between two such attractive girls?" I protested.

"Simple," she said. "Just pick one." I looked at the two dark, smiling faces with flashing eyes. If only it were that simple.

There was no escaping the fact that marriage was in the air. Paul and Sheryl, a young English couple who arrived shortly before Christmas, will remember Caqalai for the rest of their lives. It was there on the beach early on Christmas morning before Sheryl had risen that Paul scratched out a message in the sand in the Fijian language. He had involved me in his plan as his consultant, knowing that Sherry had taught me some of the most important words and phrases. When Sheryl rose and came out for an early morning swim she looked at the message in bewilderment. "What does it say?"

Paul took her hand and got down on one knee. "It says, 'I love you. Will you be my wife?'"

Tears of joy filled her eyes, and she threw her arms around him. "Oh yes! I will."

Sherry's teaching had proved effective, even if not quite in the way she had planned, but Cupid had found work on Caqalai at last – and he wasn't finished yet.

After dinner, everyone met for the kava drinking ceremony. As people went off to bed and the crowd thinned out I noticed Susie gradually moving closer to Ben, one of the local boys, who was sitting in a corner grinding kava with mortar and pestle. With his good looks and dazzling rakish, smile I reckoned things were looking promising for him. Then I too went off to bed.

Now before I left Scotland, I had visited an old friend – my former doctor, now retired – who had worked in Fiji for some years. Aware of the possibility of picking up some tropical disease I knew he could give me expert advice based on first hand experience.

"Stewart, I'm going to Fiji. What are the most likely health risks, and what can I do for protection?"

His reply took me by surprise.

"Gonorrhoea. And you know what the protection against that is."

"Abstinence?"

"That's not what I had in mind," he retorted.

"Well, bearing in mind my age and track record, I wouldn't have thought that likely," I protested.

"Don't be so sure. Age is irrelevant. The cultural attitudes to sex are very different there. You may not go out looking for it, but it may well come looking for you, and you might find it hard to resist. Take a supply of condoms anyway."

So I did, just in case I might be overpowered some dark night by a lusty maiden who wouldn't take no for an answer. However, the condoms were still lying unused in my backpack, and it didn't look as though they would be needed, but Cupid still had some magic to conjure up that night.

I had fallen asleep quickly, and was deep in slumber when I was startled by a voice breaking through the barrier of sleep; a loud whisper calling, "John. John. Wake up!"

Through the haze of my mosquito net I could just make out a dark human form silhouetted against the slightly lighter darkness of the open doorway: ever the optimist, I was still remembering to leave the door of my bure open at night. Was this my luck changing at last? Who could it be? Dauni? Sherry? Fanga? I fumbled under my pillow for my small torch and flicked the switch. My fantasy dissipated with the speed of light. It was only Ben, naked except for a skimpy pair of briefs.

"What's the matter?" I mumbled.

"John, could you give me a condom?" he hissed.

"Eh? Och aye, sure," I muttered. I reached for my backpack, ripped open the 'virgin' pack of prophylactics, pulled one out, and passed it to him.

"Thanks John." And without another word he sprinted off into the darkness.

I lay back on my bed and began to laugh, remembering Stewart's words. I'd carried those condoms half way round the world, half-hoping (well, okay – 100% hoping) that I might share some torrid nights of passion with a nubile, sun-bronzed maiden under the swaying palms of an idyllic Pacific island, and here I was supplying a testosterone-laden young buck from Fiji with the means of satiating the erotic desires of the nubile maidenhood of Australia.

NOT quite as Stewart had predicted.

Then I suddenly became intrigued. Why had Ben come to *me* for one? The young guys were surely a more likely prospect. Maybe I had a bit of street-cred here, right enough. It's all about perception – not so much what you do as what people imagine you to have done. But I had done nothing. Teasing was all I got! I stopped laughing and began to bash my head in anguish against the pillow. Why should the young ones have all the fun?

I wasn't too old!

Chapter 20
Maybe Some Day

It was quite unlike any other Christmas. The entire population of the island, two boat-loads of relatives who had come from neighbouring islands to spend a few days, and all the visitors assembled in the dorm for a church service on Christmas morning. A minister had come over from the mainland; he was a rotund, jovial fellow who spoke with such sincerity and conviction that, even though it was all in a foreign tongue, it was impossible not to feel a sense of inspiration in his message.

When his sermon was over, Dubai indicated to me that I was expected to speak. Again, whatever I said appeared to be well-received, and at the end of the service several of the islanders came to me to thank me for my words, both Sherry and Dauni hugged me warmly, and the minister engaged me in conversation for quite some time afterwards.

A feast was served in the dining area. Roast pork, chicken, tuna, shark, barracuda, and all sorts of fruit and vegetables were laid out for almost fifty people. How the women had worked this miracle quietly and unobtrusively with such limited facilities over the last few days defied understanding. It was a feast fit for a king. Visitors and relatives were served first. The island women worked in the kitchen while Kanai and the boys served the food. Only after we had eaten our fill would they sit down and eat.

Afterwards we all drifted off for a siesta or a leisurely swim. I lay on my back in the warm, shallow water, reflecting on how different Christmas would be in Lochcarron. At that moment, inhabitants there would all still be asleep, with perhaps a smattering of snow silently falling outside, clothing all the trees in crisp snow, making them glitter against the night sky – well, more likely it would be raining! Snow, in this warm, gentle part of the world, was an unknown weather phenomenon, yet they still embraced all the traditions of a European Christmas, decking the dining room with a tree and lights and decorations. The kitchen girls wore red Santa Claus hats trimmed with white fur and worked happily at their labours, singing and dancing to the sound of Christmas carols. It all seemed rather incongruous.

I had no regrets about being away from home at Christmas; the cynical commercial exploitation, the expectations seldom matched by reality, the wasteful expenditure lavished on presents, many of which would soon discarded... all of that annoyed me. These people had little more than a roof over their heads, shared a room with three of four other people, owned few personal possessions, yet they gave so much – not in any material sense, but in friendship and hospitality.

I once asked Sherry why, with so little, everyone seemed so happy on this island. "We have no need of material things," she replied. "We live with God."

And that they did, for entire family assembled each morning and evening for prayers, led by Kanai. The sound of hymns, sung with passion, could be heard drifting through the trees from their quarters.

We regard Christmas as a time for families to be together; that's fine and as it should be. But, for me, there was an immense void caused by the death of my wife. We were not all together as a family, and never would be again. The premature death of wife, mother, and now grandmother, had denied her the opportunity to see her grandchildren growing up. And for me, Christmas with the family seemed to only emphasise that sense of loss. I had found it had become a depressing time of year, and I wanted to be away from it all.

What was so refreshing for me now was to be with people I had only met a few days previously; and, in our self-chosen exile, we had been drawn together in a genuine spirit of goodwill. There wasn't a shop in sight, no TV with glitzy, packaged, self-proclaimed merriment, no radio, no newspapers, no rain, no snow, no biting frost, no burst water pipes... The spirit of Christmas with its plea for goodwill towards all men (and women, mustn't be sexist!), was evident in the example of the islanders who had embraced us with such affection. Its message of hope for the future lay in the potential of these bright, cheerful, young travellers who had filled me with optimism. I had no regrets about being here. It had been an uplifting experience.

My leg had gradually been improving. Most of the pain and swelling had subsided and, although still unable to raise my heel, I was able to hobble along with a flat-footed, limping gait. The time had now come for me to leave the island. After dinner on my last night, the boys sang all the usual songs, but the final one was special, moving, haunting, as in harmony they sang, "I'm going back to my homeland, maybe some day I'll come back again...".

Yes, maybe some day I would come back to this island paradise now so indelibly fixed in my memory.

Alberto, Paul and Sheryl, and the portly minister were also leaving in the morning. The whole family and all the visiting relatives turned out to say farewell. Their departure song in Fijian, so often heard before, was never so moving as then. By the time they finished I was struggling with my emotions. Kanai and the boys all filed past, shaking hands with me and muttering quiet, sad farewells. Dubai, my Fijian 'mother' and all the ladies followed and hugged me.

As Dauni held me close, she whispered in my ear, "Please come back, John."

"Aye, I will," I murmured.

I climbed on to the boat and Kanai fired up the engine. Everyone ashore started waving and I waved back. Tears began to roll down my cheek. Then Dubai did it again.

"Hey, John! Swing those hips, baby!"

She started clapping her hands and whooping and the others all joined in. I got the arms going, the body snaking sensuously, the hips made like a washing machine, and a great cheer broke out ashore.

Dubai called out to Kanai and he turned back. She had forgotten something. As the boat went in close she ran into the water with a bucket and a bag of flour, tipped the flour over the minister's head and then poured half a bucket of sea water over him. Everyone erupted in fits of laughter. The poor man looked like a snowman, but took it all in good part. Can you imagine that happening to a minister in Scotland?

As we turned out again she started the clapping and whooping once more, "Swing it John, swing those hips baby!" And I was into the aerobics again. About 100 metres out I stopped. The boat was called back in again.

"What is it this time?" I asked Kanai.

He grinned. "They want you to do another encore."

I swung those hips once more, and this time we were finally allowed to leave. They stood there on the beach, all waving, diminishing in size, never stopping until we moved round the island and they were at last out of sight.

As we left Caqalai behind, a heavy shower of rain swept across the lagoon, obliterating the island from view. A curtain had at last been drawn on that idyllic stage on which so many dramas had been enacted, on which romance had flourished and, for some, had blossomed.

Not for me though. I was still single. And celibate. But I could still hear the voices of Mopsje and Bill, harmonising sweetly in their song, 'Maybe some day, I'll come back again.'

Chapter 21
Melbourne

After life on a Fijian island with a population of twenty-five, Melbourne was a bit of a shock to the system. I gazed at tall buildings and wide streets thronging with people, shops, trams, buses. I was back in the 21st century and not too comfortable with it.

I caught a tram to the youth hostel, bought some food, had supper and went to bed longing for the soft lapping of the waves outside my door, the gentle glow of an oil lamp, and the rustle of the breeze among the palms. I needed a few days to acclimatise.

I'm not a city person, but Melbourne is not too bad, and I tolerated it for a couple of days. Its compact downtown area is more suggestive of the intimacy of a big town rather than a city with the colourful Victoria Market bustling with people, bright shop fronts, well tended gardens along the river side and restaurants to match the tastes of the cosmopolitan mix of people on its streets. Each evening I dined out, sitting at a table on the pavement watching the world walk past; Orientals, small in stature, but so neatly proportioned, bulky Australians, Asians, Europeans, but not a single aboriginal did I see anywhere in the state of Victoria. Melbourne has a 'British' feel to it. There's even a Scots' Kirk. After attending the church service there I was invited to the hall for a cup of tea.

"Where in Scotland are you from?" asked the lady who served me.

"Och, you'll probably never have heard of it. I live a wee village in the highlands called Lochcarron."

"Oh, I've heard of it alright," she replied. "My great grandparents were married in Lochcarron Church. Hey Willie," she called to her husband, "come and meet John. He's from Lochcarron." And so I was welcomed into the brotherhood of the kirk.

Melbourne's eclectic architecture intrigued me. A sprinkling of venerable late 19th and early 20th century buildings sits amongst a mix of pre-war art deco, post-war austere functional and more elegant tower blocks of the late 20th century. A mere infant compared to European cities, it is a thrusting upstart, challenging concepts of visual harmony and style. A walk through the rectangular array of streets in the city centre led me to the river from where this jumble of structures can best be viewed.

There, on the riverbank, was the most arresting sight of all. The Victoria National Art Gallery. It is, frankly, provocative. A bizarre, angular building, its exterior appearance was initially shocking. It looked like something knocked up by ham-fisted navvies working without a square or plumb line from the reconstituted sections of the hull of a battleship painted in the grotesque grey, blue and black hues of wartime camouflage. Yet inside, it was marvellous. I'm not much of an art gallery person, but this one offered an absorbing selection of works of art, and its recognition of the work of living artists was commendable. I found the work of the aboriginal painters and sculptors particularly captivating.

I sat outside later, having a drink in the sunshine, and looked askance at this weird building. Words such as 'beautiful', 'elegant', or 'graceful' were not coined for this mishmash. What kind of a mind could have conceived such a creation? What kind of statement was the architect trying to make – and why?

I recalled then a conversation with a former pupil, now an art teacher, who was appalled at my lack of appreciation of art: "Think of a work of art as a statement. To understand it, as with reading a book, requires participation, some effort on your part. You have to open a book, read and think about what you have read; and it may take several hours to appreciate what the author is trying to say. Give the same consideration to a painting or sculpture. Stand back and let your mind work on it."

So I did. I gazed at this building in wonder and the more I gazed, the more the wonder grew. It was like looking at a woman whose wildly eccentric appearance may not conform to conventional concepts of physical beauty yet, as your acquaintance grows, you come to realise she has a caring nature, a captivating smile and an interesting personality; that her outward appearance, in contrast to her subtle inner beauty, is challenging your preconceptions, compelling your curiosity to look beyond the superficial and find the essence of the real being, and is asking you to examine your own sense of who you are.

As I sat there, cogitating, it dawned on me that I was having an educational experience. This building was making me think, making me examine myself, and my attitudes – and was this, after all, not partly why I was travelling the world? As a teacher, I had tried to encourage my students to think critically, examine perceived wisdom, be prepared to step outside the known parameters, challenge the status quo. I actually found myself beginning to like this remarkable structure as it worked its magic on me. It has left its imprint in my memory as the most enduring image of Melbourne. It didn't generate the instant emotional response of the Sydney Opera House – surely the most remarkable piece of architecture of the 20th century – but I have no doubt that the building will establish itself as another Australian architectural icon. It seemed an appropriate metaphor for that sometimes shocking but nevertheless endearing characteristic of the Aussies: they just don't give a damn for convention.

Sitting there, watching the people stroll by, you could see it in the way they dressed – especially the men. I became quite absorbed by it all. I don't know what they feed on, but there are a lot of big guys in Australia. By comparison, I felt quite undernourished and scrawny. They were not just tall, but big-boned and bulky, tending towards being overweight, heavy limbed and cumbersome. Many of them don't enhance their appearance by the way they dress: almost uniformly, it seems, they sported baseball caps, shorts that drooped to well below knee level, and sleeveless T shirts that exposed armpits that were hairier than a wombat's belly.

This unparalleled display of sartorial inelegance was complemented by what I began to recognise as the Victoria Walk, a peculiar amble characteristic of the male of the species *Homo Sapiens Victoriae*. They accentuate their glaikitness (a most aptly descriptive Scottish word) by slouching. The shoulders droop slightly forward (never a good old-fashioned square set of shoulders in sight here), arms hang like redundant appendages from their sockets, the hands dangle with knuckles facing forwards, open palmed with the fingers hanging limply and as uselessly as the rest of the arm. Imagine a man nailed to the wall and hanging from a point somewhere between the shoulder blades forcing everything to droop and sag forward, and you have the picture.

And the legs get only marginally more deployment than the arms. When walking, the feet aren't lifted off the ground, as the rest of the world walks, rising on ball of the foot, swinging the foot forward, then heel down. Here the foot is merely raised a few millimetres, dragged forward and scuffed down again in flat-footed fashion. It presents a most un-athletic, unintelligent looking, knuckle-dragging aspect – and this in a land renowned for its worship of sport.

Had this only been observed among spotty-faced adolescents, I would have thought nothing of it, but here it was characteristic of all ages. This struck me as strange in such a fine city where I would have expected to see some slick dressing: but this is Australia, where things happen that don't elsewhere. Not everyone looked like this, of course.

There were exceptions. They were probably visitors.

However, as with the Art Gallery, the visual aspect camouflaged much of what lay behind the façade. It was hard not to like the Australians. They displayed warmth and rough-hewn friendliness, and have a propensity in conversation for conjuring up the most delightfully colourful and descriptive phrases. Like the Americans, they have adapted the English language and shaped it to reflect their own image: brash, colourful, larger than life, and downright irreverent.

The bus drivers all used PA systems to keep travellers informed, but with some friendly wisecracking as well: "Welcome aboard ladies and gentlemen. Are you all happy this morning?" Now wasn't that nice?

"Yes!" we all called back.

"Good. Well, you lot sound a helluva lot cheerier then the shower of miserable bastards I had on board yesterday." I almost choked. He would have been sacked for that in the UK.

Another example of this 'irreverence' came one hot day when I was, along with another backpacker, waiting at a bar for a drink to be poured. A local red-neck, with a Crocodile Dundee-style hat, came up to the bar and, without the courtesy of waiting his turn, called out to the barmaid, "Pour me a Foster's, Sue."

The barmaid raised her eyes from the pump and retorted, "You'll have to wait till I've finished serving these two gentlemen."

He turned. A pair of ice-blue eyes set in a wrinkled, tanned-leather face regarded us with some bemusement. "Gentlemen? In this bloody place? They must be lost."

And at a New Year's Day race meeting, the commentator announced over the PA system, in that characteristically tense, earnest voice reserved for the line-up at the start: "They're all in now and they're under starter's orders..." Then, as the horses burst from the traps, he exuberantly proclaimed, "And it's Royal Flush in the lead! Jeez, he's off faster than a bride's nightie!" Then towards the end of the race, when the horse was coming down the home straight so far ahead of the rest of the field that there was nothing left to comment on, "And with one furlong to go, it's Royal Flush ahead by ten lengths – so if you put your money on him, you might as well go the bar now and celebrate."

I had little interest in the races, but I loved the commentary.

Cities can be among the loneliest places on earth as people go about their own business ignoring each other, and Melbourne suffers from this as much as anywhere else. No cheery greetings of "Bula" or "Kia Orana" from complete strangers here. Even in the hostel the attitudes were different. It was a different class of people. The Australian cricket team was in the process of humiliating – yet again! – the England cricket team, and the hostel was filled with supporters of each side. One of the sad trends in this peculiar game, a sport once reputedly synonymous with gentlemanly behaviour (I can't speak with any authority on this, never having attained the status of either a gentleman or a cricketer), has been the increase in loutish behaviour on and of the field.

Now why anyone should wish even to cross the road to view anything so unspeakably dull as a cricket match is beyond my comprehension, yet here were hordes of beer-bellied, loud-mouthed Englishmen – appropriately labelled the Barmy Army – who had travelled half-way round the world to watch their team receive a drubbing from more beer-bellied, loud-mouthed Aussies masquerading as cricketers. Crude verbal exchanges between at least one Aussie player and the Barmy Army had reached such a pitch in Melbourne that it was rated the most important news item on TV and in the newspapers. Maybe it would have been overlooked in Sydney where such behaviour is normal, but Melbourne is perhaps the most genteel of all Australian cities.

I had never seen or heard anyone, of any nationality, behave offensively in a hostel until now. The loutish, foul-mouthed behaviour continued even there. I was incensed by one guy leaning back on a chair with his feet, in grubby sweat-stained trainers, resting on a table used for dining. I decided to try telepathy first to see if I could alter his behaviour – I had used it so often as a teacher. I fixed my eye on him and concentrated hard. Somehow it caught his attention. My eye moved marginally and focused on his feet. A few seconds later, the feet came off the table. Really, it works! These guys weren't threatening anyone – they were just boorish.

Sleeping opposite me in the dorm was one grossly overweight, shaven headed, beer-swilling, amorphous mass who, after drowning his sorrows each night with the lads (and a game of cricket goes on for at least three days, so he had plenty of sorrows to drown), grunted, snorted, sniffled, dribbled, belched and farted continuously in his sleep. Having expelled all residual bodily gases and juices through his various orifices, on wakening he was actually quite pleasant.

The other backpackers were coolly polite, but made it clear that they had their own agenda and mixing with a stranger wasn't on it. The only guy who was prepared to engage in conversation was Harry, a genial seventy eight year-old Queenslander, who told me he came over to Melbourne for three weeks every year in the height of summer to escape the oppressive humidity in Brisbane. It seemed odd to me that he should want to exchange one large city for another for three weeks. Why not go to a pleasant, airy seaside resort? Did he have friends or relatives in the area to visit?

"No. I don't know anyone here. I buy one of these runabout tickets for the transport system. They're great value. You can use them on the trams, buses or trains and go anywhere within the city transport limits. So every day I take a tram to the station, jump on a train or bus and see where it takes me, have some lunch and take the train or bus back. Most days I have no idea where I am going, but I get all over the city that way and see the suburbs."

Now that was an attraction that had escaped my notice!

He continued: "Even found myself right out at Applecross Beach the other day. Beautiful it was; and I had an ice cream there. Then I managed to get a train that took a different route back to Pitt Street, so that was a bonus. I had a great time. You should try it."

And he was serious. Now I enjoy travelling by rail, but the prospect of sitting all day in a train watching the back yards of the suburbs of Melbourne flash past for three whole weeks, was not high on my list of priorities. However, it was interesting enough for Harry to come back each year for more. It seemed absurd to me, but he enjoyed himself and that's what mattered. He was a real gentleman.

Two days in Melbourne was enough for me, so I took a train to Warragul, a small town about sixty miles to the southeast of the city to visit Helen, a girl I had taught in Germany. We had become re-acquainted through the Internet, and on learning that I planned a visit to Oz, she had insisted that I call on her. I hadn't seen her since 1972.

And on the way there I saw the suburbs of Melbourne from the train. Harry would have been pleased.

Chapter 22
The Victorians

"Mr McMillan!" Helen's cry greeted me as I stepped out of the railway station. She hugged me warmly. I had wondered how this reunion with an ex-pupil from thirty years ago would work out, but based on our email correspondence, I felt optimistic. Of the thousands of pupils a teacher encounters, some are remembered for their outstanding ability, some for mischievous behaviour and others because of their lively personality. Helen was in the latter category: vivacious, effervescent and chatty, she was a girl who always managed to get the last word. Now in her mid-forties, she hadn't changed in that respect.

The time lapse since we'd last swapped banter was irrelevant. We took up again as though it had been yesterday, and three decades of gossip consumed the next three days. Her husband, Graeme, with his cheerful and jocular manner, ensured that there was no discomfort in fitting into this household.

Helen was the first of three ex-pupils I had been invited to visit. I had never regarded this as odd, yet so many people I had met on my travels had expressed surprise.

"You mean an ex-pupil actually wants to see you again? Can't think of any of my old teachers I would invite to stay with me."

Living in small communities in Scotland, I was accustomed to meeting pupils and ex-pupils socially. Some had invited me to their weddings, and in later years I taught their children too. It hadn't appeared odd to me that I should be invited to stay with others on my travels, and I was looking forward immensely to meeting up later with Andrew in Sydney and Cecily in Queensland.

But first, my plan was to explore the state of Victoria and do some diving. Graeme and Helen offered me the use of their twenty year-old Volvo, as this would offer much more flexibility than the limited public transport system. The car had automatic transmission, so my injured leg would have no work to do, and I accepted their offer with gratitude.

Much of Victoria's rural landscape is similar to that of the UK, with cattle and horses grazing in fields fringed by hedgerows. I was on my way to Sorrento, one of the many holiday resorts along the coast of Port

Philip Bay, Melbourne's summer playground. Now, at the height of the school holidays, it was jam-packed with holidaymakers, most of whom flocked into the campsites bordering the shoreline. In my youth, camping was something you did when hiking among the hills or kayaking, finding a spot by a stream where you could pitch a small tent for the night and cook a simple dinner over a fire or on a stove. This was different, a strip of coastline on which thousands had descended like locusts. It was clothed with caravans, chalets, tents, cars, bicycles and trucks, all within touching distance of each other. So grossly overcrowded were these campsites, they would have been condemned as a breach of human rights had they been refugee camps. In a peculiar way, the absurdity of it all appealed to me. It was a reversal of what I thought was the essence of camping: peace and quiet to commune with nature, some personal space, and privacy from the maddening crowd.

Here was population density on a third world scale, and most of it had come from Melbourne, just an hour's drive up the road, where they had air-conditioned bungalows with a quarter acre of leafy land around them offering at least a measure of privacy. Yet they swapped all that for concentration camp conditions, with their neighbours literally within arm's reach. It just shows how sociable the Australians are.

This was not my ideal sort of place, but I'd heard the diving was good and booked a diving trip at Portsea, a village at the mouth of the bay. They are quite proud to tell you that it was here in 1967 that Harold Holt, the Australian Prime Minister at the time, rashly plunged into the sea for a swim and a few seconds later disappeared abruptly within yards of the shore. Maybe it was a shark that took him, maybe he just got sucked under by one of the notorious tide-rips that are common here, but no trace of him was ever found. They built a fitting memorial to him in Melbourne: a swimming pool. The Aussies have a black sense of humour.

The area just outside this almost landlocked bay is littered with wrecks, but with spring tides and a fresh breeze whipping up a lively sea, diving there was ruled out so we dived within the more sheltered water of Port Philip Bay. Even there we could only dive at slack water, as the tidal currents are very strong. After the tropical temperatures of the seas around the Cook Islands and Fiji I had expected the south coast of Australia to be a bit cooler – but this was as cold as the sea in Scotland. Even wearing a thick wet suit I was gasping. However, the body soon acclimatised, and I was rewarded with the exploration of some surprisingly colourful sponge gardens.

However, the best bit was swimming with a pack of seals. Before we entered the water the skipper told us, "Don't be afraid. They like company. When you get in the water just behave as if you were bloody daft – that shouldn't be too much of a problem for you lot. Spin yourself around, dive, turn somersaults, blow bubbles and you'll find they'll imitate your actions. And just a word of warning to those of you who've already pissed in your wet suit – bull seals are sexually aroused by the scent of urine. There's no point in trying to deny it, we'll soon see who you are." No amorous approaches were made to me. Honest.

Basking on a man-made structure in the bay, the seals' curiosity was intense as we prepared to enter the water. As we approached, they plunged in too, diving with us, holding themselves suspended vertically, tail up, and peering at us with endearingly beautiful eyes, spiralling around us with joyful exuberance. They were as playful as puppies. It was a delightful experience.

That evening I received an email from Cecily. Her son and daughter from her first marriage, both in their late teens, were living just a few miles away with their father and she was really keen that they should meet me. I agreed to meet them next morning and then have lunch with them. I was delighted that Cecily should want to meet me again, but that she should be so keen that her offspring, now young adults, should also meet me, really enhanced the compliment.

I wondered how they would feel about this: two teenagers having been cajoled by a mother into meeting her old teacher didn't sound like the ideal recipe for a fun outing for them. I needn't have worried. I felt instantly at ease in their company, and the conversation never flagged. At one point I had turned from speaking to Adam to face Tobi and gasped. Her elbow rested on the table, her chin was cupped in her hand as she listened, her eyes intent on me. It was the eyes that gripped me: they were the eyes of her mother thirty years ago. On leaving, Adam shook my hand and said, "I can see why Mum thinks the world of you."

The ferry took me across Port Philip Bay to Queenscliff where I took the coast road southwards. Just inland from here is Winchelsea, a small town of no importance, except that it was here in 1859 that a man called Thomas Austin decided that having a few rabbits about the place to shoot at in the evening would improve the quality of life immeasurably. So he imported twenty-four rabbits from England and released them into the bush. Now rabbits seem to exist to do only two things: eat and reproduce – both of which they generally pursue with considerable enthusiasm and success. Australia, having been isolated from the rest of the world for many millions of years, didn't have a single predator that recognised a rabbit as part of the food chain, so the rabbits lived happily ever after, and went forth and multiplied... and multiplied... and...

And thus it was that in twenty years of chomping merrily on the local herbage, the entire state of Victoria had been picked clean, leaving little fodder for the sheep or cattle. The rabbits hopped happily on into New South Wales and South Australia and beyond, and, like furry locusts, devoured everything in their path. In the 1950s, after almost a hundred years of devastation, myxomatosis was introduced from South America as the solution to the problem. Although only about one rabbit in every thousand survived, they were the ones with a natural resistance to the disease and re-established a population of rabbits for whom the disease was no longer a threat – and now there are millions of them again. It is one of the world's great ecological disasters... and all the result of the monumental folly of one man.

I wanted to be near the sea, and so I took the road south – the Great Ocean Road, one of Australia's most scenic routes. Lorne, a small holiday resort with a beautiful golden sandy bay, nestling snugly against some steep wooded hills was my destination. The hostel was a series of chalets clinging to the side of a steep wooded hill with well-tended gardens adorned by the presence of beautiful white cockatoos.

I had not made a reservation, but the receptionist glanced at the list and said, "I've only got one bed available tonight, but I'm afraid it's in a mixed dormitory." She looked me straight in the face, arched her eyebrows and asked innocently. "Do you have any objection to sleeping with five girls?"

"I can handle that, no problem," I asserted confidently, maintaining a straight face. Mixed-sex dorms are common in Australia. Nobody gives a hoot. You just pile in and go to sleep.

Arriving at the dorm, I introduced myself to the only girl present, a young teacher from Melbourne. On hearing that I had been head of a school, she started asking questions about managing difficult kids, as this had been a real problem in her school. Well, that was something I knew a bit about. Throughout my career I seemed to have developed a reputation for handling difficult delinquents, potential perverts, psychopaths, robbers, rapists and arsonists. Somehow, I seemed to be able to establish a rapport with them. Her interest was intense. We started talking at 4.00pm, and three hours later she interrupted me and said, "I'm getting hungry. Would you like to join me for dinner?" Well, I don't often get invitations to dine with a pleasant young lady, so I joined her. We were still talking at 1.30am.

She joined me for breakfast, during which she invited me to take a trip into the forest with her to view a spectacular waterfall a few miles away, and again we talked about education.

I was planning a lengthy drive that day so, with some reluctance, we parted company after lunch.

"This has been fantastic," she said. "I have learned more from you in a few hours than I have in four years in teaching. I'd love to have worked with you, John."

That gave me a nice wee glow. She passed me a piece of paper with her address and telephone number on it. "If your are ever in Melbourne, give me a call." Then she hugged me, and I glowed some more.

Chapter 23
The Art of Seduction – Aussie Style

The weather in Victoria is like British weather – changeable. The temperature was a blistering 32°C when I left Lorne; two hours later it had dropped to a shivery 18°C.

Along the route, I had stopped to view the Twelve Apostles – a magnificent series of sea stacks strung out along a stretch of spectacular cliff scenery, lofty pinnacles and towering blocks of rock left stranded as the sea unrelentingly eroded the cliffs behind. The sky had clouded over, a chilly wind blew in from the sea, and the coastal vegetation looked remarkably similar to the scrub and heather of the north of Scotland. It would have been beautiful a few hours earlier; now it was bleak. It was hard to believe I was not back in Scotland.

This unforgiving stretch of coast is littered with 1200 shipwrecks, many of which had been packed with immigrants. There was a sense of pathetic poignancy that, after having endured the privation of six months or more at sea in the confined space of a sailing ship, the hopes and lives of hundreds of men, women and children were wrecked with the ship within a few miles of its destination. The seas pounding against precipitous cliffs offered little chance of survival on this inhospitable coast. Yet it has an undeniably awesome beauty.

A few miles further on I picked up a couple of backpackers. They had just alighted from another car as the rain came on. This was too much like Scottish weather to leave them standing. I couldn't ignore the fellowship that binds world wanderers. The boy was a hairy Englishman with a pair of bongo drums, his girlfriend an attractive French Canadian. She was a music student who was about to return to Quebec to pursue her studies. The boy intended to keep drifting on around Australia. They were sleeping in a tent, and although interesting company they smelt a bit musky. I dropped them on the outskirts of Port Fairy, opened the car windows – despite the chill – and headed into town to find the hostel.

It is a really quaint little place, with a lovely harbour in a tidal creek. It is described as an historic town (although the description 'historic' is applied to anything over about 70 years old in Australia!). With its timbered shops, and with balconies covering the sidewalks, it had more of a frontier town appearance than I'd seen anywhere else. Take away the cars and you could be living in the last century. I liked it.

The following day, I turned inland to explore the Grampian Mountains – being a Scot, I could hardly ignore a place with a name like that, could I? Not that it was the only place adorned with Scottish place names. I drove through Hamilton, along the Glenelg Highway, and through Dunkeld. It was like being back home. The Grampians, a cluster of rocky mountains with steeply wooded slopes, offered a refreshing change from the miles of gentle rolling farmland; I even broke my journey to view one its tourist attractions signposted, 'Scenic Waterfall'.

After limping along a rocky trail through the forest for twenty minutes, I came upon a sheer rock face, bone dry save for a slight oozing of moisture among some green slime away up at the top. A dripping tap would produce more water, and what oozed over the top had all evaporated long before it reached the bottom – in fact, long before it had even left the top. The riverbed below the 'waterfall' was a sun-baked jumble of rocks, with not a trace of moisture anywhere.

I felt conned, and hobbled back through the forest to the car park, passing other suckers with cameras intent on photographing this mighty cataract. I never said a word to any of them. Let them find out for themselves. Well, I had passed plenty on my way in and not one had told me there was not a drop of water to be seen! Besides, the walk would do them good.

Hall's Gap is a snug village in a narrow, steep sided valley with a distinctly Alpine feel to it. After dinner at the local hostel, most of the residents were in the TV room watching the film *Lord of The Rings*. Never having been an enthusiast for the works of Tolkein, I settled quietly in the common room to read. Some girls arrived, a couple of Aussies and a bouncy Maori, and sat chatting opposite me. The Maori girl left, but breezed in a few moments later and announced gleefully that a lady in her dorm, who had been touring the wineries, was bringing down some wine. So, too, were the two German girls in the dorm. So they could have a 'Girls' Night'. I looked up from my book, coughed ostentatiously and said, "I take it that's my hint to leave."

The Maori girl clasped her hands over her cheeks in horror. " Oh no! I didn't mean to be so rude. You must stay."

"Och no, if you're planning an all-girls' night it would be quite improper of me to stay and spoil it for you." I stood up to leave. She blocked my exit, her eyes pleading.

"No. Please. You're making me feel terrible." And I was enjoying it too! I played up a bit more – well, why not?

"No, no, no, I couldn't stay where I'm not wanted. I'll just take my book and go and sit in the dorm – alone."

"No. Please. Please. We want you to stay and join the party, don't we girls?" There was a chorus of approval. She pressed on. "Get him a drink, Lisa."

A glass of wine was thrust into my hand, and Lisa joined forces against me. Both girls now had their hands on me forcing me back into my seat. Well, not wanting to spill the wine, and with my leg still not in top shape, I lacked the power to resist their efforts. So, with a display of feigned reluctance, I agreed to stay. Just to make them feel better, you understand! To assuage their guilt they then lavished attention on me, keeping my glass full and chatting with me. What had started as a quiet, solitary evening was turning out to be very sociable indeed – and it became livelier still.

Lisa had found some music, turned up the stereo, and the dancing began. Despite my protests, I was hauled to my feet. They outnumbered me six to one, so I had little chance of repelling their advances. Anyway, it would have been impolite of me not to perform my gentlemanly duty so I selflessly put aside personal considerations and allowed my hips to sway to the rhythm of the music. I had no rest for the remainder of the evening. A few other guys came as far as the door, but hadn't the courage to join in. The manager looked in, reminded Donnalee – the Maori girl – of the curfew on noise at 11.00pm, shook his head in disbelief, and retreated to his office. We boogied on till the wee small hours, when the girls began to drift off. I gathered the glasses and took them to the kitchen to wash up.

Lisa joined me, and we chatted comfortably. In the space of the few minutes it took to wash seven glasses the conversation changed from being lightly superficial to something more personal.

"I'm really glad you stayed, John," she told me quietly, "it made the evening so much more fun."

"Och, I fair enjoyed it myself," I remarked lightly, laying the last glass on the drainer.

"You're a very unusual man." She picked it up and dried it.

"Oh, in what way?" I dried my hands and leaned back against the work surface and regarded her with interest. She was an attractive, vivacious girl, dark haired, probably of Mediterranean origin.

She laughed lightly. "You're not what I would have expected of a retired headmaster. You have such a sense of fun, and to go backpacking round the world and do all the things you've done, especially after having lost your wife... Well, not many people would do that."

"Well, I look on retirement not as old age but as second youth."

"That's a great attitude." She hung the tea towel on a rail to dry and confronted me. "Have you never considered re-marrying?"

"No."

"Any relationships since your wife died?"

"No."

"Why not?"

I shrugged my shoulders. "I'm not against the idea, but I find it difficult to imagine myself in another relationship, so I haven't been out looking for one – and a queue hasn't exactly been forming at my door."

"You should think about it, John. Don't close your mind to it. I think you are ready for a relationship now."

"Oh, I keep an open mind, but to be honest, at my age it isn't likely."

"How old are you? If you don't mind me asking?"

"Sixty one."

She tilted her head and smiled. "You look much younger."

"Flatterer."

"No, I mean it. And you have a young attitude to life."

"Aye, well, I suppose mixing with young people all my life has helped, and travelling gives me the opportunity to enjoy the company of bright young people. That's one of the things I like about it."

"Why are you travelling, John?"

"Several reasons, I suppose. I enjoy meeting people, experiencing different cultures, trying new activities like scuba diving and escaping from the Scottish winter."

"Are you running away from something?"

"Well, I hadn't thought of it like that, but I suppose it would be easy to become miserable sitting at home all winter. I don't mind being alone, but there are times when your thoughts get ambushed and then you feel the pain of loneliness. This is much more fun and no more expensive."

"I think you are running away from something, John."

"Oh? What?"

"I think you are running away from a relationship – or at least, the possibility of one. You don't seem to me to be the kind of person who wants to be alone for the rest of his life; you're too sociable for that. You mix so well and obviously like people. Maybe you're afraid of getting hurt again if it didn't last, but I think you should consider sharing your life with someone. You have a lot to offer." This was becoming provocative, and I decided to change the focus. It was my turn now to ask the questions.

"Hey, you're not a psychologist are you? What do you do?"

"I'm a sales manager."

"Ah, a career girl?"

"Yes, so far, but it's time I found a soul mate."

"You don't have anyone, then?"

"No. I've had three relationships in the past ten years, but none of them worked out – and now time is running out for me."

"How old are you?"

"Thirty-four." She looked at least ten years younger and I told her so. "Thanks, but it's beginning to worry me. I need to find that special person before it all passes me by."

"I would have thought your chances were pretty good." She was a very attractive girl.

She shrugged her shoulders. "Maybe, but it hasn't happened yet. I'm still looking for the right guy. What are you looking for John?"

"I'm–" I began, as the kitchen door flew open and Donnalee burst in.

"Oh, you've done all the washing up! Good. I just came to say goodnight. I'm going to bed now. Thank you for being such a good sport, John. It was a great party." She threw her arms round me and bid me goodnight. Then she turned to Lisa, "Right, coming up to the dorm?"

Lisa flicked a hesitant glance at me and said, "Eh, yes, I suppose so." She paused for a moment to hug me. "Thanks John. Meeting you was something special. Goodnight."

That night, I lay in bed and pondered. What had stimulated such an interest in my reasons for travel? How did she come to the conclusion I was running from the prospect of a relationship? I couldn't recall anything I had said that was of any significance or that should pique her curiosity, yet it had happened, and all so quickly. Yet again there had been the assertion that I should be sharing my life with someone – so it wasn't peculiar to the Fijians. Was I giving out subliminal messages? And what would have happened if Donnalee had not returned? This was all too much of a female thing. Relationships rarely feature in men's talk. Thoroughly bamboozled by it all, I drifted into sleep. I had to leave early in the morning. I didn't see the girls again.

Cecily – who had been following my itinerary with interest and apparently had friends all over Australia – had suggested by email that I should try to visit Berry Bridge Vineyard. One of the partners in the business, Iain MacDonald, was an old friend of hers. It sounded like a pleasant diversion, and as it was within a couple of hours drive I headed north again. This was deep in the heart of rural Victoria, an area of farms and vineyards baking in the sun. Virtually every river was dry, the grass a dull ochre; it was a landscape parched after weeks of drought. There were few towns, and the roads off the main highway were mere gravel.

Iain was away in Tasmania. However, his partner, Rod, on hearing that I had come all the way from Scotland, insisted that I stay awhile.

"Hey, I can't let you go back to Scotland without giving you a cup of tea," he said, as though it were just a couple of hours drive away. I seldom refuse a cup of tea, so we sat on the veranda and talked. By midday I reckoned I should be on my way, but again he wouldn't let me go. "No, no. You're staying for some lunch. I'm enjoying the company."

He prepared a delicious salad lunch and opened a bottle of the vineyard's own Shiraz, a very pleasant wine indeed. As I was driving, I only took one glass. We sat on the veranda talking for another couple of hours before I finally had to drag myself away to continue my travels, and Rod had to drag himself away to pretend he was doing some work. I doubted that he would do much: he had supped my share of the wine.

It had been a very pleasant interlude, sitting in the shade with interesting company, sipping fine wine and looking out over the rows of vines that had produced the grape. It seemed to me to be the perfect gift to take to Graeme and Helen. I asked if I could buy a couple of bottles.

He looked at me pityingly. "John, you're only a bloody backpacker, mate. You can't afford to spend money on this kind of wine. This is a small vineyard aiming at the quality end of the market. This stuff sells at $32 a bottle! No, you just go into a liquor store and buy a couple of $5 bottles to take to your friends."

I laughed and took no offence. I loved the outspoken bluntness of the Aussies. I fired a salvo back. "Maybe I am only a backpacker, but I'm not your average Antipodean, impecunious, scruff. I am a gentleman backpacker who appreciates fine quality wine and hospitality, and these friends of mine deserve the best. Besides, if this drought continues, you're going to need every dollar you can get – so open up your cellar!"

He raised his eyebrows, shrugged his shoulders, and without another word capitulated in the face of my assertiveness and unlocked the cellar. I enjoyed doing business with him. I had enjoyed my visit to Berry Bridge very much. Cecily had dealt an ace card again.

In the morning, I took the road back to Warragul. Helen was having some friends over for 'a bit of a barbie' that night and having brought some quality Berry Bridge wine, I was allowed to join them.

As it happened, the girls were all drinking vodka, so Graeme and I were left with the onerous task of consuming the wine. Now, guys don't often share confidences like girls do, but there comes a point, usually somewhere near the end of the second bottle, when their heads lean closer together, they become very matey, and begin to talk from the heart. I therefore soon found myself responding to Graeme's curiosity about what I got up to on my travels through Victoria. He listened intently, and when I described my conversation with Lisa he shook his head sadly, put his arm round my shoulder and said with that depth of feeling that only the inebriated are capable of, "You need help, mate."

"Eh? Why?"

"You need to learn how to close a deal."

"What are you talking about? What deal?"

"John, I've only known you for a few days, but I can see you're a fair dinkum sort of bloke. You're a good conversationalist, very sociable, in fact damned good company, and I can understand why Helen was so thrilled to see you again. Your coming here meant a lot to her, and to be perfectly frank about it, for an old guy you're... well, you're actually quite presentable!" I had to laugh. "No, seriously, John, I mean it. No one would ever guess you're sixty-one. You hardly look a day over... sixty! But look at it this way, you're a bright, intelligent bloke yet you've wandered across the Pacific islands and squandered any number of chances with all these women in Fiji. Here, you've had two nice Aussie girls lusting after you, yet you've failed every time to close the deal. You did all the groundwork, but you didn't get it all together in the end. Get my meaning?"

"But we were only having interesting, intellectual conversations," I protested.

"Bollocks! They were panting after you and you didn't even notice! Now John, I know you're a product of a different culture, a different age even, when you had to court a girl for at least three years and put a wedding ring on her finger before you could climb into bed with her. But you're in Australia now, in the 21st century. We do things differently here. Stimulating, intellectual conversation is all very well, but there comes a time when you've got to break the flow and say, 'This is all very interesting, but are we spending the rest of the night at your place or mine?' That's what I mean about closing the deal."

Now, maybe he's right. Maybe I am thick, but I still had grave doubts about his conclusion and I dismissed the idea that I could ever adopt the courtship rituals of *Homo Sapiens Australis*, the dominant characteristic of which seemed to be a distinct lack of subtlety or sophistication. You'll find polar bears in the outback before you'll find any trace of subtlety or sophistication in the Australian male when he's on heat.

"What happened to the art of wooing? And in any case," I argued, "how could I possibly invite a lady to share a night of passion with me in a backpackers' dormitory with five or six other people listening in – and if they were Aussies, more likely cheering us on?"

He looked at me sagely and said quietly, "Find a nice secluded spot outside and put a blanket on the ground."

I shook my head in disbelief. "What? In a country crawling with poisonous snakes and spiders all prowling about looking for a meal in the hours of darkness? Anyway, I don't have a blanket."

Helen's parents, who had also settled in Australia, had been in touch and insisted that I visit them on my way through New South Wales. I was to take the car again, leave it with them and take the bus on from there to Sydney. While I packed in the morning, Graeme busied himself with checking the car. I tossed my pack into the boot and gave Helen a farewell hug, then shook hands with Graeme.

"All systems checked and in working order," he announced and opened the door for me. "By the way," he pointed to a travel blanket folded neatly on the back seat. "Just in case you get lucky."

"Aye, that'll be the day," I growled.

And in case you're wondering – I never did get the chance to use it.

Chapter 24
More Reunions

DO NOT BRING FRUIT INTO NEW SOUTH WALES proclaimed a large roadside sign. I had a banana with me so I pulled over and ate it in case a patrol car stopped and searched me. I don't know if they do such things, but the sign was compelling. Anyway, these Aussies are all big guys, and I saw no point in upsetting them. As I munched on my banana I read the small print on the sign. It seems that fruit flies are the problem. They can leave eggs undetected on fruit, and when the flies emerge they breed, which in turn can inflict colossal damage on the fruit crop. Fruit flies are not all the same, apparently, and incomer flies may well be immune to sprays used to control the local flies.

They are now very fussy about such things in Australia, and failure to declare any foodstuffs on entering the country can lead to hefty fines. Even the soles of your feet are examined at the airports for traces of soil or any other organic matter which might harbour organisms. Harsh lessons have been learned about interfering with the balance of nature – they haven't forgotten about the rabbits.

Another sign, which I jubilantly ignored, proclaimed the good news to all northbound travellers that the next McDonald's fast food restaurant was only 126 kilometres ahead! Now isn't that clever marketing? Imagine Ma, Pa and the kids wearily driving along the highway. "Yippee! Are we nearly there yet, dad? How far to go now Dad? Don't forget to stop Dad." That sign ensures that for the next hour and a half, the children's digestive juices will be flowing, and father's resistance is going to be steadily eroded away. But a Big Mac does nothing for my digestive juices.

Eventually, the forests around the state border gave way to rolling hills and farmland, and I turned off the highway to seek out Helen's parents who lived in a small village. I had now driven over two thousand miles in Australia, but where were all the kangaroos? Dead at the roadside appeared to be the answer. At night they are a real hazard to motorists – and themselves. The road verges were liberally sprinkled with the carnage from the night before. In ten weeks in Australia I only saw one live kangaroo in the bush (come to think of it, I never saw so much as a single rabbit!), but I saw plenty of dead kangaroos.

Rural New South Wales was quite attractive, and I had to see more of it. Dotted with pleasant coastal towns and sleepy villages, the place had a Devonshire feel to it. Every village had second hand bookshops and antique shops. No matter how small the community, someone was making a living from selling antiques and second hand books. Like 'historic' buildings, 'antique' is a relative term. Seeing three antique shops in one village, all within a few yards of each other, I had to stop to see what they were selling. One or two items may have been a hundred years old, but much of it was familiar to me as the kind of crockery, furniture or brassware in common use in my youth. I didn't need to be reminded that *I* was an antiquity, so I moved on.

The other kind of shop that appeared in every village sold what I would call New Age trinkets: wind chimes, tinkling bells, strange star-shaped decorations, candles and incense burners, hookahs, magic carpets... that kind of thing. Eastern mysticism is fashionable here. Signs advertising land for sale – Lifestyle Plots – were everywhere.

'Escape the rat race, become a Lifestyler and live the quiet life in the country with your cats, wind chimes and smell of incense, wear hippie clothes and perhaps cultivate a few cannabis plants in a quiet corner of the woods. Live the Australian dream!' the signs should have displayed.

The economics of it all was beyond me. I couldn't fathom out how they made a living selling junk antiques, second hand books and trinkets to one another. But just about everything about Australia defies understanding. It is a fascinating country.

After enjoying a couple of days of excellent hospitality with Helen's parents, also last seen in Germany thirty years before, I took the bus to Sydney. It was an eight-hour trip, the early part of which was illuminated by the monologue of an intellectually challenged young lady who was acquainted with the driver and kept up an incessant commentary on events of stupefying inconsequence.

"What d'ya have for breakfast, Roy? I had scrambled eggs and toast, Roy. Mmm, scrummmy they were, Roy. I'm going to see my cousins today, Roy. Two girls and a guy, Roy. They'll all be at the bus stop to meet me, Roy. How's that for a welcoming party, Roy? Not one, but three of them, Roy. I'm such an important person it takes three people to meet me, Roy. These horses are still in that field, Roy. They're at it again, Roy. They were at it last time I was here, Roy. Did you see them, Roy? They're always at it, Roy. They spit at you if you go near them, Roy. They spat at me last time I went up there, Roy." This went on incessantly for two hours. I closed my eyes and tried to shut it all out by going to sleep. Whoever heard of a horse spitting at you? But maybe she was right. This was Australia, after all. When I woke up, she was gone.

Sydney harbour is magnificent. Quite apart from its two world famous icons – the Opera House and the Sydney Harbour Bridge – it has one of the world's greatest natural harbours, allowing large ships to come come right into the city centre. It bustles with life: ferries, freighters, cruise liners, harbour tugs and yachts are constantly on the move, creating a dynamic pastiche of colour, style and ceaseless energy. It is the kind of place where you can sit all day and gaze and never get bored. People of every nationality throng its streets. It is a brash, vulgar and, at times, elegant city. Sydney is typically Australian.

Here, there is a sense of history, albeit fairly recent. Just over a century ago the Cutty Sark tied up at its wharves to load wool and make some of the fastest passages ever logged by a sailing ship. Just to the south of the city lies Botany Bay, reputed to be Captain Cook's landfall.

The company in the central Youth Hostel in Sydney was a bit more entertaining than at Melbourne. At breakfast I met a couple of elderly Americans from Seattle, both in their seventies, who immediately introduced themselves and included me in their conversation. Jack was lean, mean and athletic looking and an enthusiastic traveller. Bob was portly, of homely appearance and remarkably similar in looks, voice and mannerisms to James Stewart, the genial Hollywood film legend. He was not enthusiastic at all about travelling outside the USA.

"I allowed this guy to talk me into coming to Australia for six weeks," growled Bob in his slow drawl (here was another graduate of the American School of Slow Talking). He shook his head slowly. Everything he did was done slowly. "Biggest mistake of my life. Too hot. And too many flies. I hate the place. Can't wait to get home."

Although close friends for many years, they fell out over almost everything. Flying between destinations, they argued so much they couldn't bear the sight of each other by the end of the flight. They met for breakfast and dinner, but went sightseeing separately each day.

"It's the only way I can stop myself from killing him," muttered Bob.

Back home, they both owned RVs – recreational vehicles, for the uninitiated. These large articulated motor homes are as big as an average house in the UK, and have extending sides to make them even bigger for overnight stops. The two old-timers always set off together for a bit of fishing and shooting in the mountains on the Canadian border. Despite the enormous size of the RVs, they each had to take their own to keep the peace. Jack always took the lead as Bob was such a slow driver.

"John, he drives so slow grass grows in his tyre treads," Jack informed me. "We gotta plan on takin' a whole week for a weekend fishing trip. I tell you, John, this guy's so slow no one knows for sure if he's still alive. When he dies no one will notice the difference!"

Bob bristled at the insult and frothed at the mouth as he tried to spit the words out with some venom. "L-l-listen h-h-here," he spluttered, pointing his finger at Jack like a revolver. "Y-y-you wait! N-n-next time we're heading up north I'll show ya! I'll come at ya so fast, I'll suck ya up the intake, chew ya up into little pieces and spit ya out the exhaust!"

Jack shook his head and laughed. "It ain't possible. He carries so much stuff in his RV he can never get it to go more'n thirty. He has so much stuff packed in there, he has to sleep on the sofa in the lounge 'cuz he cain't get into the bedroom. It's like a warehouse in there, piled high to the ceiling."

Bob laughed. He had to admit that he was a hoarder. "I jest like to make sure I have everything I'm gonna need."

"Everything you're gonna need?" howled Jack. "Y'ain't needin' any o' that stuff. Y'aint never used it yet!"

"But I might one day!" he roared. Jack shook his head disdainfully as Bob explained to me, "I like to take a few things with me, John – just a few things to make life more comfortable. Y'see, I hitch up the RV to the truck and I got a boat on a trailer and I hitch that to the back of the RV. Then I gotta take my motorcycle, so I have a derrick fitted so I can hoist the motorcycle up on to the back of the truck, and I got a canoe that sits inside the RV..."

"This guy takes more gear with him than the US Army and that's only for a weekend fishing trip," screamed Jack. "And his house is the same. He pays $500 a month to hire a warehouse to store all the things he can't get in the house. He keeps buyin' – he jest won't throw anything away."

"Aw, shut up!" snapped Bob, and changed the subject."Where're you goin' today?"

"The zoo," snapped Jack.

"Good. I hope they feed you to the lions! I'm goin' out to Bondi Beach so I won't have to suffer lookin' at you. See lots of pretty bodies there instead." And he gave me a wink with a twinkling eye.

"What about you John? Where're you headed for today?

"Oh, I'm taking the train out to Pendle Bay, about sixty miles north of here, to meet up with a former pupil."

"Hey, that's cool. Have a nice day!" And they meant it. I loved them.

Andrew met me at the station and recognised me immediately, even though I had taught him twenty years before. He now managed a team of statisticians analysing trial data for a multi-national pharmaceuticals corporation. He had been one of my most able pupils and a friend of my sons so we had much to talk about. We spent hours sitting on his balcony overlooking a beautiful bay, sipping cool beer and watching the surfers.

It was very illuminating to hear the things he remembered as we reminisced. Much of what you say as a teacher simply trips off the tongue. It may be inconsequential to the teacher, but just a few choice words scattered, like seed, can have an astoundingly significant effect on your students, arousing interest in the subject or influencing career decisions and laying the foundations of a lifetime's work. It was an education for me to listen to his articulate observations on my teaching style and how I had influenced him and so many of his peers. The knowledge that a simple remark can have such a profound effect on the lives of others is a wee bit scary, but it's true. It was how I was inspired to enter the profession by my mathematics teacher.

The following day, as he drove me into Sydney to catch my plane, we encountered one of the many bush fires that had been sweeping through New South Wales in the last few days. We were lucky: the wind was blowing the flames and smoke away from the highway. Hundreds of acres of bush around Sydney had already been scorched, yet the amazing thing is that although the trees are blackened new growth appears on their charred branches and trunks after a few months. They survive the fires.

As my plane rose above Sydney, the entire sky away to the west was obliterated by smoke. Four hundred homes were consumed by the blaze that day in the suburbs of Canberra.

Australia – beautiful, diverse, wild – can also be a harsh place to live!

Chapter 25
Home Brew and Hairy Legs

Queensland is my favourite of all the Australian states. It has a fantastic climate, glorious beaches and lush forests with more different species of tree per hectare than you'll find in the entire North American continent and Europe put together. At least that's what the Queenslanders tell you. There is a downside to all this of course. It is populated by some of the most deadly venomous and voracious creatures on earth.

Before I left home, my younger son very thoughtfully gave me a book entitled *Healthy Travel in Australia*. Maybe it was part of a plan to get me to change my mind, for it was not comforting bedtime reading. The word Healthy in the title could be replaced by *DON'T*. Australia is home to more things that will bite, eat or sting you to an agonising death than anywhere else in the entire world. It has the most venomous of just about everything, including the world's ten most deadly snakes. If they don't get you, the funnel web spider, the blue ringed octopus, the paralysis tick, the stonefish, or the box jellyfish just might! They are all said to be the most lethal of their kind in the world – and Queensland has probably the greatest concentration of most of these.

The golden rule is: Don't Touch Anything! Even furry caterpillars can knock you out with a nibble, and there is a type of cone shell with a venomous proboscis which will go for you if you disturb it: imagine, being attacked by a sea shell! There are estimated to be about 100,000 crocodiles waiting for silly tourists to offer themselves for lunch – and would you believe it, some of them do.

But don't let all that put you off, for it is a marvellous place to visit. You simply need to exercise a little common sense, a commodity sometimes lacking among tourists.

Cairns, its most northerly city, is the gateway to the Great Barrier Reef, and as a qualified diver, exploring the reef was my primary mission. I also hoped to meet Cecily sometime before journeying back to Brisbane. She lived some distance from Cairns, but had arranged for her parents to meet me at the airport and look after me for a day or two before I went to sea. They lived in a valley a few miles inland from Cairns, helping out with their son Nick's bush-trekking on horseback

Above: Fijian *bure*, my island beach home for three weeks.

Above: Moai, giant statues on Easter Island, half-buried at the quarry where they were carved from a sheer rock face.

Above: Cook Island sunset, Mauke island.

Left:
Hats worn by Cook Island ladies for church, made from woven pandanus leaves, each one unique.

Right: Island survival skills. The coconut tree provides food, drink and materials for shelter, building boats, clothing and medicine.

Right: Diamonds in the sunshine, droplets from the tail of a Humpback whale.

Left: Gentoo penguin rookery, noisy and smelly.

Below: The Scot in the Antarctic

Above: Los Quernos (The Horns), Chile, with tree sculpture.

Above: Glacier lake, Mt Fitzroy Argentine.

Above: MV Explorer among the brash ice, Antartica.

Above: Moai, complete with eyes and top knot, restored on a ceremonial *ahu* at Hangaroa.

Above: Perito Morena Glacier, moving at 1.7 metres per day - probably the fastest in the world.

Above: Outrigger canoes on Mitiaro, Cook islands; dugout and plywood versions.

Above: Torres del Paine National Park, Chile. The guanacos in the foreground are humpless camels: no need to store water in humps in this wet climate.

Above: Idyllic lagoon, Rarotonga, Cook Islands

Above: It was well worth the effort to see this magnificent panoramic view of Mt Fitzroy, Argentine.

Right: A *falle*,
Traditional
Samoan house.
Privacy has no
meaning here.

Left:
Seaspray, a
veteran
Scottish-built
schooner in
the Mamanuca
Islands, Fiji.

Right:
Homesick?
No way!

business, preparing lunches and transporting clients to and from Cairns. I hadn't seen Bruce and Shirley for thirty-one years when Bruce, then a major in the Australian army, was attached to a British regiment in Germany. I was welcomed with great warmth. And, with a lot of catching up to do, Bruce and I spent many relaxing hours sitting talking out on the veranda and supping his ice-cold home brew.

This relaxing atmosphere was conducive to the telling of stories, and the two of us sat and entertained each other with long convoluted tales, as old men do. What better way is there to while away the hours in the late afternoon when all the work is done? When Bruce launched into a tale, ever considerate of my lack of knowledge pertaining to certain matters, he inevitably had to provide me with many essential snippets of background information in order to set the story within a context that I would understand. That was very helpful and really quite interesting for me. I was learning. Now, maybe it was something to do with the effect of the home brew, but I had the vague impression that some of the stories were hijacked along the way, meaning we never actually got to the end of them. Maybe it was because somewhere in the telling their beginnings had been lost in the mists of time, but that was of little consequence and we were quite happy to ramble on incoherently.

Shirley would come and join us once she had the dinner in the oven and could relax for a few minutes, but she lacked the advantage of having swilled a glass or two down her throat and was struggling in her pitiable state of sobriety trying to make sense of what we were saying. Now there is only so much a sober and sensible woman can tolerate, and so after a few minutes wallowing helplessly in confusion she had to reach out and touch Bruce on the arm in a most kindly and considerate way to interrupt the flow and say, "Bru darlin', would you hurry up and get to the point!"

Startled by such interruptions, Bruce would   look at me blankly. "Yes. Umm. Er, what was I talking about, John?"

And I would have no more idea than he had. It was all so endearingly familiar. I know exactly what it feels like, and was just as guilty, but Shirley was far too much of a lady to interrupt my own tortuous tales. Or if she did, I was too inebriated to notice. And before I forget what the point of *this* story is, it is that I enjoyed Bruce's stories very much. They were full of interesting and illuminating references to his distinguished military service, from which he retired with the rank of Colonel.

Nick joined us for dinner and invited me to accompany a party of tourists on a trek into the bush next day. I had only been on horseback once before and was a trifle uneasy. I didn't really trust horses, and this was tropical rainforest in North Queensland with the possibility of encountering so many things that might spook the horses, causing them to eject the rider. I had no desire to provide an easy meal for a snake, crocodile or spider. Nick dismissed my concerns. The rivers up here were quite safe, he assured me. The crocodiles mostly inhabit the estuaries, and snakes generally clear off when they hear the disturbance before they get trampled under horses' hooves – and you don't need to worry about them dangling from trees waiting to snap at passers-by either. Nick said he would take the lead so they could take a bite at him first, and that he could sweep away any spiders' webs. That made me feel better. Australians do delight in proudly telling you the most horrific tales of all the creatures that will eat you or sting you to death (and there are plenty, as I have said), and then dismiss it all as nothing to worry about. They overdose on machismo here. Anyway, in my quest for further adventures, I agreed to go.

My mount was a pleasant looking cuddy called O'Malley. I patted his nose, looked him straight in the eye, and told him who was the boss in this partnership. I was radiating my 'I'm the Headmaster' aura. He looked me straight in the eye for a moment. He knew I meant business and nodded his head in agreement. So that was that sorted out. Okay, so maybe he was just clearing away the flies, but it gave me a feeling of reassurance. I'm sure he understood. He did look quite intelligent, more so than many of the delinquents I had to deal with in my teaching career. I mounted him, but as soon as he moved I realised just what a mistake I had made.

Everyone was wearing jeans – well, everyone except me. I had been wearing shorts for months now, and it never occurred to me to dress differently for riding on horseback. But a horse has four legs, and all move independently of each other. Therefore, with everything moving in apparently contradictory motion, your legs rub against the saddle – and, believe me, bare skin wears out quicker than cowhide. The stirrup straps slide back and forward against the saddle and clamp voraciously on to the hairs on your legs, uprooting them painfully (the hairs, that is, not the legs – thankfully!). This is a particularly cruel method of defoliation as although they only pull out a few hairs at a time they catch and tug painfully at all the others to ensure that you will continue to suffer over a long period. By the end of the trek my inner legs had become raw, pink flesh screamingly sensitive to any touch, like sunburn. But, dour Scot that I was, I endured the pain in silence.

Apart from that, it was a pleasantly relaxing excursion through the forest. I loved the bit where we went splashing along a riverbed for a short distance. I had seen the cowboys do this in western films, and before long I was talking to O'Malley in a John Wayne drawl. The horse seemed to understand it too. We got on just fine together. After a short break by the riverside we made our way back for Shirley's delicious salad lunch washed down with Bruce's home brew.

Nick's twelve year-old daughter had been staying with Cecily, and she brought her home the following day. After a gap of thirty-one years, we met at last. She had been an outstanding pupil. Now a woman in her mid-forties, she had the same mental acuity and mischievous sense of fun. Three very pleasurable hours drifted away as we sat on the veranda and talked until she had to leave for home.

As I waved her off, I marvelled at the power of the Internet that had enabled me to be re-united, 12,000 miles from home, with three of my most memorable pupils. It gave me a nice wee glow again, one that more than matched the glow on my hairless legs!

Chapter 26
The Great Barrier Reef

Cairns is a mecca for backpackers. It is crammed with hostels, dive shops and tour operators offering adventures exploring the rainforests, white water rafting, kayaking, diving, snorkelling, sailing, and so on. Everything is made easy for the visitor here. The hostels all offer advice on where to go, what to do, and they will also arrange bookings, often with discounts, for all the excursions available. The streets are lined with inexpensive restaurants where you can sit and watch the adventure-seeking youth of the world stroll by. Very attractive some of them are too, but the main attraction here is the Great Barrier Reef.

A World Heritage Site, this incredible series of coral reefs extends for some 1250 miles along the east coast of Queensland. Visible from space, it is the world's largest living thing, the habitat of billions of polyps which secrete a hard blend of calcium carbonate and protein to form the coral that provides them with an external skeleton for support and habitation. Successive generations build on the skeletal remains of the old, and so the coral develops into rock-like formations. There are over three thousand separate reefs and over six hundred islands providing food and shelter for over fifteen hundred species of fish and four thousand varieties of shellfish. The incredible beauty and variety of its marine life is astonishing.

Glass-bottomed boats offer a glimpse of what lies beneath the surface of the sea; snorkelling is fine in the shallower water, which is where the most colourful corals are to be found; but the reef can only be fully appreciated by diving. You can explore much deeper, examine in detail the strange coral pinnacles, swim through dark tunnels and deep canyons lined with gently waving fronds of soft coral where you may encounter huge crayfish, large wrasse, malevolent looking moray eels or perhaps a turtle having a leisurely feed. Fish of every size and shape, clothed in the most amazing colours, mingle in submarine coral cities. Here, the diver has the capability of flight, soaring at will, like a helicopter among skyscrapers, up and over their towering high-rise blocks of coral, or down among traffic of yellow-streaked fish in the shadowy canyons between. You can glide along sunlit, sandy streets between coral formations pulsating with electrifying colours, feel the powerful thrust of water expelled by a giant clam snapping shut as a hand hovers above its vice-like jaws, or swim in convoy with a turtle, imitating the graceful and effortlessly efficient motion of its fins.

No matter how long you gaze, the childlike wonder grows. You inhabit a surreal world, alluring, mysterious, utterly enchanting, populated by the most astonishing creatures; some fast, some slow, some stationary, some beautiful, some bizarre in appearance. Yet all, in their infinite variety and dazzling colour, are supremely adapted for life in this silent, submarine world where the only sound is the rhythmic hiss and bubble of air passing through your regulator as you breathe, a reminder of the privilege bestowed upon you: that you are a transient being here, that you belong elsewhere. It is a world that defies the power of imagination to visualise, so beyond anything you have ever witnessed before: it offers something akin to a spiritual experience, for here you have returned to your primeval roots, the primordial sea from which life on earth originated countless millennia ago.

I enrolled in a course to gain my Advanced Diver's Certificate. A three day course, it combined classroom work and study on board a specialist diving vessel out on the reef, including deep dives down to 100 feet, night dives, underwater navigation by compass, underwater photography and exploration. The dive boat offered excellent air-conditioned accommodation, plenty of good food, and all the necessary equipment.

Starting each day with a 5.30am wake up call, we had to be in the water for a deep dive at 6.00am. A pack of dark heads bobbing around in the water like seals, we released air from our buoyancy jackets and followed the instructor. Descending slowly into the depths, we grouped together on the sandy bottom 100 feet below to perform some simple exercises. We were asked to do some simple calculations on an underwater clipboard to demonstrate how the mind is slowed at this depth by nitrogen narcosis. An egg was broken, yet the pressure of water around it kept it entirely intact as we tossed it around the group like a rubber ball. A closed plastic bottle taken down was completely crushed by the pressure. It was then filled again with air, and when released it shot up like a shell from a gun, the air expanding rapidly as pressure decreased until it exploded, a reminder of what can happen if you hold your breath as you ascend. Your concept of time diminishes and fifteen minutes at this depth seemed like only two or three – another important lesson.

Then we began the slow ascent, slanting upwards along the coral wall, exploring its life forms in the increasing daylight. As the sun rose higher in the sky it illuminated our world, like an artist at work, splashing colour on a previously monochromatic backcloth. Shoals of fish darted, glinting silver, blue, green, red and gold. Large wrasse with blunt noses glided silently past, quite unconcerned, rays flapped their wings in elegant sinusoidal motion and soared upwards and away from us. Reef sharks prowled with lazy effortlessness, but kept their distance. Recumbent among the rocks lay the elegant spiral beauty of large triton shells. A startled octopus, its tentacles oozing over the rocks, withdrew shyly into a dark chamber. Giant clams with beautiful, intricately patterned, multicoloured membranes between their vice-like open jaws, shut tightly as we passed over them. No one complained about having to be roused so early. This was well worth getting out of bed for.

After breakfast, we were underwater again, in shallower water this time, practising navigation techniques. Then around mid-day the boat moved on to another reef and the exploration began again.

Night dives were a different experience. Supplied with waterproof torches we descended into an eerie, gloomy world. When artificial light was shone upon the coral it reflected colours different from its daytime appearance and, in contrast with the surrounding darkness, seemed to burn all the more brightly, like the embers of a glowing fire. As on land, the sea also has its nocturnal creatures, and now we had glimpses of species which were absent during the day. Sharks loomed silvery-grey out of the darkness, but darted away with a quick flick of the tail when a torch beam shone on them. The distant lights of other divers glowed mistily in the gloom, like car headlights in a fog.

Underwater photography presents challenges. Light under water is much less intense, so care must be taken to get reasonably close to the subject with the sun behind you when shooting pictures. I was so excited at the prospect of capturing vibrant images and started shooting pictures till Nick, one of my diving buddies, came across and took the camera from me and turned it round. I had been taking close-up pictures of my own face! That went down in the course notes as one of the silly things *not* to do.

In three days we were kept busy with dives, lectures and homework exercises, so there was relatively little time for socialising – a great pity, as there were lots of shapely, bikini-clad girls wandering about between dives. We always dived in groups of two or more: your diving buddies look after you, you look after them, just in case anything goes wrong. Safety is paramount. You are always checked out and back on board again with time, air pressure in your tanks, and length of rest periods between dives recorded. This is strictly enforced. A few years ago, a couple were left behind at one reef. The crew had failed to notice their absence and the boat returned to Cairns, about thirty miles away. It was fully two days later before anyone realised that they were missing. No trace of them has ever been found. Hollywood's interpretation of that story resulted in the film *Open Water*.

My diving buddies were Nick, a twenty five year-old Dane and Jamie, a twenty one year-old Canadian. During the three days afloat we became close friends. I would hate not to be on friendly terms with people on whom my life may depend. This action-packed three days of living and learning in close proximity to other students had the flavour of life at university, where the work is intense and relationships develop quickly under pressure. All too soon it was over, but we were reluctant to sever the bonds of our new-found fellowship. We had established a dependence on one another in our undersea explorations, laughed and teased our way through study and relaxation periods, opened up our lives in discussion as we relaxed on deck and at meal times, and the experience had left its mark on each of us.

On the way back to Cairns, we arranged to meet again at O'Brien's Irish Pub to celebrate out success: we were now Advanced Open Water Divers. Some of the others who had been on the boat joined us: a Dutch couple and a French couple, Els, a twenty one year-old Belgian girl, and Ingrid, an eighteen year-old Dutch girl. The two couples decided to have an early night, but the rest of us were in no hurry. Nick suggested that we should go on to the Woolshed, a popular nightspot. Of course, I'm too old for that kind of thing, but Nick would have none of it and, as in Rarotonga, I was dragged along with them.

It was bedlam! The place was heaving, packed solidly with bodies. Girls were not only dancing on the floor but on chairs, tables... in fact, anywhere there was a bit of surface to gyrate on. I could only stand and stare, lost in wonder. Jamie, Ingrid and Els soon had endured enough of this, and had the sense to leave. But I was curious. I was interested in observing this strange form of social behaviour. From an intellectual standpoint, of course. I knew you'd understand!

A cry disturbed my reverie: " John! How are you?" It was Jules and Sarah, two English nurses who had also been on the dive boat, but had left a day earlier than us. After chatting for a few minutes – well, shouting at each other is more accurate as the music was so loud – Sarah leaned towards me to speak. I bent down to listen. "I just love hearing you talk, John. Your Scottish accent is wonderful."

That took me aback. "Really? I thought it was as common as muck."

She leaned forward again. I bent down once more to listen, and could feel her lips caressing the edge of my ears. "Oh no! It is so attractive. Think of Sean Connery. Who could ever say *he* sounds common. I could listen to you all night."

Well, this was becoming interesting, I thought, but just as Graeme's advice about closing a deal entered my mind and I was about to offer her the chance to do just that the music changed and Jules grabbed Sarah by the arm. "Come on, let's dance," he yelled, hauling her into the press of bodies writhing on the dance floor. I hadn't been included in the invitation. In my day, men invited ladies to dance. Now they go it alone. I shrugged my shoulders.

Besides, I didn't have a blanket to put on the ground!

The place was so tightly packed that it was virtually impossible to dance anyway. The crowd was so dense that all you could do was stand there surrounded by girls and their writhing bodies rubbed against you and your eyes went all glassy. If you let your hands fall by your side, in front, or behind you and turned your palms outward, it was inevitable that some pert little bottom would wiggle its way into your hands. It was so effortless. And nobody seemed to notice. So I just stood there on one spot with my hands dangling and without a hint of invitation, or even the slightest vestige of embarrassment, beautifully rounded female buttocks oscillating to the rhythm of the music were constantly thrust on to my palms.

Sad, isn't it, what an old man has to do to get a thrill.

Now you don't really believe that... do you?

Chapter 27
Diagnosis and Dismay

In the lingering euphoria that followed, I just had to get diving again, so I snapped up a great deal at almost half-price: a five-day diving trip on what is regarded as the best part of the entire reef. However, talking to Nick and Jamie about it that night, they both urged me to see a doctor about my ankle, which was still rather swollen since the incident on Fiji – perhaps more so. Then Rod, the hostel manager who had been expressing some concern about it since I arrived in Cairns, looked at it in the morning and ordered me to get to a doctor at once. Although not in any pain unless I stretched the ankle, it had now been six weeks since the injury had occurred in Fiji and I thought, right enough, that it was taking a bit of time to heal properly.

So I went to a doctor, who asked the usual embarrassing questions like, "When did this happen?" When he heard my tale, he shook his head and rolled his eyes and sent me to have an ultrasound scan. Another doctor there looked at the picture and asked me how and when it had happened, and he too shook his head and rolled his eyes.

Then he told me: "The Achilles tendon is completely severed. There is a three centimetre gap between the ends, and if you don't have surgery soon the gap will widen further. It may then prove impossible to repair the damage, and you'll never be able to lift your heel again. Your calf muscle will become redundant and will deteriorate through lack of use, and you will be physically impaired for the rest of your life. You'll become a decrepit old man, a mere shadow of your former fit and agile self, and you'll be scuppered for diving and sailing and dancing – or even standing holding your hands by your side and allowing pretty young ladies to press their pert little bottoms into them for you'll not even be able to get to the dance floor 'cos you'll be bloody well crippled!"

Or words to that effect. Australian doctors do have a rather brusque bedside manner.

I was then despatched to see a surgeon, who also shook his head and rolled his eyes and – well, you know the story by now! He said, "I can operate tomorrow, but you'll be cemented into a full-leg plaster cast for at least three weeks, then we'll change that to a lighter cast. You will be completely immobilised for at least three months, and then you can go home. And by the way, it will cost you $2100 – and that doesn't include the post operative consultations or my fee for this consultation."

Maybe he detected a change in my colour when he mentioned the cost, for he then went on a different tack. "Or, you can wait perhaps six months to have it done under Australia's reciprocal health care arrangements with the UK, but since your holiday is now completely buggered..." His words not mine! As I said, they are quite brusque. "...why don't you just go home and have it done in Scotland for free, like all the other tight-fisted Scots' gits?" Or words to that effect. I reckoned he realised he was on a loser this time. I left to consult my insurers.

They would generally only support private treatment in an emergency, otherwise I had to be treated under the aforementioned reciprocal health care agreement. Having tramped merrily around Australia for six weeks, gone horse riding and completed fourteen dives with a broken Achilles tendon rather spoiled my chances of being treated as an emergency case. With only five weeks of my trip left, the most sensible course of action was to abort the trip, return to Scotland and recuperate from surgery at home. So that was that. Forget going on to Bali. Go home.

Still, looking on the bright side, at least I wouldn't have to sit around a backpackers' hostel totally incapacitated for three months gnashing my teeth as I watched all the others go out to play, telling me what a wonderful day out they'd had diving, rafting, kayaking, bungee jumping or boogieing the night away at the Woolshed packed with pert little bottoms. Oh no, much better by far to be at home in chilly Scotland instead of lying about in the tropical sun with bronzed young ladies all hovering around me, lavishing sympathy and care and attention on me, helping me to my feet and inviting me to put my arm over their shoulders while they clutched me and helped me get to my dorm to tuck me in bed at night and feeling my leg to see if it was getting any better...

Well, being a strict and devoted Calvinist all my life and doomed to endure pain and suffering in order to remain virtuous and achieve eternal life, there was no option really but to abort the trip and go home. Bruce and Shirley, on hearing the news, immediately offered to care for me, but three months of me in plaster, inactive and grumpy was too much to inflict on anyone.

Of course, I was disappointed, but you've got to trim your sails to suit the wind, so I got on the Internet to see if there were any seats on flights home. I was lucky. I got one on a flight the following week.

My diving excursion had to be cancelled, but I could still fit in a short trip to Cape Tribulation where Captain Cook ran the Endeavour aground. The area had other geographical features called Weary Bay, Mount Sorrow, Mount Dismay, Cape Disappointment, Cape Catastrophe – all very apt in my present circumstances. It was Cook who gave them these names. He was 12,000 miles from home with a big hole in his ship and he was forced to beach her up a creek for seven weeks for repairs with hordes of unfriendly aboriginals and hungry crocodiles milling around. He wasn't feeling too cheery either. Compared with his predicament, I couldn't really complain.

It was hard to be gloomy for long here. Our bus driver had a fund of entertaining stories about the horrors lurking around Cape Tribulation. "Now, you can't fail to be impressed by all the lovely beaches we have here in Queensland. But just ask yourself one question: why are they all empty, with not a single swimmer in sight?"

We pondered, but he supplied the answer: "Well, the reason is this: October to May is the stinger season, when the beaches close to river mouths and creeks are populated by box jellyfish, which breed in the estuaries. You don't want to go meddling with those little monsters. Even a dead one can sting you. Don't even think about going for a paddle along the shore. If you get stung, you can count the seconds till you depart this life. And if you get beyond ninety you are not lucky, you are in hell – because the pain is said to be beyond anything man can conceive. A year or two back, one young and very stupid backpacker ignored all the warnings – you can't just miss them, they are posted everywhere, so he must have ignored them and went for a swim at the height of the stinger season. Within a couple of minutes he got stung and started screaming in agony. His mates dragged him out of the water. His back looked liked he'd been whipped with barbed wire, and even though there were paramedics on the beach to administer first aid, he rapidly went comatose. They pumped enough morphine to kill a horse into him, yet he was still screaming blue murder even though unconscious. He died within a few minutes. So that explains why, with all the beautiful beaches around, you don't see anyone swimming."

Well, that shut us all up. But there was more to come.

Our route took us across the Daintree River by ferry. Large warning signs tell you that these are crocodile-infested waters. This was a cue for another story from the driver. "Now look at all these signs. You can't fail to get the message. Right? Wrong! In spite of the fact that people make a good living from running boat trips along the river to let the tourists see the crocodiles, a group of tourists who'd had a bit of a party one night decided it would be fun to have a bit of a skinny dip in the river. Now, a girl called Beryl – she was only up to her knees in water – bent down to skim the surface of the water with her hand when she suddenly disappeared. Taken by a crocodile! Not even a scream was heard, it all happened so suddenly. She was found by a search party a couple of days later beside a large, well-fed crocodile. It was his last meal, for they shot him.

"Now there are two lessons to be learned from this story. First, virtually every crocodile casualty is alcohol related – and it's not the crocodile that's been drinking. It has only behaved as nature intended. Secondly, given a choice, a crocodile will always select the smallest person around as its prey. That's the easiest target, and the meat is usually more tender and easier to digest. The men in this instance had all been in deeper water swimming and one guy even felt the crocodile brush against him as it made its attack run. So, guys, the moral of this story is, if you plan on swimming in crocodile infested water, take your girlfriend with you. The crocodile will always go for her first!"

I love the Australian sense of humour.

The Daintree Forest is another World Heritage Site. Plants have survived here that became extinct elsewhere in the world millions of years ago. It is a biological time warp, a dense steamy forest with trees covered in straggling creepers, populated with pythons which grow up to ten metres long, and numerous other snakes and lizards, tree kangaroos, cassowaries (oh, the cassowarie is a large emu type of bird with razor sharp claws that can kill a man – well, everything else does, so why not the cassowarie too?). There are large vociferous frogs that croak deafeningly through the night, millions of insects that chirrup in the trees so loud it feels like you are in the middle of a huge sports stadium with screaming fans following your every movement, deadly spiders, and a stinging tree that won't kill you but makes you wish you were dead. It is the kind of place in which you could easily visualise dinosaurs prowling – and you wouldn't be a bit surprised if you met one.

It is not difficult to get lost either, our driver told us. "Now another word of warning if you plan to go bush walking. People get lost here all the time." I had deduced by this time that Australia seemed remarkably adept at reducing the world's population! "So if any of you plan on going walkabout, make sure you tell the people at the hostel. Fill out one of the safety forms with details of your route and when you expect to return, and leave it with them."

We all nodded obediently, thinking it sage advice – until he went on: "Not that it'll do you much good. One guy went off a few years ago on what should have been a six-hour hike up Mount Sorrow. No one bothered to check the safety sheets, and even though he'd left his tent pitched in the grounds of a backpackers' hostel, it was *three weeks* later that they realised he was missing. He's never been seen since."

There was still a vestige of adventure left in me, so I went walking in the jungle (well, hobbling is more accurate with my bad leg), with all these thoughts in my mind. I did not wander far, and stuck strictly to the sign-posted paths and boardwalks that had been laid across the swamps. The fact that you are reading this now is proof that I am still alive after strolling casually in the company of all the horrors lurking there. I began to wonder if the driver had made it up, for all I saw was one sluggish terrapin.

Back at the hostel we were warned not to leave any food lying around in the kitchen because it encourages nocturnal visitors, like snakes. They don't have windows, just holes in the wall to keep the place cool. As a result, it is not a good idea to go wandering into the kitchen for a drink of water in the dark. It wasn't too inviting outside, either, with Golden Orb Spiders' webs, a metre in diameter, suspended between the eaves and the nearby trees. The spiders' bodies were as long and thick as my little finger, and their legs would have spanned my entire hand if laid on the palm, but they were beautiful, with golden rings circling each leg. They are said to be harmless. The forest comes alive at night with all sorts of rustlings in the undergrowth, bats fluttering around, and toads and frogs belching at each other. The noise is amazing. It wasn't the sort of place to go stumbling around in the dark. I took a book to bed and had an early night.

I took a sea-kayaking trip next morning. We set off from a beautiful bay with soft white sand and not a jellyfish in sight. It was a perfect day, cloudless without a breath of wind, with the surface of the sea like glass allowing us to view the coral below and observe turtles and rays swimming underneath us. Our guide led us round Cape Tribulation and we beached the boats for a picnic. He then took us for a short walk up a shallow creek among the mangroves to visit the resident crocodile. From about fifty metres away we watched him as he watched us, motionless as a log. Had it not been for the guide pointing him out to us, we could have wandered along blissfully unaware that he wasn't a log. This was not a place for the uninitiated to go stumbling around either.

Not far from the hostel lived the bat-woman – a woman literally festooned with bats, all clinging to her shirt. She ran a bat sanctuary, and told us about the bats' lifestyle and the research programme currently being undertaken there. The bats were big, with bodies the size of a weasel and wings about eighteen inches long, and as they were stroked and fondled, they snuffled like young puppies. The wings were beautiful to touch, delicate and smooth as silk. Bats, like tarantulas, sharks and wolves, have been much maligned by ill-informed writers and hollywood film makers in their quest for scaring people. These creatures were beautiful, cuddly and affectionate.

On my return to Cairns for my final night I wanted to say farewell to my diving buddies, and wandered out to see if I could find Jamie and Nick. O'Brien's Irish Pub was the most likely place to find them. As I went in I heard a cry, "John, John! Over here!" It was Els and Ingrid. "Come and join us."

I sat down at their table and gave them the news. On hearing I was leaving in the morning, Ingrid immediately called up Jamie and Nick on her mobile phone. They arrived a few minutes later. They were all so sympathetic. We talked for a while and exchanged addresses and I issued an invitation to visit me in Scotland and come sailing with me. I left to go to the toilet. When I returned, Jamie and Nick both put their arms around my shoulders and said, "We've just been talking about you, John, and your fantastic lifestyle. You know, for such an *old* guy, you're really quite young at heart!" I felt another wee glow, which helped to ease the ache I felt. They, too, had cared, and I hoped that I might be privileged to meet them all sometime in the future.

I left Cairns at 8.00am the next morning. Forty-two hours later I walked through the door of my house in Lochcarron, Scotland.

Now I had to see my own doctor.

Chapter 28
Sharks and Falling Coconuts

Seven months after leaving Australia, I was on my way back. During that time I had spent twelve weeks with my leg in plaster following surgery to repair the broken Achilles tendon. I healed very quickly. Amazingly, I had suffered no pain as a result of the operation. When I regained consciousness I asked the nurse what the tube plugged into my arm was for. "That's your morphine pump. Just squeeze this button here with your finger and you'll get a shot to keep the pain under control."

"I don't feel any pain."

"Oh, but you will when the effects of the anaesthetic wear off."

At night, when she came round doing her checks she looked at the reading on the morphine pump. "You haven't taken any morphine," she scolded.

"I don't need any," I retorted. She drew me a pained look.

"You don't *have* to suffer, you know."

"But I'm not suffering. I don't need it. You might as well take all this damned plumbing out of my arm. It's just getting in a fankle when I turn round to sleep on my side."

"Of course you need it. You've just had major surgery. You've been cut open and had bits of you pinned together and you've been sewn up again. You're bound to feel pain. If you don't like taking morphine, I can give you some paracetamol tablets instead."

"But what for?"

"For the pain!" She was getting exasperated with me.

"But I-don't-have-any-pain." I hammered the words out – I was getting exasperated with her. "Now will you kindly disconnect all the plumbing and let me get back to sleep."

She placed her hands on her hips and tilted her head. She didn't have to say anything. I could read the body language: 'Oh, I would love to give this one a right good slap'. Aye, she's determined to get me to feel pain one way or another, I thought. We squared up to each other and I glowered back. She could read my body language too. She knew she couldn't touch me, not with my leg in plaster from hip to toe, not just after an operation. I held the ace card. She cracked. "I'll have to ask the doctor." The tube was taken out. I never, at any time, felt even a slight twinge of pain after the operation. Maybe the Fijians with their bush medicine know something we don't.

I had been warned by the doctors to take things easy for at least a year – and definitely no single-handed sailing that summer. That was a major blow, but if I had to be beached all summer I decided to turn the enforced convalescence to some advantage. My kitchen was in need of major surgery, too, so I spent some time working on a new design. I started assembling units while still using crutches, but when the plaster came off my leg I got busy with the demolition work, taking it right back to the bare walls and bare rock underneath with a few days of invaluable help from my son. The re-construction took up most of the summer, but by early October I was desperate to get on the road again.

I wanted to take up that cancelled diving trip from Cairns to some of the more remote parts of the Great Barrier Reef. I also had plans to go to Antarctica and since I had to go to South America to get there I could fit in some trekking in the Andes. And between Australia and South America lay the Fiji, the Cook Islands and Easter Island, another place I had long dreamed of visiting. My patched up Achilles tendon seemed to be doing fine, so I got the backpack on again and flew from Scotland to Cairns, stopping only to change flights at London and Hong Kong.

My first night back in Australia was spent visiting Bruce and Shirley again at Cairns. I had enjoyed their hospitality so much on my last visit, and they had insisted that I should stay with them again. On my arrival, Shirley suggested an afternoon nap, a sensible suggestion after thirty nine hours of continuous travel. A few hours later, the delicious smell of a barbecue drifted through my bedroom window and brought me to my senses again. I then enjoyed a delightful evening in their company. Bruce dropped me off in town next day, and the dive company minibus picked me up at the Youth Hostel.

MV Taka was a new, purpose-built dive boat. It entered service towards the end of 2003, specialising in trips to some of the most remote, pristine parts of the Great Barrier Reef and to Osprey Reef, some 200 miles out in the Coral Sea. Twenty five divers had assembled in the ship's lounge for the pre-cruise briefing, and I gazed around the faces. I get gut feelings about people, and studying the faces and body language I noted those I felt I'd most likely bond with during the trip.

The social interaction began at dinner that night, and I found myself surrounded by most of those whose company I had anticipated I would enjoy. In the days that followed we spent a fair bit of time together on deck in the sun, resting between dives or chatting in the lounge in the evenings. That first night we steamed steadily northwards for about 250 miles, arriving at our destination around 11.00am the next morning. On our approach to the reef, my attention was caught by a splash in the sea ahead of us. Dolphins? I gazed ahead. A black body and fin broke the surface in that characteristic leap.

"Dolphin ahead!" I shouted.

Everyone rushed to the bow to see them. A pod of nine dolphins had arrived and were gleefully jostling for position in the pressure wave just ahead of our bow. In the crystal clear water we could see them all pushing and shoving for the best position to slide down the pressure wave, like surfers, but underwater. Absolutely delightful to watch, they stayed with us for maybe twenty minutes or so. It was an uplifting start to the day.

This part of the reef is well beyond the range of most of the boats operating out of Cairns. Our position was much further north than any other settlement along that coast, so the reef has not suffered the same damage as many of those closer to areas of human habitation. Here, the highlight was the feeding of the giant groupers, sometimes called potato cod, a fish around five feet long with a body as thick as a human torso yet so tame here and amiable. Discovering one resting under a coral overhang, I signalled to my dive buddy, Eric, to come and have a look and moved over to let him in. The huge fish gazed at him with as much curiosity as he gazed upon it. It seemed to like the look of him and began to move slowly towards him. Eric backed off. The fish still came forward slowly, inexorably advancing towards him, its face no more than about thirty centimetres from his. Its jaws appeared big enough to swallow his head. They gazed into each other's eyes. There was no hint of any aggressiveness in its behaviour, indeed with its huge pouting lips and its big eyes looking directly into his, I thought it had fallen in love with him. Eric confirmed later that he had been thinking along the same lines and was beginning to feel nervous in case its amorous looks were a prelude to an attempt at procreation.

Later that day we had a fish-feeding session during which the divers sat around in a circle with the divemaster and a bucket of food in the centre. A giant cod swam up to him, gently took a morsel and moved away allowing another leviathan to come up for a nibble. Swimming between the divers, these enormous fish caressed themselves against our bodies. I am not comfortable with the idea of feeding the fish. I believe you should affect their behaviour as little as possible, but it was on the itinerary and it was an interesting diversion.

We did four dives each day, the last one usually a night dive. As you don't have the same range of vision at night – virtually only that afforded by the torch beam – it is interesting how you begin to notice all sorts of small details of reef life that you tend to miss during the day. Tiny shrimps, their orange eyes like gemstones reflecting the beam of the torch, hide among the staghorn coral, and when you get close they propel themselves backwards with a flick of the tail and the velocity of a bullet, certainly much faster than the eye can take in. Crustaceans leave their rocky cavities and move about the rocks and ocean floor in search of food. Much of the coral appears a different colour in the artificial light, adding another dimension to the experience.

The limited visibility generates a certain excitement, in that you come upon things unexpectedly. During the day, visibility here is around forty metes and you can see so many fish at a distance; at night, you see only a few metres ahead in the beam of your torch. What is lurking beyond, in the gloomy darkness, you just do not know. And then, as you rise above a coral wall, a grey shape suddenly emerges from the gloom on the other side, and you find yourself face to face with a large shark. It is as surprised as you are, doesn't like the look of you at all, and with a flick of its tail veers off quickly to be consumed by the darkness once more. Large trevally hunt at night and they know that the light from the divers' torches will pinpoint the smaller fish they prey upon. So you find them swimming in your company as they await your beam picking out their dinner. With the small fish a bit dazzled by the light, the trevally dive upon them from the shadows beside you with lightning rapidity. We try to reduce the unfair advantage we offer the trevally by avoiding keeping the beam of light on small fish for too long. A limit of three hits per diver had been recommended by the divemaster.

It had been a superb first day, and as we ate dinner that night the anchor was raised and the ship got under way again to leave the Great Barrier Reef (we would return to dive more sites on our way back) and steam 200 miles out into the Coral Sea. Osprey Reef, a coral crust which has built up around the crater of an ancient submerged volcano, was our destination.

We dived four sites along this reef, which is quite outstanding in the quality of coral and the range of marine life it supports: turtles and sharks, barracuda and moray eels, unicorn fish, trevally, tuna, red bass, literally hundreds of different kinds of fish of all sizes and in the most brilliant colours. We dived on a garden of giant clams, their jaws a full metre across, with the most beautifully coloured, abstract patterned membranes covering the gap between the two huge corrugated shells. We spiralled around coral pinnacles rising thirty metres from the shelf like mountainous stalagmites festooned with multi-coloured growths, and explored reef walls, fissured with long, dark caves and canyons, one of which had trapped an old anchor estimated to have lodged there around 150–200 years ago. On Steve's Bommie – a coral knoll about eighteen metres down – a memorial plaque has been placed to commemorate a guy called Steve who loved free diving (i.e. diving without breathing apparatus – the specialist activity of such men as the Pacific pearl divers who can stay down at amazing depths for several minutes at a time). Well, poor Steve overdid it on one occasion and blacked out underwater doing what he loved doing, but would never do again, and his friends placed this plaque on one of his favourite spots on this remote reef 200 miles out to sea. It is not the kind of thing you expect to find at the bottom of the sea and it had a certain poignancy about it. Osprey reef is, quite simply, fantastic.

It was here we saw the sharks being fed. The divers all perched, like seabirds on a cliff face, on ledges at around twenty metres depth and the fish, knowing this gathering was the prelude to a feast, gathered around in great numbers as we waited for the boat with the food to arrive. I was intrigued by this. How did they manage to communicate with one another? Somehow, word seemed to get around that food was on its way, and thousands of fish assembled around us. On my way down I saw a couple of sharks, but by the time everyone had assembled I had counted no fewer than FIFTY sharks, all circling above us. Like aircraft waiting permission to land, the sharks cruised in circles, mingling with hundreds of other smaller fish, some giant groupers and a passing turtle. The sea was thick with fish.

The feast consisted of several large tuna heads with holes drilled in them and a chain threaded through, thus forming a sort of giant tuna head kebab. The ship's boat arrived above and lowered the chain into the sea. The effect was electrifying. Sharks dived on it from all angles, tearing at the fish heads, shaking them from side to side much as a terrier would play with a rag doll. Huge groupers barged in like fat torpedoes, their snouts butting sharks sideways to get at the food. Opportunist red snappers dashed in to snatch at fragments of fish flying from the rips and tears of the sharks and shot out again before being crushed among the writhing bodies of the big fish. From this melee of writhing, snapping, tearing jaws, a shower of smaller fragments was sprayed around like snowflakes for the little fish to snap up: crumbs from the big boys' table. It was mesmerising.

In the middle of this melee was Paul, our fearless crew cameraman, filming the action close up with his video camera, and Ty, the divemaster, taking still pictures for the record of our voyage. As the frenzy began to subside and there were only a few fragments left, a huge moray eel raised its head from a hole in the coral just below the boys with the cameras and hooked its teeth into the last fish head. With its tail firmly anchored in its hole in the coral it then retreated, trying to pull the tuna head in with it. The hole was just not big enough, and the head jammed at the entrance. Tugging at it seemed to excite the sharks once more and two or three dived in another frenzy on the fish head, tearing it away from the eel and another round of shaking, wriggling and snapping followed.

When the frenzy had subsided, we were free to go exploring the reef. On sandy beds under ledges in the coral wall lay several hyperventilating sharks, exhausted by their efforts. Divers approached close up to take pictures. The sharks tolerated them. There was no aggression from the fish, just a kind of 'leave me alone guys, I need a post-prandial nap' attitude.

Many people express concern about the danger of swimming in waters populated by sharks. Let's put it in perspective. Look at a coconut and compare that with a shark. Which is more scary and why? It is a fact that far more people are killed every year by falling coconuts than are attacked, let alone killed, by sharks. There are very few sharks even capable of biting a human limb. Many of them have jaws designed for eating in other ways, like sifting through coral sand, or filtering plankton from the sea – and human limbs neither attract, nor are capable of, being eaten by such mouths. We don't go around chewing up trees because our jaws are not up to the task, nor are our digestive systems capable of digesting wood. It's the same with sharks. Biting a human would be inconceivable for most of them. They are beautiful creatures.

Yes, a few incidents occur from time to time, maybe four or five worldwide annually, when an occasional great white or a tiger shark may snap at arms or legs when they confuse swimmers with seals, but they don't go around hunting for human beings for lunch. You are more at risk of having a fatal accident in your own home or in your car.

So give the sharks a break and forget the sensationalist stories portrayed by films like *Jaws*.

Okay, I know it's hard, but try.

Chapter 29
Adrift in the Coral Sea

Despite the various attractions of this excellent reef, the most memorable dive of all was the one we had to abort. The reef follows the shape of the leaf-shaped crater. A narrow shelf spreads out from the reef wall for about fifty metres to the drop off, a precipitous wall descending to the ocean bottom around 1,000 metres below. We were diving at the north end of the reef, near the pointed end of the leaf shape, and were warned to stay clear of the point as the current runs strongly round there and we could be swept out to sea.

Out there, the deep water is home to large tiger sharks, one of the very few species that might be curious enough to have a nibble. A strong current was running, but using the mooring rope as a guide line to the shelf at around eighteen metres depth, we should have no problem getting down, and only a short distance from there, clearly in sight ahead, was the reef. Once there, we could explore its canyons and caves, sheltered from the strength of the current. Simple.

We did our buddy checks on each other: air supply turned on, tank pressure checked, regulator working, emergency air supply working, buoyancy vests working, emergency kit stowed in pocket. The crew checked each of us off the dive list as we entered the water. I entered first and made my way along a surface rope streaming from the mooring buoy to help us get there easily. There was quite a current. Eric followed.

On reaching the mooring buoy, I signalled to descend, and he returned the signal. I pressed the button in my buoyancy vest and slipped below the waves with the hiss of escaping air. With one hand on the mooring line, the other squeezing my nose while I blew it to equalise the pressure on my ears, I made my way steadily down. I could see the seabed clearly below me and looked back up to check that Eric was following. He wasn't. I arrested my descent.

Still at the surface, he was struggling with his buoyancy. Sometimes, the buoyancy vest traps a pocket of air and you need to angle one shoulder down to get a vertical run to let all the air out. I made my way back up to help. That's the role of the buddy – stay close to your partner and give assistance when required. Using my negative buoyancy to lower his right shoulder, we got him tilted and all the air hissed out. He signalled to descend.

I slipped again below the surface and dropped towards the bottom. Looking up, I could see him still above me having yet more trouble getting down. I ascended again. He was descending, but very slowly, and he was still fiddling with his buoyancy apparatus, but to no avail. I released my grip on the mooring line to help check all the air was out. He let go as we worked on it. The buoyancy vest was definitely empty, and we both descended, but still very slowly. Of course, having let go of the mooring line while we struggled with his apparatus, the current had taken us back towards the stern of the ship, now visible above and slightly ahead of us. We should have been forward of the bow. I indicated that we should swim towards the reef rather than waiting for the bottom to come into sight. The shelf here is narrow and visibility that day was not too good. We did not want to miss it altogether.

We swam forward. At least, that's what we appeared to be doing. By now, the ship had disappeared from view and there was no sign of either the shelf below or the reef wall ahead of us. Still we swam in the right direction, descending all the time, but at the same infuriatingly slow rate. I couldn't understand what was wrong with Eric's buoyancy. The current was strong and we had no visual terms of reference to see whether we were making any progress.

A gradually deepening blue void surrounded us. I checked my dive computer: 17 metres. The shelf bottom should be right there below us now. It wasn't. It was time to neutralise buoyancy, to stop descending, level out and find the reef. We swam harder in the direction of the reef hoping that we would pick up sight of it, or the shelf, at any moment.

We didn't.

With startling suddenness, a strange, eerie flash of light pierced the blue gloom. It glowed like a bluish diamond for a few seconds and then dimmed. It was amazingly beautiful. It was followed by another... and then another... And yet more! They were all around us. The most intensely beautiful, faintly bluish lights were flashing everywhere. We were immersed in a sea filled with sparkling gems: diamonds, or perhaps more accurately, pale blue sapphires. The night before we had been lamenting the fact that we hadn't had a view of the sky at night, for away out here at sea, far from any artificial light, the southern sky on a cloudless night offers the most amazing display of stars. This more than made up for it. It was like floating in space *among* the stars. Their beauty was indescribable. It was a sight so breathtaking it had to be shared. I wanted the whole world to see what astounding beauty there was down here in the depths of the ocean and how tranquil it all was. What a beautiful, peaceful place. I had found paradise. I could die a happy man after seeing this. I could die quite happily here and now. I wanted to hear the silver tongues of choirs of angels, singing serene harmonies to accompany these most wondrous sights around me as I made my euphoric way towards the gates of heaven.

Something then triggered in my brain and jolted me out of my euphoria. I had studied zoology as an ancillary subject in my degree course at university. The wondrous illuminations were light-emitting plankton, creatures which, when agitated, emit flashes of light. But these weren't the tiny, almost microscopic, dinoflagellates I have seen so often when sailing at night in Scotland. These were much bigger, the size of a finger nail and so brilliant in the intensity of light they projected.

A realisation hit me: light emitting plankton of that size tend to be found in deep water!

I checked my dive computer. The figures were flashing rapidly now: 33 metres... 34 metres... 35 metres... We should have touched the shelf bottom at no more than about 18 metres. The implication dawned on me: the current, flowing off the shelf, had swept us out and down, like being carried over a waterfall, and we had missed it completely. Our buoyancy was now decreasing as the tiny air pockets in our wet suits were compressed by the increase in pressure at these depths, and with the strong down current we were actually accelerating towards the floor of the ocean, 1,000 metres below.

Two more words flashed into my mind: Nitrogen Narcossis. At certain depths, the nitrogen levels in the blood build up and can induce a feeling of euphoria. People become irrational in this condition, and often do silly things, like taking their mouthpieces out, thinking they can breathe seawater. I wondered how it was affecting Eric. Would he go crazy and go carousing off into the depths, and how would I get him up if he did? If I followed him, I could go off my head too. I wasn't a kick in the backside away from it already with my thoughts of pearly gates and choirs of angels and dying in a sea full of sapphires. There was no time to waste.

I reached out and touched him, pointed to the dive computer on my wrist, and signalled to ascend. He checked his computer and signalled his agreement. We pumped more air from our tanks into our vests to counteract the strength of the downward pull, and slowly began to rise once more. The beautiful lights died out at around 28 metres. We kept on climbing, slowly – too fast a rate of ascent could give us the bends.

We hovered at 5 metres for a standard three-minute safety stop, then eased ourselves back to the surface.

The sea was now quite lively, with a fresh breeze whipping up a fifty centimetre chop, the waves obscuring our view of the horizon. *Taka* is quite a big vessel, three decks high, and easy to see on the expanse of the ocean – but it was nowhere in sight! I couldn't believe this. I checked my dive computer to see how long we had been down. It registered only eleven minutes. We couldn't have lost a ship that size in such a short time. It couldn't have left the area, because this was the start of the first dive of the day. Reason kicked in again. Our eyes were virtually at sea level and the sea was throwing up waves which must be preventing us from seeing the ship.

I pumped more air into my buoyancy vest to raise me further out of the water and kicked hard with my fins to gain some extra height, turning a full circle as I did so. It worked. As I rotated, the ship came into view above the waves, but a long way off. In spite of constantly swimming hard towards the reef, we had been swept in exactly the opposite direction a good 500 metres in only eleven minutes.

"Over there! Let's swim for it," I called to Eric. It was to no avail. The current was too strong, and we were simply reversing further out into the Coral Sea. The divemaster's warning came into mind. Out here was the territory of the big tiger sharks – one of the few species that just may be tempted to have a nibble. It wasn't a very comforting thought. I remembered seeing recently a clip from that film Open Water, about the couple who'd been left behind in these waters and had never been seen again. The film clip showed them surfacing to find the boat gone and in its place was a large, black circling fin. I looked around. There were no fins – and this was no time for such thoughts either.

The mathematician in me took control. The probability that, in the enormous expanse of the Pacific Ocean, there were tiger sharks in exactly this spot seemed slight – let's say a 1-in-1000 chance; and, even if there were, that they would be sufficiently aggressive to have a bite at us? Say also 1-in-1000. As I said before, most sharks are just not interested in us. Then the total probability of our being attacked by a shark was a million to one in our favour. That made it more comforting. Like eating porridge, or a good portion of green vegetables, a little sprinkling of mathematics is good for maintaining a healthy attitude mind.

I just hoped two things: one, that Eric hadn't been thinking of the sharks, making him panic. And two, that I hadn't been counting chickens!

But this was no time and definitely no place to panic, so I called out to Eric, as calmly as I could manage: "It's a waste of time swimming. Let's inflate the sausages." No, I wasn't imagining things – 'sausages' are long plastic tubes carried in our pockets that, when filled with air, rise erect from the sea. The bright orange colour attracts the attention of the lookouts posted on the dive boat.

That's the theory anyway.

However, all the divers should be ahead of the boat, and we were a long way astern. I just hoped the lookouts would be looking all round, just in case. We got the big balloons out of the pockets and filled them with air from our tanks, then lay on our backs, and for good measure blew our whistles for all we were worth. I wondered if sharks' sense of hearing was as acute as their sense of smell. I hoped they were as deaf as posts!

There was an amusing side to it. There we were, lying on our backs holding what looked like enormous condoms sticking up in the air. Again to make light of things I called out, "Hey, Eric! It's the first time I've had a two metre erection." He grinned. It worked and helped ease away the fears. He confessed to me later that he was really concerned at that point and making light of the situation was the best medicine.

A few moments, later we saw the ship's boat pull away from the stern and turn towards us. It was soon alongside, heaved us each a line with a handle on the end and then towed us, like a couple of logs, back to the ship. The divemaster was waiting. He checked us back aboard on the dive list. And then we had some explaining to do.

I told him that we'd had a problem with Eric's buoyancy and, in attempting to solve the problem, we had floated free of the mooring line. Mistake. We should have kept at least one hand on the line. The current did the rest. But after that point we'd done all we'd been trained to do. We stayed close together. We kept in constant communication. If we had been a bit affected by nitrogen narcosis, we still were 'compos mentis' enough to make a proper, safe ascent. We'd tried to swim back, but on realising we couldn't we'd deployed the safety signal. The crew of the boat were keeping proper watch and we were picked up safely. The training and the teamwork had been effective. He studied me carefully and paused for a moment to let all this sink in. "Yeah. You're right," he conceded. Then he turned to Eric. "But what was the problem with your buoyancy?"

Eric looked a bit sheepish. He'd felt a bit cold in the water the day before and decided to put on an extra wet suit. A wet suit is really a layer of tiny air bubbles, and what he had done had therefore increased his buoyancy considerably. What he should also have done was add extra lead weights to his belt to counteract the increase in buoyancy. That bit he'd forgotten. He looked at me so shamefaced and began to apologise.

I reassured him. "Och, anybody can make a mistake. It could be my turn tomorrow. What pleases me is that we stuck together and remained a team throughout. We kept in touch and did all the right things to recover from a hazardous situation, and that's a good lesson. It was a learning experience neither of us will forget! And down there we saw some of the most beautiful sights any human being could have been privileged to witness."

Chapter 30
Back Among Friends

Fiji has over three hundred islands, and on my second visit I fulfilled a desire to sail among a few of them on a schooner – *Seaspray*, a beautiful, eighty year-old vessel built in Scotland. It achieved fame as the star of a TV series made in Australia in the late 1960s about the adventures of a widowed journalist who travelled the Pacific with his three children.

Cruising among the outer islands of the Mamanuca group under a cloudless sky, we dropped anchor off the island where Tom Hanks's film *Castaway* was made. Ashore, the sand was so hot on the feet you could hardly stand on one spot; even worse, the heat stored in the black, volcanic rock made it unbearable to walk on. However, the sea was lovely: it must have been very close to body temperature as there was so little sensation of temperature change when you entered the water. The snorkelling was good, with some superb coral teeming with brilliantly coloured fish.

At nearby Malolo we had some time ashore to visit a typical island village and shared in a kava drinking ceremony with the local chief. The custom on such occasions is always to seek the chief's permission to enter the village, and the visitors are expected to offer a gift – usually some kava root. On this occasion, we were invited to consider offering a cash donation to improve the resources of the local school.

After the welcoming ceremony, we were free to roam the village and buy trinkets from the villagers: shells, hand made jewellery, hats, woven mats, and tapa hangings (a sort of parchment with traditional patterns dyed on them, which are made from tree bark).

The standard of housing is very basic. A few of the older houses were traditional bures, but gradually they are being replaced by more modern houses of concrete block construction, basically a concrete box with a tin roof. Windows had no glazing; they were simply holes with wooden shutters hinged above, which could be drawn in stormy conditions. Doors were always left open to encourage air circulation, and it was evident that the houses had little in the way of furniture – often no more than mattresses laid on the concrete floor with little else. Concrete, rather than wood, is preferred for the floors as it is cooler. Cooking was generally done outside over a wood fire set close to a rack with pots and a sink. Plumbing was elementary, usually just a standpipe with a tap.

This short voyage among beautiful islands was executed in dreamlike conditions, ghosting along at a leisurely pace with only a few degrees of heel to the wind. *Seaspray* is a beautiful old lady, possessed of all the elegance of a bygone age, with the graceful and sleek lines of a true thoroughbred.

My main reason for coming back to Fiji was to return to Caqalai, the idyllic wee island I had lived on the previous year, to visit Kanai and his family. I took the bus round to Suva and onwards to Korovu to catch the boat, but I had left it too late. The entire family had left the island just a month previously. Kanai, Dubai and the younger children were now living away over on the far side of Motoriki; no one knew where the girls Dauni, Sherry and Fanga, or Mopsje and the older boys were now. The old chief had died, and it was the new young chief and his wife who were now running the island resort.

I'm a sucker for the simple life on a wee island with dusky maidens dancing attendance on me, so I stayed for five days. Because of my injury the previous year I hadn't been very active. This time I made up for it, exploring the island – that only took about half and hour – exploring Leluvia, a neighbouring island, and snorkelling. The snorkelling was outstanding, with some of the most vibrantly coloured coral gardens I have ever seen. The outer edge of the reef, layered with multicoloured coral growths, tumbled away into the dark blue depths. It was endlessly fascinating and always delectably warm.

As had happened the previous year when we went over to Motoriki for the church service, the chief asked me to speak on behalf of the visitors. To my surprise, most of the congregation not only recognised me, they even remembered my name. When the service was over I received the most heart-warming welcome. The minister's wife hugged me tightly and beamed at me.

"John, this is wonderful. You have travelled all the way round the world, but God has brought you back to us again. It means a lot to us."

To my astonishment, the chief ordered a special kava drinking ceremony to celebrate my return. I felt like the Prodigal Son. We all retired to the village hall, and I was given the place of honour, seated cross-legged on the floor in my kilt, immediately opposite the chief. It had proved to be quite a homecoming after all.

I had planned to spend the next two weeks in Samoa, and on my return from Samoa I had few days before I was due to leave Fiji, so I decided to head out to the Yasawa islands to relax for a few days. I was so disappointed that I had failed to make contact with my Caqalai friends from the previous year and thought I'd never see any of them again. However, at the airport I picked up a brochure and flicked through it. My attention was drawn to an article entitled *Coconut Bay*. It described the small resort 'owned by Sherry and her family'. That sounded familiar. I remembered Sherry telling me the previous year on Caqalai that her family owned a small resort on one of the Yasawa Islands. If Sherry were there now I could perhaps get news of the others from her. I went into a tour office at the airport and asked them to phone Coconut Bay and ask if Sherry was on the island. The Coconut Bay phone was out of order. However, the tourist office tried a neighbouring resort and they confirmed that Sherry was there. They agreed to pass on a message telling her that she had a guest called John coming for a couple of nights. It would be a surprise for her. I took the ferry to the islands next morning. As events unfolded, there were even more surprises for *me*.

The small motorboat came alongside the ferry to take me ashore and I gasped when I saw the helmsman: it was Mopsje, who had ferried me to and from Caqalai the previous year. Once he had the boat lashed alongside, he looked up and reached out to catch my baggage. I stuck my hand out and shook his, grinning. "Hi Mopsje!"

"John!" he gasped. He was speechless. So was I, such was my delight to see him again. It was only a short distance to the shore, and a welcoming party awaited my arrival. The boys were playing their guitars and singing and Sherry was among them, looking out towards us. Then she recognised the newcomer. She screamed and ran back up the beach and rushed into the kitchen. When she came back out she was dragging Dauni behind her, and they both rushed down the beach. So she was here too! I couldn't believe this. I jumped out of the boat and waded ashore into their open arms.

"How did you know we were here?" asked Dauni.

"I didn't." I explained the events of the past three weeks, my going to Caqalai and the disappointment to learn that they had all left, about going to Samoa and then finding the leaflet that led me here. They were astounded I had come all the way round the world and found them again.

"Oh, John," asserted Dauni confidently, "you can't ignore this. It's the hand of God guiding you back here to marry me!"

I laughed. "Well, maybe He did guide me here, but I'm not so sure about the marriage bit."

Sherry and Mopsje had become husband and wife since last year and were now expecting a child. Later on, as I lay on a hammock reading, another girl walked past. She stopped dead in her tracks, staring at me. "Excuse me. Is your name John?"

"Aye." I looked at her closely, then realised that she was Niko, one of the kitchen girls from Caqalai. She told me that Anna, another of the kitchen girls, was also there. Having been reunited with five of the young people who cared for me so well last year, I just had to stay for longer than the two nights originally booked.

To change my flights and get more cash to cover the cost of my extended stay necessitated a trip back to the mainland. Mopsje and Sherry were going over to the hospital for a routine check on her pregnancy in a couple of days, and Dauni was going too, so I went with them. It was voyage of forty miles over open sea in a small open boat – in a thunderstorm! The two girls and I lay on an improvised mattress of lifejackets on the floor and covered ourselves with a tarpaulin while Mopsje stayed at the tiller and got soaked. I wondered what it would feel like if lightning struck us.

We made it without being incinerated.

We went to Dauni's sister's house in Lautoka. She and her husband and children had come to Caqalai at Christmas the previous year when I had played my spoons on the children's knees. That had ensured my immortality and recognition was instant: "Did you bring your spoons?"

This reunion called for another celebration, and that meant more kava drinking. I feigned great enthusiasm and joined in the fun. They were so hospitable and insisted that on the night I had to leave Fiji I was to come to their house again for a feast and kava, and they would drive me to the airport for my 4.00am flight to New Zealand.

Next day I got my tickets altered, we gathered some groceries for the island and shipped the supplies back to Coconut Bay. I could now relax and enjoy myself among friends.

Chapter 31
Faith and Hope

I enjoyed being in Fiji again. It is definitely more interesting when you stay longer in one place. I got to know the island and the rest of the local people, and with a group of other tourists visited the secondary school on the other side of the island. The teacher asked us to introduce ourselves and talk a little about where we came from and what we did. The kids sat and listened politely. Several of our group mentioned rugby as one of their interests. Rugby is very popular in Fiji. It doesn't excite me at all.

I mentioned that in my youth I had played a fair bit of football. Proper football. The beautiful game. Where the magic is performed with the feet. And to demonstrate I began to mime the art of ball juggling with feet, knees, head and shoulders, as you see top-class players like the Brazilians do. But I was doing it without a ball. Big, white-toothed grins broke out. The kids were fascinated by my every flick or nod and the sensuous movements of leg, head and shoulder. They gazed in astonishment at the artistry with which I kept this non-existent ball in the air. For the climax of my party piece, I flicked the ball up from foot to head, nodded it a couple of times, then bounced it off my left shoulder on to my right knee, which gave it another flick up; then, as it dropped towards the floor, I swung my right leg round behind my left and volleyed the ball neatly with my instep before it reached the floor, sending it into the middle of the class. Except that there was no ball.

So engrossed were they by this display of artistry that the absence of a ball was of no consequence, as evinced by the fact that when I propelled that non-existent ball into the crowd, one boy was so tuned in that he reached up and caught it, like a good goalkeeper! And that brought him a spontaneous round of applause. Even the other tourists clapped their hands. That's the power of imagination. It's one of the first principles of teaching: stimulate the imagination and you capture their attention. Then the learning really begins.

Before we finally left, the kids sang for us, unaccompanied. They had no need for music. One senior girl hit the first note and the rest all followed, singing heartily with beautiful harmonies. In common with the other people in the Pacific, music is in their soul. We waved goodbye and filed out. "Goodbye" they called out and waved. Then one girl called out, "Goodbye, *John*." Another followed suit, and then there was a chorus of, "Goodbye, *John*."

My no-ball juggling had made quite an impression. It could never have been so good if I'd actually had one! Okay, I had conned them, but I had them with me. What mattered was that they believed in something they could not see and, by that simple act, I knew they believed in me as a teacher. That's faith. Now, take me to the sea and I'll show you how to walk on water!

I spent so much time in the sea, scuba diving, snorkelling and skin diving, that I found caves in the reefs that the even local boys didn't know were there. They went out to the reef to fish, spear fishing mostly in order to feed us, whereas I had the time to explore. I collected a few bloody scrapes on my shoulders to prove it too, but the caves were beautiful. The colour of the rock inside is a muted, dark pink, encrusted with marine growths, shellfish and soft corals. The light is a soft, bluish glow and fish peer at you with wide-open eyes as they lurk in the shadows. The sunlight filters through the water, is beamed down through holes in the coral, and reflects off the white sandy bottom to create an ethereal, soft, turquoise hue, gently illuminating the colours, shapes and forms of the marine life clinging to the cave walls and roof.

Exploration of these caves involved first checking that they were navigable all through and that there was a clear way out. I checked the exit hole in the reef from the top, and having satisfied myself that I could get in, through and out in one breath, I dived to the bottom, usually about six metres down, swam into the cave and then up through the exit hole in the reef much farther back. This proved entertaining when taking snorkelling parties out. They watched from the surface as I dived to the bottom and disappeared into the reef. Some were so intent on watching the mouth of the cave, they failed to see me emerge from a hole a few metres across the surface of reef until I swam over and tapped them on the head.

"Where did you come from?" they cried in astonishment.

On the other side of the island we dived on the wreck of a US fighter plane, a casualty of World War Two. The crew of two had been rescued by a local girl who had witnessed the crash, swam out and dragged them to the shore. That girl was the mother of our boatman. We found a group of manta rays, their wings flapping like giant birds cruising in the narrow sound between Naviti and Drawaqa where the coral on the

Drawaqa side was probably the best I have seen anywhere. I learned to spearfish with the local boys using a piece of rubber inner tubing like a giant elastic band and a long rod sharpened to fine a point at one end: simple, but effective. When hunting bigger fish, we went scuba diving down to around thirty metres with a proper spear gun borrowed from the dive centre along the bay.

I led groups through the bush and over the hill to the next bay for picnics of freshly speared reef fish, cooked on an open wood fire, and did demonstrations of coconut gathering and husking. It all started with being asked by the Fijian boys to do the talk about the coconut palm and all its uses because I knew all the facts and my English was better than theirs. Then, when they saw I could climb a coconut tree as well, they thought it would be a good idea to let the visitors to see that even a white man could survive here. Having shinned up the tree and brought down the nuts they suggested I might as well complete the entire demonstration by husking the nuts and cracking them open. I did, while they lay back and relaxed.

Now maybe it was tribute to my age, wisdom and maturity, but I found myself cast into the unexpected role of counsellor to damsels in distress. The Fijian boys had a good thing going there. Every day new girls came to the island to stay for just a few days, so there was an endless stream of attractive young ladies for them to charm and impress with their finely toned muscles, their abilities as hunter-gatherers and their skills at volleyball, at which they always out-performed the visitors. Each night they played their guitars, sang love songs and performed some traditional dances.

With this heady cocktail of skill, virility and ethnic charm, combined with the moonlight shimmering over the lagoon and the whispering of a soft breeze among the palms... Well, it's hardly surprising that the young ladies often succumbed to their amorous advances. It was usually a quick fling for a couple of days and then they were off again. Perhaps that's why these chaps were too tired to climb coconut trees!

Just occasionally, however, the romps with the local guys became a wee bit complicated, and when the girls needed someone to listen to their romantic problems, well, Papa John was always there. It gave me some interesting insights into the backpacker lifestyle. I must have been the only *virgin* backpacker around! I didn't have nearly so much fun in *my* youth.

And it wasn't only the girls. Late one afternoon, I was approached by one of the young Fijian stallions. A real smooth operator, he had just returned from an afternoon walk along the beach with one of the girls.

He looked around furtively and muttered, "Can I have a quick word with you, John? Could you lend me a condom?" Here was exactly the same thing happening to me again as had happened last year on Caqalai!

"Aye, sure," I replied, and fished one out from the same stock – still unused by me!

"Thanks, John, I was sure I could count on you." And he shot off with a big grin on his face. But why did he come to *me* to ask for one? He too believed in me. A couple of hours later, as I sat down for dinner, he came in, smiled at me, winked and flashed the okay hand signal used by divers. He looked like a very happy man. His faith in me had been justified, his hopes realised.

It was a beautiful evening and I was sitting on the beach watching the magnificent sunset over the bay on my last night on the island. Chiko, an attractive Japanese girl, came and sat beside me. A few days previously she had sought my advice on a problem she was having with a local guy she had become involved with. He had fallen for her in a big way, and now wanted her to stay and marry him, but she was only having a bit of holiday fun. I let her talk to ease her mind and let her decide for herself how to handle the situation, and she had left feeling much better. We had become good friends. Now she sat on the beach beside me, and together we watched the sun slip below the horizon in a blaze of golden glory.

"That's a sight I'm going to miss when I leave," I muttered ruefully.

"I'm going to miss *you*, John. I don't know what I'll do without you."

"Och, thanks. I'll miss you, too."

She reached out and touched my arm, stroking it gently.

"You're a really cool guy, John."

"Oh?" I was getting quite steamed up. All this 'really cool' stuff and stroking my arm, where was this leading, I wondered? She continued, "I would like to keep in touch with you, John."

"Och aye, no problem. I'll give you my email address."

"That's cool, but I would like more than that. Have you ever thought of visiting Japan?"

"Aye, I have."

"Would you would like to come to visit me in Okinawa?"

"Aye, why not?"

"Oh, John, that would be so cool!" She squeezed my arm with delight, her eyes sparkling in the dying light of the sun. "You could stay with me and I could show you around and be your interpreter."

Well, this is getting better and better all the time, I'm thinking. This girl has obviously had enough of these rampant young Fijian bucks and has found that the more mature man has something else to offer, a bit of wisdom and understanding, good conversation, tenderness. Maybe she had ditched her Fijian beau and was ready for some vintage quality experience now. Maybe, as it's coming to the end of my time here, she's keen to make the most of the time left, otherwise she might be left with regrets, wondering what if...? This was beyond my wildest hopes. My faith in her good judgement was being validated.

I reached out and touched her arm tenderly, stroking it, mirroring her touch on mine and, looking intently into her dark brown eyes, I murmured softly, "Sure. I would love to come and spend time with you in Okinawa."

Her eyes glistened with emotion; her breath exhaled in short, excited gasps. "Oh John, that would be wonderful! I'd really love that, because I want you... to be the grandfather I never knew!"

Grandfather!*Grand*father!!

Well, everything drooped after that.

Why can't I ever read the signs properly?

Is there no hope for me?

Chapter 32
Pilgrimage to Villa Vailima

As the plane took off from Fiji, a kaleidoscope of colours unfolded below. The deep blue of the ocean's depths, the browns, reds and golden colours of coral reefs; lush, green islands fringed with white beaches, and lagoons whose waters glowed with turquoise luminescence. I marvelled at the risks taken by the first European ships to navigate these uncharted waters, for scattered liberally among Fiji's three hundred or more islands lie even more coral reefs – beautiful, but deadly to the unwary mariner.

Samoa consists of two large volcanic islands – Upolu and Savai'i – with a sprinkling of tiny islands close by. From the air, the volcanic nature of Savai'i can be clearly seen with well-defined craters and extensive lava fields. The last eruption was in 1911: it lasted for six years. Upolu is more heavily forested. On both islands, most of the population live along a narrow coastal strip in a series of villages. Apia, the capital, is the only city in Samoa.

I had decided to spend two weeks exploring the two main islands with a couple of nights on two of the adjoining small islands. The main attraction in Apia for me was Villa Vailima, the former home of the Scottish novelist Robert Louis Stevenson. The last four years of his life were spent in this imposing mansion house, which he built on an elevated site overlooking the city. The author of such classics as *Treasure Island*, *The Strange Tale of Doctor Jekyll and Mr Hyde* and *Kidnapped*, he had been dogged by ill health, and had spent the previous two years cruising among the Pacific islands in a schooner with his wife and extended family of in-laws. He fell in love with Samoa, settled here and built this fine house.

Known locally as Tusitala (The Storyteller), he won the respect and affection of the Samoans to the extent that his memory is still cherished there. I visited Villa Vailima and Stevenson's grave on top of a neighbouring hill. This was not an easy climb. A very steep hill and covered in jungle, climbing it was energy-sapping in such a hot climate. The fact that Samoan coffin bearers carried his body to his lofty grave demonstrates the depth of feeling they had for him.

On the grave are the words he composed as his own epitaph:

Under the wild and starry sky
Dig the grave and let me die
Glad did I live and gladly die
And I laid me down with a will

This be the verse you grave for me
Here he lies where he longed to be
Home is the sailor home from the sea
And the hunter home from the hill.

With only a short time here I negotiated a personal tour of the islands through a small local agency. The benefit was that I would be picked up by minibus each day and dropped off at my next destination where accommodation and food had been booked for me. This saved a lot of hassle as the public transport system on Samoa is notoriously unreliable. Buses run according to the whims of the driver, who may own the bus, and he sets his own timetable. If he meets a friend who is about to go out for a day's fishing and takes a notion to accompany him, then he'll leave the bus and all his passengers to fend for themselves and join his friend in the canoe for an afternoon's fishing. True. Passengers have to wait for another bus, which will come whenever *its* driver decides. With my limited time I preferred not to experience that aspect of local culture.

My arrangements worked very efficiently. It was the same driver each day, one for each island. He was informative and knew everyone and we became known to each other as the days progressed. Driving around the island you pass through a series of villages. Some are modern concrete block bungalows, but the traditional falle (a house without walls, basically just a roof supported on posts,) is still very much in evidence. The whole concept of privacy seems to have eluded the Samoans, as there are neither exterior nor interior walls. It looks quaint to see furniture sitting there, with TV, cookers and fridges. I wonder to what extent this contributes to the nature of the Samoans: a people who are very open and honest, among whom crime is virtually unknown, and material possessions are accorded much less importance than in western society. In the poorer falles, the only furnishings were a few mats and a mattress. The kitchen is sometimes an external shelter with earthen floor and an open wood fire. Families eat using their fingers, usually seated cross-legged on the floor.

Samoa, in terms of housing and customs, is still more traditional than any of the other island groups I visited. Religion exerts a powerful influence. Each evening at around 6.45pm a bell is rung in each village. This is a signal that it is time for family prayers, and if visitors are walking in the village at that time they are asked to respect this custom and sit down by the roadside until the bell is rung again after about twenty minutes to signify that devotions have ended.

My first day took me around the east end of Upolu where I was picked up by a small boat and ferried out to Nu'utele, a tiny rocky island where I would stay overnight. I was greeted warmly at the beach by Fa'anati, a pleasant twenty one year old girl who took me to my falle and prepared my bed and mosquito net for me, interrogating me as she did so. "Travelling alone? No wife? Do you have a girlfriend?"

I decided to play the same game. "Have you got a boyfriend? No? Surely there must be plenty of young Samoan men who would love to go out with you?"

"They're no good. Too lazy. My father doesn't want me to marry a local boy. He told me to get a foreign husband. They take better care of their wives than Samaon men."

I recalled Ray's similar words about Fijian women preferring European men. She then invited me for a cup of tea. Her cousin, a woman in her thirties, joined us and started asking exactly the same questions.

"Why don't you marry a Samoan girl? Fa'anati there would like a husband. She is a good cook and would take good care of you. She's very good at massage. Take her round the island and let her give you a massage." Was 'massage' a euphemism for something else?

I began to break out in a sweat – and it wasn't the tea that raised my temperature – and changed the subject.

Fa'anati beat a tattoo on a large wooden drum to summon the guests to dinner that evening. I had dressed in my kilt, and when I walked across to the dining area a cheer erupted from the other guests and the two boys who also worked on the island. In response, I started my Maori warrior dance. Fa'anati's eyes lit up, she passed the drum sticks quickly to her brother, leaped over the barrier into the dining area and began to dance along with me, her hips shaking to the rhythm of the drums. When the music stopped I planted a kiss on her cheek. She giggled shyly and went off to serve dinner.

After dinner the staff went back to the mainland leaving only the owner and his wife on the island with the guests. As I walked down to the beach with the boys to see them off, Fa'anati's brother sidled up to me and whispered, "We'll bring your girlfriend back later, John."

"Eh? What girlfriend?" The boy looked at me like I was thick which, it must be obvious by now, I am. Very.

"Your girlfriend," he hissed. "Fa'anati!"

"Oh. Is she my girlfriend?"

"Of course," he muttered. "She told us she likes you so we'll bring her back later tonight so you can be together."

"Oh, that's very kind of you," I mumbled. It was all I could think to say. They all piled on to the boat and pushed off. As the engine roared into life I waved. They all waved back.

"See you later, John," the boy called out and nodded to his sister. Fa'anati turned to look at him, then she looked back at me and blew me a kiss. I blew one back. She beamed and waved to me.

The moon was just rising over the horizon. The sky was perfectly clear. It was going to be a heavenly night. With silvery moonlight shimmering over the lagoon, dark swaying palms overhead and the gentle swish of the waves whispering along the beach, it was a perfect night for romance.

But not for me.

The boat did not return and I fell asleep with my fantasies. I reckoned the boys were just pulling my leg. I left next morning, but before I did so Fa'anati gave me a big hug and slipped me a piece of paper with her address and asked me to write. I began to wonder what might have happened if I'd stayed around a bit longer.

The next night I slept in a falle built in a tree above the beach. In the family who owned it were three teenagers, two boys and a girl who were always hovering around me full of questions. They were keen to improve their English, they helped me with the Samoan language, and one of the boys obtained an outrigger canoe for me to try out. They were fun. Normally they brought the guest's dinner from the house kitchen over to the falle, but that night I was invited to join the family in their own home for the evening meal and to join them in their evening devotions. Every night without fail they sit on the floor and conduct a short religious service. That evening there was a Bible reading by one of the sons, a prayer led by another, and singing led by the daughter. Both parents and grandparents were present and all sang heartily. It was an occasion marked by simplicity and sincerity.

Before dinner was served I was invited to offer a short prayer of thanksgiving before eating. A small bowl of water was brought to me to wash my hands and the food was then served. Afterwards, the guitars came out and I joined in with my spoons. The kids had ordered me to bring them. The grandparents, both looking very infirm and lying weakly on their beds, had to be helped to eat, but on hearing the clatter of the spoons they both forced themselves upright and beamed with delight. The grandmother's hands clapped in time to the music to the extent that her loose fitting nightdress slipped off her right shoulder revealing a long sagging breast, but she didn't give a hoot. She was enjoying herself.

When my bus driver arrived to pick me up next morning I was still packing my rucksack. He chatted with my host, who told him of the events of the evening before. As we drove off, he told me, "John, you certainly made a great impression there. You are the first tourist ever to have been invited to join them for devotions and the evening meal in their house. That is a great honour."

At the next village, while out walking and taking some photographs, a woman called me over. I wondered if I had caused offence by taking pictures without permission but no, she was charming and friendly and was simply curious about me, asking the usual questions leading to the inevitable, "Why not marry a nice Samoan girl?"

This woman, with the help of her niece, was preparing food in her cooking falle – a simple earth-floored kitchen with an open log fire and a wooden fence round it to keep the pigs out. Having satisfied her curiosity about me, she was also responsive to my questions about her lifestyle and culture. My preference for doing something rather than just sitting around amused her, so she let me help in the preparation of the food. Her husband showed me how to grate the coconut to make coconut cream, and this was added to a large stewpot on the fire with the hunks of pork the woman and her niece had been chopping. Vegetables were added, and the mix was then left to stew for a while. They were as delighted with my interest in their way of life as they were curious about mine and took great pleasure in having their photographs taken.

Of course, having learned that I was an eligible bachelor, she suggested I should marry her twenty-two year-old niece, Tina, who didn't seem at all put out by the idea. But I had to move on next morning. I began to regret the fact that I was on a tour. How much more interesting might it be if I were to stay put in one village, become absorbed in the community, allow interactions to take place and see what happens. Like Robert Louis Stevenson, I might never have left.

To my surprise, I was invited to join them for dinner. I felt a bit hesitant as this was clearly an impoverished family. Only a month before, their falle had been destroyed by a cyclone and had not yet been rebuilt. They were sleeping in the husband's parents' falle. But they would not take no for an answer, and so again I was treated as an honoured guest. The woman would not eat until I had finished. Her duty was to remain in attendance, serving me food till I had eaten my fill, waving a leaf about to keep the flies off me. These honest, humble, god-fearing people really impressed me: in material terms they had so little, yet spiritually they were rich.

Snorkelling so far had been rather disappointing in Samoa. Most of the shallow water coral was dead. It had suffered from the recent cyclone, but that wasn't the only reason. I wondered if the crown of thorns starfish had been responsible for the devastation I witnessed, but I never saw one, maybe because they had cleaned the place out already. I arranged a couple of dives with a local operator who took me to a very good site off the south coast. We dived down thirty metres to the bottom of a tall coral pinnacle, and spiralled our way round it, ascending slowly back to the surface, examining the marine life. This was a rich habitat with a good range of plants, coral and abundant fish life. Two large sharks spotted us and diverted seawards. We swam round behind the pinnacle again, and encountered them once more. Crouching behind some coral we watched. Gently scouting around, their movements were effortless and graceful, their bodies sleek and streamlined. As soon as we revealed ourselves, they gave a flip of the tail and disappeared into the gloom. A turtle casually flipped its leisurely way across in front of us, quite unconcerned about our presence, a shoal of sleek tuna darted swiftly past. It was wonderful to be in the undersea environment again.

That night I walked along the beach to a neighbouring resort to see a demonstration of traditional fire dancing. I was just approaching the resort when the drums began, the signal that the show was about to commence. Dancing with flaming sticks, that part of the show is performed on the beach, so the dining room was open-sided and the audience were all seated facing outwards.

As I approached, a woman in traditional costume had just completed a few words of welcome and retreated to the shadows. The audience sat in the bright light of the dining room peering into the darkness as they waited for the fire dancers to appear. But instead of Samoan fire-dancers, a Scotsman wearing a kilt emerged from the gloom. I strode across the sand into the light, through the open side and into the dining room. People gasped and turned to gaze in wonder. I'm used to that by now and purposefully made for the bar.

The manager approached me. I wondered if he was intent on throwing me out again, but no, he grasped my hand, shook it warmly and introduced himself. He was from New York. "That was one of the most remarkable entrances I have ever seen," he cried. "The woman faded into the shadows and, like Brigadoon, you emerged out of the mists in full highland dress. It was stunning! Where did you come from?" He then insisted that I take a seat in the dining room to watch the show.

As usual, they invited a few of the visitors to dance with them, and after an entrance like I had made, it was inevitable that I would be one of them. I had never seen Samoan dancing before, but I did my best and improvised, injecting a bit of Cook Island style dancing as well. The crowd loved it, and when we had finished, my dancing partner, her eyes glowing, shook my hand, kissed my cheek and murmured, "Hey, you're cool!"

The manager was already waiting at my table with another glass of beer in his hand. "John, please accept this with the compliments of the house for your outstanding performance. Your presence has enhanced the entertainment considerably."

"Och, that's awful kind of you," I muttered modestly. "Cheers." I needed a sup. Dancing in the tropics is hot work, especially when wearing a kilt.

A short trip on the ferry took me to Savai'i. It's a slightly larger island than Upolo, and its high volcanic interior is uninhabited. My new minibus driver met me at the jetty and took me a short distance to the resort. My falle was still being prepared for me, but I was in no hurry – I had the company of two charming young ladies at reception who entertained me with conversation. Leaning against the counter with one arm resting on its surface while chatting to the girl on my side of the desk, I became aware of a hand gently stroking my forearm. I turned and there was the girl on the other side of the desk utterly engrossed in stroking the hairs on my arm. I paused in my conversation, and that broke the spell. She suddenly withdrew her hand and apologised.

"Och, there's no need to apologise at all. I was enjoying it," I protested. I reached out, took her hand and placed it back on my arm. "Now you keep caressing me for as long as you like."

She laughed. "Oh, it's just so strange to see such a hairy arm. Men here don't have hairs on their arms like that. It's lovely and soft to touch."

"Well, be my guest. Stroke away," I commanded. She was beautiful, and had one of the most endearingly soft smiles I had ever seen. I would have been delighted to have her stroke me all night long, but her work intervened and this delectably sensual welcome was over. I was the only guest in the entire resort that night. The owner, a Samoan woman who had lived in New Zealand for many years, came over with her husband to join me for dinner. They were good company too, and on leaving to catch up on the paperwork, they instructed their young staff to keep me entertained. The girl from reception who'd stroked my arm came over and joined me again, much to my delight. Another day here and I could have fallen in love with this girl. Whether she would have fallen in love with me is best not debated!

A long drive over the extensive lava fields took us to a village built around the edge of an old, low-level crater about 200 metres in diameter. Here was an example of turning nature's creation to good advantage. The floor of the crater was perfectly flat, so the Samoans had created a rugby pitch down there. The inner slopes of the crater provided a grass terracing for spectators, and almost every house in the village faced inwards and looked over the crater, offering a view of the games as well. Brilliant.

My plan had been to dive a couple of sites around the coast of Savai'i, but this coast had been badly affected by the cyclone. In several places high seas had breached coastal roads, houses had been destroyed and boats damaged. Trees had been stripped of their foliage. Palms stood forlorn, as bare as match sticks, every frond and nut having been stripped off by the wind. Recovery work was in progress all along the coast, but no dive boats were yet operable so my plans were scuppered. The next few days were spent in uncharacteristic idleness.

All across the Pacific the people are very musical. During dinner at one resort, three musicians played guitars and a single-string base made from a plastic bucket and a broom handle. These guys were very good. I asked if I could join in with spoons. No problem. The audience clapped like mad and wouldn't let me rest after that. I belted out some blues on harmonica, and then another Samoan now living in the USA joined in on guitar. He was another ace player, and his wife was an excellent singer. One of life's great pleasures is when a few musicians come together like that, completely unrehearsed, and provide entertainment that delights an audience. Our jam session went on till 1.30am. Before leaving I apologised for keeping the waitresses up late. They had kept me supplied with free beer all night, my reward for providing entertainment. "Oh, there's no need to apologise. We're looking forward to more of the same tomorrow night."

"I won't be here tomorrow night. I have to move on."

"Oh no! Can't you stay for just one other night?"

"Sorry, but my arrangements are made. I would love to stay but I am expected at another resort tomorrow."

"You'll have to come back. It was the best night we've had for years."

Once more I was regretting my decision to keep moving on. But there was no way of knowing. It was all a gamble. On my last day on Savai'i I had plenty of time before I caught a late afternoon flight back to Upolo. My driver had no other pick ups that day, so I had a chance to explore the landscape a little. He took me on a trek to a beautiful waterfall where we went swimming in the pool below the falls. Its cool fresh water was perfect for swimming, so refreshing.

Later, we went to a spot on the coast where the lava flow ended in the sea. This part is famous for its blowholes. The sea is funnelled up lava tubes and the spray ejected from holes in the rock some distance back from the water's edge with considerable force, rather like a geyser. Such is the power of the jet of spray that it can propel a coconut about thirty metres up into the air.

My mind drifted back half a century. I recalled reading RM Ballantyne's classic story *The Coral Island* when I was about ten years old. It had been one of the first stories I had read of life in the South Pacific, and it left powerful images in my mind. One part described such blowholes, and I began to wonder where Ballantyne got his inspiration. Had he been here too, standing at this exact spot in the middle of the 19th century? In my travels I had already traced much of Robert Louis Stevenson's route, visited many of the places associated with Captain Cook and now, I wondered, was I following in the footsteps of another writer whose images had sparked my longing to see the South Pacific islands so any years before. Such is the power of literature.

The story had inspired the creation of permanent images in my young mind, but this required some effort on my part. I had to be involved in the creation of these pictures. They had become my own personal property, and were possibly different from those in the minds of other readers of the same story. Had I only seen TV or film dramatisation of these stories, would the images be so powerful? I have my doubts, for then they would have been the creation of someone else's imagination.

I enjoyed my visit to Samoa very much, but my journey round the islands had reinforced the message that a rolling stone gathers no moss. I'd had to make a decision between staying in one place and wondering what was around the corner, or having a quick dash round the islands but running the risk of missing out on something good at any one place. Dashing around you may see much but gain little. My experiences in Fiji and Rarotonga had taught me that there was more enrichment to be gained from lingering awhile in one place, savouring the lifestyle and culture of its people. From that may come greater understanding.

Chapter 33
Travelling in The Kilt

On my first visit to the Cook Islands, I regretted my decision not to bring my kilt. The Cook Islanders' respect for ancestry and tradition, their desire to retain their traditions in music and dance, and the trouble they take over making traditional costumes, left me feeling I had betrayed my own culture. The kilt is a Scottish icon that is recognised worldwide, and most people seem to like seeing it worn.

Complete strangers have approached me and called me sexy, cute, handsome, manly... – and who am I to disagree? That never happens when I wear trousers. I had reasoned that as most of the travelling would be in the tropics, it would be uncomfortably warm wearing the kilt, so I left it at home. Big mistake. Air conditioning is standard in planes and airports, and at times it can be rather cool, so wearing the kilt while travelling is quite comfortable. Of course, it is too hot to wear it during the day in the tropics other than for a short time, but it can be quite cool at night, so for a night out the kilt is just fine. Wearing the kilt on my subsequent travels has added another dimension to the experience – it is a great ice-breaker. People talk to you when you wear a kilt. It is a key that opens opportunity's door, leading to all sorts of interesting situations.

At Motueka, New Zealand, I was striding along the main street, kilt swinging jauntily, when an attractive, willowy woman emerged from a shop in front of me. Her eyes and her arms opened wide and without a word of introduction, she wrapped herself around me and hugged me tightly. Now this is the kind of welcome I can't get enough of. I had been told the New Zealanders were very friendly and things were indeed looking promising.

"You must be from Scotland," she murmured softly in my ear as she held me close.

"Now how did you know that?" I mocked gently, my lips caressing the lobe of her ear.

"I love men in kilts." This was getting better all the time. "My mother was a MacPherson," she murmured, still holding me close.

"My great-grandmother was a MacPherson," I said.

She leaned back, still clinging to me. Her eyes opened wide again,

"We are related!" Cue another lingering, body-clutching hug!

I was beginning to enjoy this and, hopeful of some encores, murmured in her ear, "This is nice. Tell me the names of your other ancestors. Maybe we're related some more."

Perhaps I had been pushing my luck, or maybe it was the incredulous stares of the people on the street wondering where all this was leading to – as indeed was I – but she released me from her clutches and looked me straight in the eye. "You are coming home with me for lunch." My pulse quickened. This was really becoming interesting. Then she spoiled it all by adding, "My husband will be delighted to meet you."

I couldn't complain, though, for she served up a delicious seafood lunch with stirring pipe-band music playing in the background. It was an encouraging welcome to New Zealand, but it would never have happened had I not been wearing the kilt.

There are, of course, always the inevitable requests for information regarding what is worn under the kilt, to which the standard response is, "Nothing is worn, it is all in fine working order." It does become a bit tiresome though. Just imagine the ruckus if men started asking every woman who wore a skirt if she was wearing any knickers. The cry of 'pervert' would resound around the world. But somehow it's fine for a woman to make such personal enquiries of a Scotsman in the kilt. Come on girls, play fair.

Again in New Zealand, I had gone into a pub which advertised Three Course Meals – Choice of Roasts – as much as you can eat for $12.00. Well, that's not the kind of bargain any hungry Scotsman can ignore, so I went in and joined the queue.

Wearing a kilt inevitably aroused some interest, and I noticed two women gazing at me in wonder, their heads close together as they discussed my attire. After finishing my first helping I rejoined the queue for more, and one of the women immediately rose and sidled up close behind me. She got really close. So close I could feel her hot breath on my ear as she panted, "Go on, let's see what's under your kilt."

Now maybe I'm old-fashioned, but I thought that was a bit forward. However, exercising some diplomacy, I replied, "I'm flattered by your interest, but how would you feel if I came up behind you and asked to see what was under your skirt?"

"Oh, that's no problem," and she lifted up the front of her skirt to reveal a fine pair of strapping thighs and rather saucy underwear. I couldn't help noticing. "Right, I've done my bit. Now it's your turn!"

I had to think fast. "Och, haud oan the noo, hen." (I think better in the vernacular!) "You can do that because you're wearing something under your skirt – if I lifted my kilt I could be arrested for indecent exposure."

"You're kidding."

"Why ask if you won't believe what I tell you?"

"So, it's true then?"

I looked her straight in the eye: "You're looking at the genuine article here. The real McCoy!"

She paused, regarded me with some doubt, then eyed me up and down, slowly and lasciviously, and said, "Well, if it takes a skirt that long to cover it, you must be one hell of a guy!"

Chapter 34
Return to Rarotonga

Returning to Rarotonga proved to be a delightful 'homecoming'. Here, you step off the plane onto the tarmac – there are no long caterpillar tubes to guide the passengers blindly from air-conditioned aircraft cabin to air-conditioned terminal building. Instead, as you walk across the tarmac to the terminal, you enjoy the deliciously fragrant, tropical breeze which caresses this island and titillates the senses. Brown faced stocky men driving luggage trolleys are waiting for the cargo hold doors to open. They look over, curious to see who has arrived, smile, nod and call out their greeting, "Kia Orana" (may you live on). Having cleared immigration, I turned to the arrivals hall.

"John! John!" I looked to my left and there was Krystina, running over to hug me and present her cheek for the usual kiss. She was waiting for her brother who was on the same flight from New Zealand, and was surprised to see me walk off it. Her mother and father came over to greet me, and behind them was Mata from Tiare Village waiting to pick me up in the minibus, all smiles and fragrance, wearing her usual head ei – a beautifully crafted crown of bright, sweet-smelling flowers. Three more beaming Cook Island ladies followed in quick succession with hugs and smiles, all seemingly delighted that I had returned. It felt good to be back.

After checking in at the hostel, I went down to a wee shop along the road for some provisions for breakfast. I almost collided with a young woman at the door. Her eyes opened wide. "John! When did you get back?" Another big hug. Fiona is the daughter of Rob Good, a Scotsman who had married a Cook Islander. "Oh, Dad and Mum will be delighted to see you again. You must go down and surprise them."

I did that the following night. Their house was only a few minutes walk away, so I put on my kilt and walked along the darkened road. Only one car passed me. It stopped. The reversing lights came on. Bet I'll get offered a lift, I thought. It reversed towards me. Bet it's a woman, I thought. Right both times. Not just one woman either, she had four lovely young ladies with her.

"Excuse me, sir, would you like a lift?"

"Thanks. That's really kind of you," I laughed, "but I'm only going another twenty yards to visit a fellow Scotsman."

"Which one?"

"Rob Good."

"Oh, you know Uncle Rob and Aunt Mary then."

I laughed again. It seems everybody I meet on Rarotonga is related to someone else I know. We chatted awhile as she explained her Scottish ancestry, and how she thought I looked so smart in the kilt. I gazed at the four girls inside, all of whom were smiling invitingly at me, and now I'm thinking, what a fool I am, I could have squeezed in there beside them instead of going in to see old Rob. However, Mary is an excellent baker and always stuffs me with goodies when I call, so I did enjoy myself – and she gave me some to take away with me too.

Next day I was gazing at a menu board outside a café, contemplating a snack for lunch when once more I heard a startled cry. "John! You've come back!" I looked up and Amina, a pretty young waitress, came forward, wrapped herself around me and hugged me tightly. And people keep asking me why I return to this island!

As usual on Thursdays, I had organised a party from the hostel to attend the Island Night Show at one of the local restaurants. We had the Polynesian feast and then sat back to watch the dance show. The MC welcomed everyone as usual, but then added, "And a special word of welcome to our friend John, from Scotland, who is back with us again."

After the show finished a young islander in his mid-twenties then came over to our table. He beamed. "I thought it was you, John. It's great to see you back. You must come out on the deck and meet the rest of the boys. They'll be delighted to see you again." I followed him out to the open-air deck extending outwards from the dining room, and three other young men looked up. Their faces broke into big grins and they reached out to slap my hand and hug me.

Tere, my old friend, was almost turning somersaults, erupting with laughter, bringing his knee up and slapping it, delightedly clapping his hands together. He then grasped mine, shaking it, hugging me and slapping my back.

He paused and looked at me again. "I can't believe it. You're here again. What a guy." And then the whole hand-slapping, hand-shaking, back-slapping and hugging was repeated. After talking with them for some time, the girls from the hostel who'd accompanied me got curious and came over. Well, this was just fine with the local lads. I'd brought a group of very attractive girls with me, as usual. Introductions over, the guys and gals got boogieing and the party really began to swing.

I planned on a three months stay this time to do some voluntary work, so I decided to buy a second hand motorbike rather than hire one for so long, and I went to the bank to withdraw cash to pay for it.

As I handed over my card for a cash advance, the girl behind the desk looked at me knowingly, her beautiful, brown eyes gazing right into mine. She smiled at me warmly. "So... you've come back again, John?" I was taken aback and looked at her more intently.

"Aye..." I muttered hesitatingly. She was quick to notice.

"You don't remember me, do you?" The words were terse, fired rapidly at me, like a burst from a machine gun. Ouch.

"Well... your face is familiar, but I'm trying to remember where I've seen it before. I'm sure it wasn't in here." I normally used the cash machine. I had only ever been inside the bank once before, and it was certainly not this girl who served me.

"That's right. But you don't recognise me at all? Oh well, I couldn't have made much of an impression, then." She feigned offence: at least, I think she was pretending. Pretending or not, she had me squirming.

"Och, wait a minute. Look, I meet so many beautiful young ladies here, it's difficult to remember them all." Well, that did no good at all.

"Oh, so you remember some of them, but certainly not me! So all that talk about being your favourite waitress meant absolutely nothing at all." This lassie really had the knife in the wound now and was twisting it. I writhed in agony. This was not going well at all. I struggled with my memories. Waitress?

"Wait a minute. I've got you now. You were a waitress at the Edgewater Hotel." (A place I occasionally frequented to see traditional dance shows.)

"Oh, so you do remember me... at last!" God, she could make a man suffer. I had to laugh in spite of my suffering. She was quick-witted and sharp with it, and was really piling on the agony. And just to set the record straight, all that stuff about the 'favourite waitress' – I'm sure I had never used a corny chat-up line like in all my life. She was just being creative, and I admired her for it.

"You're making me feel terrible," I spluttered.

"And so you should be. I was so pleased to see you, expected you'd be pleased to see me too, but you didn't even recognise me. Well..."

"Och, I'm sorry. I'm grovelling. What can I do to make amends?"

Quick as a flash, she rapped out, "I suppose you could buy me lunch."

"I'd be delighted to..."

But before I could finish, she fired back, "But I don't think I want to have lunch with a man who doesn't recognise me. There's your money now. You can go and do your shopping and forget all about me again."

I loved this girl's sense of humour, her quick wit and her play-acting – at least, I think she was play-acting! Anyway, the bank isn't really the place for making up to a girl I'd failed to recognise after I had apparently left an indelible impression on her almost a year ago. There were other customers waiting. It was game set and match to her. I took my cash and left with my tail firmly between my legs.

But my conscience was bothering me something awful. She was rather sweet in an acerbic sort of way, and very pretty too. Should I go back again and offer to buy her lunch? But it might be like walking into a lion's den. I would hate to be savaged twice.

Chapter 35
Becoming Famous

Although English is spoken throughout the Cook Islands, some children struggle with reading and writing the language, and many homes are without books. The education department budget could not afford to pay for learning support specialists, but Global Volunteers, an American organisation, had been sending volunteer tutors to help out. However, most of the Global Volunteers come for only three-week stints. I felt I could make more of a difference if I stayed for a longer period and offered a full term to give the children a little more stability and increase the prospect of developing an effective tutor-student relationship. This suggestion was warmly welcomed.

I enjoyed being back working at grass roots level, teaching in a one-to-one situation, with the benefit of no planning for a whole class. The children were aged between nine and twelve years old. Some had attention deficit disorders and could be awkward at times, but generally they were well motivated and really seemed pleased to see me. When I arrived in the mornings they ran across the playground towards me, calling out, "Papa John, Papa John."

Quite uninhibited in their expression of pleasure, they gathered round me like a rugby scrum and hugged me. Life is more informal here, yet they are always respectful.

In addition to my tutoring, Tai, an excellent young teacher I worked with, also asked me to introduce a Scottish element into their Cultural Studies Course, as a surprising number of Cook Islanders have Scottish ancestors. Some may have arrived with the early whalers and jumped ship here – and who could blame them? After many months enduring the privations of life on a sailing ship, Rarotonga must have seemed like paradise, with a great climate, an abundance of food and beautiful young women. I keep wondering why I don't stay on myself. Others emigrated to New Zealand as young men, met Cook Island girls there and eventually settled on the family land in the islands. The Cook Islands telephone directory is liberally sprinkled with Scottish surnames.

Dressed in my kilt, I made my presentation and taught them some Scottish dances. In the shade of the trees bordering the beach (I didn't even have any music at the time), I walked them through the dances first, then clapped hands to give them the timing, and they were off. They loved it. Dancing is important in Polynesian culture. They have a marvellous sense of rhythm, their timing is superb, and they picked it up so quickly. To my amazement, when I arrived next morning the entire school was dancing *Strip The Willow* on the playground. My students had been so keen they had practised in the playground and the others wanted to join in. Imagine – Scottish dance craze sweeps Rarotonga!

When the music arrived, there was no holding back, and the teachers suggested putting on a display at their prize-giving day. That was something different, and earned many favourable comments. I was also honoured by being asked to present prizes at the ceremony. The kids were so cheerful, always smiling, enthusiastic and so friendly, and it was with considerable sadness that I left at the end of the term.

Shortly after I had arrived, an open seminar On Effective Schools at the University of the South Pacific campus on Rarotonga attracted my attention. The discussion was led by an American professor, now working in Australia, whose thoughts on the subject seemed closely aligned to mine, and in the open forum I made a short contribution. This appeared to be well received, several people coming over to speak with me afterwards. One of them, a student teacher, had found my words inspiring. She suggested that I should come up to the Teachers' Training College, as she felt I had something worth sharing with the other students.

I had met Teremoana Hodges – the Principal of the Teacher Training College – just a couple of days before. She was receptive to the idea: "Of course, come and meet the students now. They'll be delighted to have some light relief. I can assemble them all in a few minutes." Soon, she had gathered them together, between thirty and forty of them. She turned to me, and said, "Oh, I don't know enough about you to introduce you. Can you do that yourself?"

"Aye, sure," I laughed and took the floor. I started by explaining that I had retired as the head of a secondary school and how I had become a world traveller. "Since my wife died a few years ago, I have had no one to spend all my money for me..." This comment brought an almighty and joyous chorus of, "We'll help you!"

That set the pattern, and from then on anything I said was greeted with amusement or some amorous suggestion. They were nearly all girls, being trained for primary education. Afterwards, Teremoana introduced me to one of her bright young students, an eighteen year old girl called Christine, from the island of Mangaia. Nearing the end of her first year, she had been selected to represent the Cook Islands at a

Commonwealth Youth Conference on Education, which was to be held in Edinburgh the following week. I was asked if I could help her to prepare, brief her on what to expect in Edinburgh, and offer some critical comment on the presentation she was arranging? I was delighted to be asked, and spent some time over the next couple of days with her.

She was a good ambassador for the islands: thoughtful, intelligent, and pulsating with energy and enthusiasm. I felt sure this girl would make an excellent teacher. On her return, she visited me to tell me what a wonderful time she had spent. Everything I had told her in my briefing had been spot on, and she found the Scots so hospitable. Wide-eyed with excitement, the words simply tumbled out. I noticed that she was sitting cross-legged. On a chair. It was an almost childlike pose and caught my attention. We take chairs for granted. After all, you can't go sitting on cold, damp ground or floors in Scotland, but here sitting cross-legged on the warm dry ground while socialising is commonplace. There is little need for chairs, and even now, when she had one, she still sat as though she were on the ground. That tickled me.

She had been so thrilled to be one of only a handful of delegates to be invited to lunch with Scotland's then First Minister, Jack McConnell.

Her eyes sparkled. "I was amazed. Why me, a girl from the tiny island of Mangaia? No one else there had ever heard of it – in fact, very few had even heard of the Cook Islands. Oh, John, when I went in to the dining room and saw all the silver on the table, I was terrified. You know John, in the Cook Islands we normally use our fingers when we eat. That's just our culture." She giggled. "Of course, I know how to use a knife and fork, but there were so many there – what were they all for? So I thought, just wait to see what everyone else does and copy them and that way I managed to avoid embarrassing myself."

At that time, thirty-six Australian student teachers had arrived on Rarotonga for one month's teaching practice. The training college had planned a day of cultural exchange to allow the Cook Island students and the Australians the opportunity to become acquainted, and share aspects of each other's culture. The students wanted me there, too, insisting that I wear my kilt. Teremoana asked me to address the students briefly at the start of the day. A TV crew were present, and that night on the local news programme a clip of my performance appeared in the news bulletin. At the hostel, the backpackers almost choked on their dinners as they recognised the kilted figure on the screen. A spontaneous cheer erupted, followed by cries of, "Hey John, you're famous! Can we have your autograph?"

A few nights later on a night out with Chris and Sonne – two Germans from Munich, who had just arrived at the hostel – we walked into Banana Court to grab some of the action. Many of the Australians were dancing, and they immediately spotted the kilt. A group of girls rushed over to greet me. They all hugged me and dragged me on to the floor to dance with them.

Oh, it's a tough life!

The German boys looked on open-mouthed, and when I rejoined them a few minutes later, Chris leaned towards me seriously and said, "John, where can I buy one of these kilts?"

Chapter 36
Hot Lips

Things livened up after that, and later I found myself dancing beside a party of ten young ladies who were having a girls' night out. As usual, the music inspired me to introduce some Cook Island dance movements in my repertoire, and this rapidly caught the girls' attention. Eyes opened wide in wonder. I don't really know the meaning of the various arm, hand and leg movements in these traditional dances, but they all tell a story – and whatever story I was telling got them all worked up. They, too, danced in traditional fashion, sidling up closer, arms flowing in movements of poetic grace, hips swaying sensuously in typically Polynesian fashion, each one following the other in quick succession. Then one lovely girl with a superb figure danced mischievously behind me and began rubbing her posterior against mine. We boogied back to back for a few moments, to everyone's delight. The others, enclosing us in the centre of a circle, were now cheering and whooping with delight.

Now those of my acquaintance, knowing how relatively shy and withdrawn I am in the social scene back home (I know you won't believe me, but it is true), may well raise a few eyebrows at this ostentatious display of exotic, and indeed erotic, dancing. Actually, it raised a few eyebrows, even here in the heart of Polynesia. But the primitive beat of the drum stirs up thousands of years of deeply rooted tradition in these girls. It erupts from beneath the thin, overlying veneer of Western culture and, when you're caught in the tide, you just gotta go with the flow. At least that's my excuse, and I had no qualms about savouring the moment for all it was worth. It was all good innocent fun.

As we made our way out, the girls were all leaving too, and a couple of them stopped to talk to me, expressed their delight with the kilt, and proudly told me they both had Scottish ancestors. I thought it an appropriate time for introductions.

"Ko'ai to'ou ingoa?" I asked. (What is your name?)

"Ko Moana toku ingoa." (My name is Moana.) "Ko'ai to'ou ingoa?"

"Ko John toku ingoa."

"Hey, that's really cool! You speak our language!" Moana beamed and wrapped her arms around my neck in a warm embrace. Mmmm, I noted mentally, a wee bit of the local language, spoken with a Scottish accent while wearing the kilt has a definite aphrodisiacal effect. I'll try that again some other time.

Then another girl came over and asked the usual question about what is worn under the kilt. Moana was horrified, shooed her away, and apologised for her shocking behaviour. She was so concerned that I might have been offended by what she regarded as such a rude question, and was overwhelmed by a need to console me – or else it was the aphrodisiacal effect of the kilt again – that she put her arms around me and hugged me closely yet again. Now, this was quite an attractive young lady who was trying to soothe my damaged sensitivities, and I could find no reason whatsoever to dissuade her by admitting that I wasn't really all that bothered by the question. Instead, I was quite happy to assume some semblance of offence. There is something nice about skin that has been anointed with scented coconut oil since birth. It has such a luxurious texture, and the silken touch of her cheek caressing mine was indeed very soothing. She murmured abject apologies while holding me close and I softly reassured her, my lips flicking sensuously against the lobe of her ear. Then, as the girls all climbed on to their small motorbikes, the usual form of transport here, they called me over for one final hug each before they left.

The second from last – the one who had asked me the 'rude' question earlier – was really very pretty, and instead of giving me the usual hug she reached out her hand, took mine and drew me towards her. Her face uplifted, she raised her other hand, placed it round my neck and drew my face down to hers and then kissed me full on the lips. And hey, this wasn't just a peck either! She lingered awhile. Well, I did too, actually – but I wouldn't want to offend her by recoiling from her embrace. You've got to follow their lead in such matters. Go with the flow. Maybe she was just trying to make amends for 'offending' me earlier. Eventually, having released me reluctantly and with a longing look (okay, maybe my eyesight isn't as good as it once was, but it looked longing to me!) I turned to Moana who was last in the queue to say goodnight.

Now, whether inspired by what she had just seen or whether she was determined to claim territorial rights to me, I don't know, but she also raised her lips to mine and gave me another, even more lingering, goodnight kiss. Indeed, such was the quality, intensity and longevity of her performance that the other girls all cheered. I would have cheered too had I not been – and I modestly admit to it – an inspirational part of the performance.

It had been a long, long time since I last exchanged lingering good night kisses with a pretty girl but, as with city buses, here two came along at once! These two incidents stirred memories of pleasures long forgotten. I have to admit that I walked back to the hostel with a big cheesy grin on my face. It's great what wearing a kilt can do for you.

I can imagine you are wondering, after such an excitingly promising encounter, where does it all go from here? Was there passion under the palms for me?

Well, about ten days later, I dropped in to the Cocobar – a popular watering hole patronised mainly by the locals (sadly, it has now been demolished). As I waited to be served at the bar, I glanced around, and my eyes met those of one of the girls who had been dancing with me that exciting night. Her eyes lit up. "John! How nice to see you again." Then she turned and beckoned to another young lady sitting with her back to us talking to a man. "Do you remember my friend?"

I looked at the back of the girl's head then moved to the side. "Moana."

"That's right. Do you remember her?" She had a mischievous glint in her eye. I drew her a look.

"I'll never forget her!"

She laughed and reached out to touch Moana on the shoulder. "Hey, Moana, look who's here." Moana turned, her eyes opened wide, not in admiration or with desire this time, but with a look of sheer panic.

"Oh, my God!" she muttered, turning away rapidly. I thought she was just a bit embarrassed, the shock of coming face to face with me again after our session of prolonged osculatory pleasure.

I sought to put her at ease and murmured, "Nice to see you again, Moana. How are you tonight?"

She turned again. Panic stricken anguish was written all over her face. With a look of desperate pleading in her eyes, she waved her hand in the direction of her male companion: "John, meet my husband!" I almost burst out laughing, but played it real cool and held out my hand.

"Hello. Nice to meet you."

"Hey... you're Scottish!" His eyes glowed as he took in the kilt and we spent a few moments chatting about it, a useful diversion, for poor Moana was in an agony of embarrassment. A few nights ago she had been having a bit of fun on a girls' night out. It was just a bit of mild flirtation, but now the poor lass was quaking with fear in case I, or one of her girl friends, would let a word slip which might cause her husband to ask questions. I felt for the girl, excused myself, and moved a safe distance away to release her from the tension that gripped her.

No – there was *no* passion under the palms for me.

Chapter 37
Immaculate Conceptions on Mitiaro

Wearing a kilt on Rarotonga had earned me a modest degree of celebrity. As a consequence, I received an invitation to lunch with Sir Appenera Short, the former Queen's Representative in the Cook Islands, and his wife Lady Maui, whose grandfather was Scottish – she was intensely proud of her Scottish blood. Also on the guest list that day was Mii O'Bryan, the queen from Mitiaro, one of the smaller islands, who also happened to be the grandmother of my young friend, the current Miss Tiare, Krystina Kauvai. Mii was delightful company, had a mischievous sense of humour, and insisted that I visit her on Mitiaro. "Come for at least a week, John, and wear your kilt," she insisted.

There were only four of us on the flight to Mitiaro, the most north easterly of the southern group of the Cook Islands. From the window of the small Bandierante aircraft, I could see the entire island laid out below me, a small patch of greenery in an infinite ocean. It had once been an atoll, but having been thrust up out of the ocean like Atiu, its fossilised coral reefs had been colonised by trees and shrubs. The depression in the centre of the island, formerly a lagoon, now contained a fresh water lake around which a fertile plantation produced fruit and vegetables. The plane dipped its wing, slipped low over the reef and touched down on the coral runway.

I was first off, and walked over to the terminal building, which was no more than an open-sided shelter filled with people about to leave the island and those waiting to pick up arrivals. I searched the faces, the crowd parted, and there was the beaming face of Mii, the queen, but known to everyone on the island by the endearing title Aunty Mii. With her arms outstretched in welcome she greeted me: "Kia Orana, John." She placed an ei, a crown of fragrant flowers, on my head, and another long neck ei on my shoulders. "Come, John, and meet the Mamas."

The small shelter was full of ladies all wearing brightly coloured cotton frocks and head eis. First to greet me was her niece, Tungane, whom I had met some weeks previously and danced with. "Kia Orana, John. Remember me, your dancing partner?" She gave a mischievously seductive flick of the hips to remind me.

"Och, aye. I'll no' forget *you*!" I assured her.

While the introductions went on, there was a spontaneous outburst of song led by one lady, to which all the others immediately responded. A couple of seconds later, the scene had switched from a rather demure gathering into one of unashamedly outrageous fun as they all swivelled their hips and sang at the top of their voices.

Surrounded by gyrating mamas, the other arrivals smiled and then joined in the fun. The attention was switched from one to another and the singing and chanting broke out repeatedly. It all looked rather bawdy to me. It was. The Mitiaro ladies are famed for their bawdy songs.

Standing there quite bemused, I felt a hand on my knee, gently stroking the hairs on my leg. Maori men don't have hairy legs as a rule, and the hand belonged to an elderly mama with unfettered, child-like curiosity, intent on exploring this strange, pale-skinned, hairy creature. I suppose I did look a bit unusual. They don't see many kilts on Mitiaro. The hand moved on to feel the texture of my woollen sock, then it began to lift the hem of my kilt.

"Hey, that's private property," I scolded gently. She turned her attention to my sporran, and began to flick the three tassels on it playfully, and a big, delighted smile lit up her face. Like a small child, she was completely overcome by curiosity. Then Mii turned round and saw what was going on. With regal authority, she smartly scolded the woman, who scuttled away to be lost in the crowd.

The mamas broke into song yet again to bid farewell to the lady mayor. Their song was about a centipede trying to crawl up your leg to bite you. One of the mamas started crawling about the floor attempting to act the part of the centipede and tried to crawl between the mayor's legs. Her voluminous physical proportions emphasised the absurdity of her actions, and the long cotton dress the lady mayor was wearing proved an effective barrier to the progress of the 'centipede' into her personal space. The dance finished with a vigorous sideways kick of the leg to thrust the centipede away.

Denied the prize of the lady mayor, it occurred to me that the centipede might seek easier targets. There was a glint in its eye as it moved in my direction. I brought my knees close together in a hurry. I asked Mii if this happened every time a flight came in. She apologised for their uninhibited behaviour, but it was a tradition here. I assured her there was no need for apologies. I had the feeling that my visit to Mitiaro was going to be full of fun.

There was abundant evidence that the lifestyle here was far removed from the lively bustle of Rarotonga. Traditional outrigger canoes lay beached at the inlet that served as a harbour. On the crushed coral roads, children played happily without fear of injury, and families of pigs roamed at will. Traffic was conspicuous by its absence: an occasional truck or motorcycle and the odd bicycle did appear from time to time, but it was an occasion when they did. A diesel generator produced electricity for the community, but it was switched off at 10.00pm. There were no pubs, clubs, restaurants or hotels, and only one small store. Visitors to the island are dependent on local families for accommodation.

I was the only tourist on the island and, being the guest of Aunty Mii, everyone knew of me. I soon became known as Papa John, a title that has stuck, and by which I am known in the Cook Islands now. The title 'Papa', indicative of maturity or authority, is used as a mark of respect.

Lunch with Mii consisted of umukai, food cooked in an umu, an earth oven. A fire is set in a hole in the ground and volcanic rocks heaped on the burning timber. When the wood burns down, the rocks retain the heat. The food, usually chicken, pork, fish, breadfruit, or taro root, is wrapped in banana leaves and placed on top of the rocks, then covered with more banana leaves, and the lot covered in earth. Two hours or so later, the umu (oven) is opened and the kai (food) is taken out. The meat, cooked in its own juices, is deliciously tender and succulent with a slightly smokey flavour. It is normally eaten with the fingers. Eating is an important part of the culture here. If you can't eat everything on your plate, your host is likely to clear your leftovers on to his or her plate and finish it for you. Even the fatty or grisly parts I had set aside on the edge of my plate were picked up by Mii and chewed and sucked with relish as she responded to my questions about her role as Ariki, the queen.

Cook Islands society is based on an association to a village and its chief, the Ariki, often referred to as king or queen, and titles of authority and land rights are passed on through both the male and female lineage. As land cannot be bought or sold, marriage to someone who has title rights to land is of considerable importance. The title of Ariki still carries considerable mana, a kind of spiritual power. They are respected in their communities, but they live unpretentiously as neighbours, and work at everyday jobs. You could find yourself out having a drink and rubbing shoulders with royalty here, as I subsequently found out on more than one occasion. The House of Ariki in the Cook Islands' Parliament, offers a consultative role in relation to matters of cultural significance and ceremonial affairs.

That night, Tungane joined us for dinner, another struggle for me so much had I eaten at lunchtime. "Come on, John, you must eat more," urged Mii. "We'll have to build you up to look like a good Cook Island boy." It's hardly surprising they are big here, but I was well and truly stuffed.

The only entertainment on a small island like that is what they make for themselves. They like to have a good time, singing and dancing, and are always laughing and joking. Tungane suggested I might teach them to do some Scottish dancing later in the week, to which I readily agreed. "But you had better make sure you wear plenty of layers under your kilt," she added with a serious look on her face. "Oh, these cannibal mamas are wild. They'll have no hesitation in sticking their heads up there to see what you're wearing!"

Unfortunately, it was the week of the government's quarterly inspections of homes. Houses must be clean and habitable, and there must be no pools of standing water outside where mosquitoes might breed. In anticipation of this, all the mamas were busy with their spring cleaning and tidying up gardens, so the dancing lesson had to be abandoned.

Next day, Mii arranged for her nephew, Niki, to give me an introductory tour of the island on his truck. The island is only about eleven miles in circumference, with one circular road and one cross-island road. Niki had left the island as a boy in the 1950s to live in New Zealand with an uncle and worked in the food industry, educating himself at the same time. Now in his retirement, he had built a home for himself back here on the family land with a richly productive garden around it. He could fish, kill chickens or pigs for meat, and eat his own fresh fruit and vegetables. He needed little else.

He took me to meet his cousin, Marguerite and her fifteen year-old grandson, Ladislav. I was intrigued by the eastern European name. He was named after his late grandfather, a Hungarian. Marguerite's first husband and her eldest daughter, Ladislav's mother, had died within a few months of each other. Marguerite, now a woman in her fifties, was busy painting her partially built new house. I offered to help, but she was running out of paint. The nearest paint shop was in Rarotonga, so work was suspended. Who knows when it will resume – there seemed to be no rush.

That afternoon, I ventured out with my camera and wandered along the shore to the small inlet that served as a landing stage. There are no real harbours outside Rarotonga. Freight is lowered by derricks from the inter-island cargo ships onto a small barge, which then struggles through the surf to bring the goods ashore. The landing ramp is a poor substitute for a beach, but this was where the children came to swim. It was better than the sharp edged coral shelf surrounding the island. I wanted photographs of the island lifestyle, and this was one place to see it.

The kids had no reservations about having their pictures taken. They loved it, and competed for my attention, calling out, "You take smiles of me, Papa John." But when they came out of the water they were stark naked. They had no inhibitions about that either. But what would their parents think if I were to take pictures of them? I explained my predicament later to Mii, who merely laughed, "Oh, that's always been the way of life here. Nobody minds." But I had no doubt about what western society would think if I returned with a digital camera full of pictures of naked children.

At 6.00am on Sunday morning I was awakened by the beat of a drum. It was clearly a wake up call, a few slow steady beats with a couple of seconds interval alternating with more swift beats. It was persistent and its irregularity cleverly defeated the desire to fall asleep again. The church was just a few yards away, and this was the signal to allow the villagers time to get dressed for the early morning service. At 7.00am the distinctive sound of Cook Islands hymn singing drifted through the early morning air – the early morning service had begun. It makes a lot of sense to start early in this climate before the heat of the sun becomes oppressive. I had agreed to attend the later service at 9.00am with Mii.

A few moments before nine o'clock we left to walk the fifty yards to the church door. The timing was perfect. Everyone else was seated. Mii, as befits a queen, made her entrance last and walked towards her personal box. She beckoned me to take a seat on one of the vacant front pews a few feet away. Two other village chiefs greeted me with handshakes and the customary "Kia Orana" and took their places on the opposite side of the church. An elder and the minister also stopped to shake hands and welcome me before taking seats below the pulpit. The elder had a list of announcements to make, including a formal welcome, "To John, our brother from Scotland. We are pleased you have come to share in our service this morning. We hope you will enjoy your holiday on Mitiaro and when you return to your homeland we hope you will take with you the abiding love of our people." Later, as he began his sermon, the minister again expressed a warm personal welcome to me, and offered an apology for the fact that he would be preaching in Maori.

While the offering was being collected, I glanced around behind me. Seated a few feet away were all the children, brown faces eyeing me with great curiosity. From among the pack of glowing brown eyes, one smiling face hissed, "Papa John!" It was one of the small boys I had photographed the evening before. As we made eye contact, he gave me a wink and a dazzling smile and the thumbs up sign as he was wont to do when having his picture taken. I grinned and acknowledged his greeting with a wink. A few seconds later, I heard the whisper again, "Papa John." Again the thumbs went up. When it was repeated a third time I felt I had to ignore it, as this could go on all through the service. Still, it was nice to be recognised and made so welcome.

Mitiaro, like Atiu, also has several limestone caves. With a high water table, most of them are filled with fresh water, and are popular for swimming. At the largest cave, the fun-loving local ladies have a tradition of gathering there in late afternoon when the day's work is done to sing bawdy songs at the end of which they all plunge into the cooling waters of the pool and have a swim. Once again I was denied the opportunity to see this because of the priority given to cleaning the houses prior to inspections.

I did, however, go exploring myself, found the cave, and went down into it. Here, down in the cool shade of the cavern on a hot afternoon, I enjoyed a luxurious swim in its crystal clear water. It was so transparent that I had to reach down with my finger to locate the surface of the water to judge exactly where it was before diving in. It was refreshingly cool without being cold, but I felt almost guilty about putting my sweaty body in such pure, clean water.

On my way back, as I passed Marguerite's house, Ladislav spotted me from the passion fruit tree where he was having a snack and called me over to join him and his two friends who were playing some music. I spent a pleasant hour or so talking with the boys. Typically, their interests were fishing, the plantation and girls, but there were few girls on the island. Most girls in their age group had gone to school on Rarotonga, or had started work there. I felt for them: young emerging adult males laden with testosterone, and the nearest available females were almost two hundred miles away on Rarotonga. But even there, meeting a girl could be complicated.

Genealogy is very important to Cook Islanders. Many of them can proudly trace their ancestors back for many generations to the original tribes who migrated to the islands; but it also has a real practical significance. In such small communities, the risk of inbreeding is high, and many young people have to go abroad to find a partner. One of the boys told me despairingly, "It's hopeless. You've got to know who you are dating. Every time I meet a girl I like, she turns out to be a cousin."

The term 'cousin' is loosely used to describe someone with whom you share a common ancestor. This can be quite complicated, as some men father children with two or more women, or women have children with different fathers. Of course, the offspring of such liaisons may not be aware of their relatives. Large families are still common. This can sometimes mean that older siblings leave home to be looked after by a grandparent, for education or for work. Even in recent times, some fail to keep in touch with their families back home, and don't even know their youngest siblings. This can lead to complications when someone turns up a couple of generations later to claim their entitlement to a piece of the family land. Then it is vital to be able to prove your pedigree.

It has long been a tradition in Polynesian society to give children away to be brought up by someone else – perhaps a grandparent or an aunt – so they'll have someone to work the plantation and fish for them and care for them in their old age; or to a childless couple so they can have a family to bring up. This still happens. Children are loved in this society, and the giving of a child is regarded as an act of unselfishness: the ultimate gift. Even without formal adoption, children are often brought up within another family, and seem quite happy to have two mothers: a feeding mother, the one who looks after them on a day to day basis who may in fact be a cousin, an aunt, grandparent or friend of the parents; and a natural mother who may live on another island or perhaps works in New Zealand and earns enough to send money home to pay for the upkeep of the child. Knowing who your 'cousins' are can be quite a complex business in this society as, in such circumstances, it becomes difficult to distinguish between cousins and brothers and sisters or just the child next door who may spend more time in your home than in his own. Yet strange as all this seems to the western mind, it does have advantages. No child is unwanted. Older siblings care for younger ones with obvious enjoyment. To hear a child cry here is a rare event.

Walking back to the village with the boys, we passed a beautifully cared-for grave, decorated with flowers and other trinkets on a neighbour's land. Even after death, relatives are revered, and it is common to see elaborate, well-tended graves within the family garden, a custom which often startles Europeans. Yet why not? The land, which cannot be sold, remains in the ownership of the family, so ancestors are cared for by future generations. I liked that.

Entering the village, the boys exchanged some cheerful banter with a young woman. "Friendly young lady," I remarked as we moved on.

The boys looked at each other and smiled knowingly. "Yes. Friendly." The words were laden with meaning, and I looked at them inquisitively. One of the boys leaned towards me and muttered confidentially: "She's got two kids – and she's still a virgin."

"A virgin? You mean, the miracle of Immaculate Conception has occurred *twice* here on Mitiaro?"

"Oh!" He doubled up laughing. "I got the wrong word in English. I mean she is an unmarried mother."

On the final night, with the usual gathering of friends present at Mii's house, she made a little speech thanking *me* for bringing so much laughter to the island. I was touched by that, but had to reply that it was *they* who had made me laugh so much.

Mii took me to the airport. Already waiting for me were Tungane, Niki, Marguerite, Ladislav and the boys, all there to say goodbye. I was crowned once more, with no fewer than three head eis, stacked one on top of the other, and two shoulder eis. Smothered in flowers, I was then heartily hugged and kissed by all the mamas, some of whom made a real meal of me.

And, of course, I was invited to come back again.

Chapter 38
Mauke Miracle

Similar in appearance to Mitiaro, Mauke was another low, flat, potato-shaped island, heavily forested with glimpses of buildings appearing briefly among the canopy of trees. We skirted the north-west of the island and flew past the airstrip. A steep turn took us over the reef and we swept in over the end of the runway and touched down. A large crowd awaited the arrival of the plane, many of whom were leaving the island after the Christmas holidays and heading back to Rarotonga and New Zealand.

As I made my way over to the crowd I spotted Tai, one of the teachers I had worked with at Arorangi primary school, waiting with a big smile and a head ei for me. She crowned me and gave me the usual greeting, then introduced me to Ta, my host, who also had an ei for me. Another young woman came forward and said, "Kia orana, John. Welcome to Mauke." That was a pleasant surprise. She was one of the students I had addressed weeks earlier at the Teachers' Training College. They pop up everywhere. And then there were others.

A wee girl came over to me, looking at the kilt, wide-eyed. "Do you play one of those whistle things?" she asked, her fingers making a passable demonstration of bagpipe playing.

"No. I'm sorry, I can't play the bagpipes," I said.

"Are you from Rarotonga? I think I've seen you there. My name's Moira. I live at Nikao." That's just along the road from Tiare Village where I lived.

A boy about ten years old joined us, "I saw you in church on Raro."

"How do you know it was me?"

"You were wearing that skirt thing," he replied confidently, pointing to the kilt. I could never fool an identity parade here.

Two teenage boys hovered nearby, looking at me intently. They approached. "Hi. Do you live on Raro?"

"Well, yes, I have been for a few months."

"Do you know a girl called Moira?"

"Moira George?" Moira was Tai's younger sister.

"That's right. She's our cousin. We met you on Raro a few weeks ago." I remembered then. I'd met Moira downtown on Saturday with her cousins, and we had been introduced. And I thought no one knew me on this island, apart from Tai!

Ta, a sturdy, athletic looking man in his forties with the build of a rugby player, took me in an old, open-top Land Rover to meet the family. His wife was a teacher and his in-laws Tau and Kuru were retired teachers. They kept a few chalets for visitors, and provided all the meals. Tau had also been a headmaster, so we had much in common. We spent a fair bit of time talking together and got on fine. He'd lived on several of the islands, but he'd retired to his family land on Mauke where he'd been the Government Representative on the island for several years. They had an ancient bicycle, probably dating back to about the 1930s, which I could borrow. It was very low geared and had a maximum speed of about five knots. Still, it was better than walking everywhere and allowed me to explore the island comfortably and visit one of its peculiarities.

On an elevated site between the two villages in the centre of the island, the missionaries built a church in the nineteenth century. It was large enough to accommodate all the worshipers from both villages. However, the people of the two villages could not come to an agreement on the interior décor, so each half is decorated according to the wishes of the respective factions. The pulpit is situated centrally, the people from each village sitting in the pews on either side. They even have separate doors. United in faith they may be, but the old tribal traditions and rivalries still simmer away under the thin veneer of Christianity.

In late afternoon I cycled down to the harbour. Hordes of kids were having boisterous fun here. Plunging in off the quay, swimming, throwing each other in, boogie boarding in on the surf that surged through the narrow entrance in the reef... The place was positively pulsating with activity. I couldn't help being infected by their enthusiasm, and so I pulled off my shirt and strolled out on to the small wharf. Moira, the wee girl I'd met at the airport, came over to advise me that the water was deep all along the wharf, so I could dive in anywhere safely. I did and she then jumped in beside me intent on continuing our conversation as we swam back to the shore. She fired questions at me in rapid succession: "What is your name? What is your Mum's name? What is your Dad's name? How old are you?"

As we reached the shallows, I turned to face her and the sunlight shone directly on my face, lighting up my eyes. She gasped in amazement, came closer and peered intently into my eyes. "Your eyes are blue!" she exclaimed. "I've never seen blue eyes before."

That surprised me, and I explained that it was quite common in my country. I climbed out and dried myself off – but I couldn't shake Moira off. She had appointed herself as my personal assistant, introducing me to everyone else. When I took my camera out, she organised groups of young posers, all of whom were all too keen to have their picture taken. They invariably giggled with delight when they saw the results on the screen of the camera. Very shortly everyone there knew me, thanks to Moira. She was eight years old.

A teenage girl then came over. She smiled at me as though she had known me for years and said, "Hello. When did you get here? Did you come over from Mitiaro?"

"No. From Rarotonga. But how did you know I was on Mitiaro?"

"You were on Mitiaro just before Christmas. You were staying with Aunty Mii, weren't you?"

I was astonished. "How do you know that?"

"I was there visiting my cousin. You came and spoke with a group of us playing volleyball one night."

I shook my head in amazement and laughed. Here I was on a tiny island with only about three hundred people living on it, about one hundred and seventy miles out in the ocean from Rarotonga, and it was infested with people who knew me. It brought home to me just how small a community the Cook Islands is, despite the considerable distances between the islands. The whole concept of neighbourhood is different here. It is impossible to remain incognito.

We traded names. Her name was also Moira. I remarked on how many girls seemed to be named Moira on this island. She laughed. "Yes, it's a very common name here. We had a Scottish doctor here called Archie Geanies. He died a few years ago. He was a real character and very popular with everyone on the island, and his wife's name was Moira. He delivered all the babies on the island for about thirty years, and just about every family named one of the baby girls after his wife."

"Ah, that explains it. So Moira George would have been one of the babies he delivered."

"That's right. You know Moira?"

I explained I had worked with Tai and met Moira through her. "You'll know the family, no doubt," I added.

"Oh, yes." She then rattled off a seemingly endless list of all their names. I was amazed.

"Wait a minute. That's some size of a family. How many are there?"

"Twelve. That's quite common here. There are lots of big families, especially among the Catholics."

Sixteen years old, she attended school on Rarotonga, lived there with her aunt, and was home for Christmas. She left me to join some friends. "Have a nice holiday. I'll see you again."

I had no doubt that would be true. It was proving to be a very small island indeed. After she had gone, a portly middle-aged man drying himself with his towel approached me and introduced himself. He was the local minister and, like all the others, his curiosity was aroused. We spent several minutes in conversation. When I left, he invited me to drop in on him anytime for a chat. Mauke was proving to be a sociable place.

"Here John, try this," said Tau, passing me a local delicacy to eat – a sun-dried banana. I'd never seen a dried banana before. It was about the size of a large date and of similar texture. It was very tasty, all the flavour having been concentrated in the shrivelled flesh, and it was only about one sixth of its original size. He took me outside to show me how it's done. The bananas are split and laid out on a white corrugated iron sheet in the sun and covered with mosquito netting to keep the flies off. Turned daily for the next five days, they shrivel and turn a rich brown colour. They are then wrapped up in dried pandanus leaves and tied tightly, each bundle weighing about 1kg. Hung up in a dry place, they will keep for years. He sells his dried bananas to retailers in Rarotonga. Thus preserved, there is no problem waiting for a ship to freight them off, and he gets a good price for them.

They have such an abundance of food here. Breadfruit – boiled or fried and served as an accompaniment to roast chicken, pork or fish – is delicious; it can also be made into a sweet pudding. Tomatoes grow in profusion, they have taro root and taro leaves, arrowroot, tapioca, pineapples, limes, bananas in abundance and the paw paw (papaya) trees produce fruit all the year round. Goats and pigs graze in the bush, fish are plentiful around the shores, and coconut trees are everywhere. It's easy to understand why so many people return to the islands and retire to a life of plenty.

Tau, now in his late seventies, was only fit for light duties, so the work in the plantation was left to Ta. On a small island like this with such a limited market for fresh produce, the community works together to ensure that everyone has a share of the market. Each year it is decided who should grow each crop rather than have a free for all, which could result in a surplus of one crop and a shortage of another. The crops are rotated among the growers. That way, everyone has some income. It is all very civilised – a nice kind of communism.

Another treat came my way at lunchtime. Kuru had prepared some uti, the scraped out contents of a sprouted coconut, and quite delicious it was, too. No matter what age a coconut is, it can be used. The young green nuts are perfect for drinking, as they are full of liquid. The mature brown nuts have plenty of flesh for eating; the flesh can also be grated and squeezed through a muslin cloth – or traditionally through a handful of fine grass – to produce coconut cream, which is used in cooking. Even after the coconut has sprouted, there is still good eating in it. The flesh is now soft and rich in sugar and makes the most delicious and refreshing thick drink with a sprinkling of limejuice. Accompanied by cabin bread, broken up and soaked in it, the versatile nut made a substantial lunch-time snack. I had no need for anything more.

After lunch, Kura introduced me to some bush medicine. She had fallen off her motorbike and her foot was badly bruised and swollen and she showed me how to make a poultice of crushed leaves to take away the swelling on her ankle. Using a wooden bowl as a mortar with a pestle fashioned from volcanic rock, she crushed a bundle of leaves Tau had gathered that morning. When the leaves had been crushed into a dark green mush she added some coconut oil with a selection of herbs, mixed it all thoroughly, and wrapped it in a cloth. This was then wrapped round her foot and tied at the ankle. The medication is known as Mauke Miracle.

Some years ago a Mauke woman had a dream in which she was given the recipe for mixing certain herbs with coconut oil as a treatment for injuries. When she woke up next morning she went out to seek the plants required and mixed the recipe according to her dream. It worked! She had a medicine with amazing properties for removing pain and swelling. Word soon got about, and an American who owned a perfume factory on Rarotonga saw its potential and marketed it as Mauke Miracle.

There are three flights per week to Muake from Rarotonga, and the arrival of the plane is a major event in the otherwise sleepy life of the island. Like many others, I went along out of curiosity. It was teeming with folk again, and once more my youthful friends greeted me warmly. A small amount of cargo – mostly food and provisions for the three small general stores – was heaped onto a couple of trucks with a handful of teenagers piled on top of that to keep it all aboard. Once again there was sadness in the air as so many people were leaving their relatives on the island after the Christmas holiday to return to their homes in New Zealand, Rarotonga or Australia. Tears flowed freely. One woman had so many friends and relatives to say goodbye to, the plane's departure was delayed to allow her to get round them all. I liked that. This was a civilised way of life.

When the plane had taken off, the place quickly emptied of people. I lingered a few minutes, absorbing all I had witnessed. The hustle and bustle of people and goods coming and going, the gleeful greetings and poignant partings, for some elderly people the last time they would see the island of their birth, was all familiar to me. So often I had witnessed the same comings and goings, the same excitement, the news-gathering, and the sadness as the ferries sailed from harbours on the islands of Scotland, brief interludes of interest, anticipation and activity in the quiet lives of the islanders. When they had all gone, the island dozed sleepily in the sun once more. I listened to the muffled heartbeat of the ocean as the surf pounded incessantly out on the reef, and to the gentle breathing of the island as the wind sighed among the palm fronds. Peace.

In the evening I returned to the harbour to watch the fun again. There was a big swell running, and I watched in amazement as the kids sat on the edge of the wharf to get battered by the huge waves that broke right over it. The concrete surface of the jetty is almost permanently wet with spray, and is covered in slippery algae. The force of the big waves erupting over the jetty struck the children on their backs, engulfing them completely, and scattered them rapidly across the slippery surface, like shot from a gun. They insisted I join them. Wee Moira grabbed me by the hand and led me over to the edge. "Come on, Papa John. It's great fun. You'll love it."

I reflected for a moment as I sat there and waited for the next big wave. Here I was, sitting half-naked among all these kids aged from about five to sixteen – and I was sixty-two – waiting to have my back pounded by tons of cascading seawater. An excited cry went up.

"Another big one!"

An intense thump, the jetty trembled and a dense wall of water erupted skywards. Then it fell and hit us. It was like being struck by a huge fist, and I was suddenly shooting across the surface of the jetty towards the rock wall at the landward end. I stopped a few feet short, dripping wet, having slid on my backside a good fifteen feet or so from the edge of the jetty. Wee Moira was right. It *was* good fun. I rushed back to the edge ready for the next wave.

I attended the church service on the Sunday and took my seat in the neutral pews in the centre, facing the pulpit. Again, I received a personal welcome from the pulpit, and as I left after the service, the minister invited me to join him at the mission house for limejuice and biscuits. He had been born on Penrhyn, the most northerly of the Cook Islands, and had served as a minister on various other islands. Making shell jewellery was his hobby, and he presented me with a Maori fishhook necklet. A fishhook is a distinctive, traditional shape carved from a piece of shell. He urged me to stay on the island and apply for a teaching post.

"Please give it some thought, John. We are desperately short of good teachers. You are the kind of person we need here. I can see it by the way you relate to the kids, they all flock round you. Why don't you try it for a year?"

It was so tempting. I had developed a fondness for this island and its people, but then I had the same feeling about all the islands I'd been to. Tying myself down to a contract for a year put me off. There would be the marking, the necessary preparation, and the inevitable paperwork – all of which I had been so glad to leave behind. I suppose I could have managed it for a year; indeed, the prospect of living the life of an islander for a whole year appealed to me very much. Just about everyone on the island was recognising me now, they would wave and call out to me. It would be interesting to stay here longer, become an active member of that community. I could really absorb the culture and learn the language. But I now had freedom of movement. I had my boat in Scotland. I had my family. I did not feel like cutting myself off from all that. So, with some regret, I declined.

I had to leave the island again the next day. I checked in my luggage and turned round and there, waiting behind me with big grins on their faces, were several of the boys from the harbour ready to shake my hand and see me off. More of the kids arrived and said their goodbyes. Wee Moira assured me she would see me on Rarotonga. A few other people came across to wish me well, and then at the last moment, the minister's wife, apologising for her husband's absence due to duty, rushed over to give me a hug.

I walked out to the plane, turned and gave them all a wave. Hands were raised in reply and cries of "Bye, Papa John" echoed in my ears as I climbed up the steps to take my seat. I liked Mauke.

Chapter 39
The Duties of Papa John

Some people might mistakenly think that life is one big holiday for me. But in the Cook Islands, believe me, the title 'Papa John' does not come without its responsibilities.

Nikki, a vivacious Scottish girl, blonde and neatly configured, attracted attention wherever she went. And she had a young Uruguayan accountant eagerly escorting her. She introduced us one evening, and then went off to the ladies' room. That was the cue for some male talk. This boy was really keen on her. Later, she engineered some time alone with me and told me she was tempted by him, loved his Latin-American charm, especially the accent, but she also had a promising romantic interest in the USA where she worked for a travel company. However, right now she was still unattached, she was on holiday, and she had this handsome young Latino panting after her. At times like this, she needed a sounding board, someone older to talk with, a father figure. Papa John was the obvious choice. She asked me what I thought. The boy seemed reasonable to me, but she would have to make her own decisions as to how she should proceed. Then, I added mischievously, "I suppose I might allow you to snog him."

She beamed, "Oh thanks, Papa John! I knew I could count on you."

Nikki had had to move from Tiare Village to another hostel because of prior bookings, and a few days later we met outside the Internet café. She was climbing on to her scooter with her back to me as I pulled in behind her. "I'd ken these legs anywhere," I growled.

She spun round and laughed, "Oh, whit are ye like?" She did have beautifully tanned and shapely legs – and the rest of the figure was pleasingly proportioned as well.

We went into a café and had a chat for a while. She was on her way home to Scotland. It was to be her last night on the island, and she had to see me on her final night out. Well, it would be a shame to disappoint the girl so, strictly in the call of duty you'll understand, I was out again that night with Lars, my young German housemate, to 'see her off' at Banana Court.

Lars headed straight to the bar to buy the drinks while I was distracted by two attractive young Cook Island ladies who admired the kilt. At least, I presume, in my modesty, that it was the kilt and not the man in it that excited their attention – but of course, I could be wrong. My modesty can be a bit overwhelming at times.

Conversation came easily, and a little of the Maori tongue eased things along even better. They were surprised that we had never met before, but then they were both married and tonight they were having a girls' night out. One of them, Tanya, was secretary to the owner of The Flame Tree Restaurant, one of Rarotonga's most prestigious eateries; she expressed surprise that I'd never eaten there. "Now, this just won't do. You really must come round some night. Just phone up and ask for me, and I'll arrange it all for you."

"Well, to eat in a place like that I'd need to have the right company," I protested. "I wouldn't want to eat out alone. Lars there is alright to go out with for a couple of beers, but for the Flame Tree I'd need to have a charming female companion to dine with."

She waved her hand around and said, "Well, what's stopping you? There are plenty of beautiful girls here." There was no denying that. It's one of the things I like about the Cook Islands.

A few minutes later I left to join Nikki and a few other friends for her farewell bash. She introduced me to Leanne who'd just arrived that day and was also staying in the same hostel on the other side of the island, but who now found herself in an unfortunate situation.

"Leanne is going to be the only girl left in the hostel in a couple of days' time. There will only be her and a Norwegian honeymoon couple so she'll have no one to go out with, but I told her not to worry, Papa John would look after her."

See what I mean? The responsibilities just keep piling up. It's a tough job, being Papa John, but somebody's gotta do it! Attractive, intelligent and instantly likeable (I mean Leanne, not Papa John!), I felt sure that the execution of my new responsibility would be a pleasure rather than a burden. I wasted no time.

"Right, have you anything planned at all?"

"No."

"Okay, on Thursday nights I normally organise a table at the Staircase Restaurant for people from Tiare Village for the Island Night Show. It's a chance to see some traditional dancing. Interested in joining us?" It would be a chance for her to meet more people.

Nikki chipped in with some encouragement, having been one of those I had taken the previous week. Leanne, smiling, said, "Okay, I'm in."

"Now on Friday night I suggest dinner at the Flame Tree Restaurant.

I've just been scolded by the owner's secretary for never having eaten there, but I need someone to dine with me."

Again, Nikki chipped in with her support. She had dined there a few days ago. Leanne beamed. "Sounds great."

Nikki beamed too. "See, I said Papa John would take care of you."

Leanne grinned. "This is fantastic. I only arrived this morning, didn't know anyone, and now all this is happening to me. I can't believe it."

I went to the toilet. On my way back, I passed Tanya. "Tanya, I've taken your advice and found myself a beautiful young lady to dine with. When you go into the office tomorrow, please make a reservation for Friday night for a table for two at 7.30." She looked at me in amazement.

"Wow! That didn't take you long! How did you manage it?"

I shrugged, modestly. "Kilt and Scottish accent, maybe?"

At the Island Night Show we had the best seats, our table fronting the small dance floor. In his welcome, the leading male 'warrior' dancer prances about and appears to shout aggressively at you, but it is all really quite friendly. He approached Leanne, bent on one knee before her, looked into her eyes, kissed her hand and uttered a few quiet words, which I presume were words of welcome. He did have a mischievous twinkle in his eye, so who knows what he said? I was sure he'd be back.

He performed a demonstration of husking a coconut with his bare teeth, quite an astonishing feat. He chose Leanne to help demonstrate cracking the nut open with a drum stick. This can be done with one strike by a skilled practitioner, but, with Leanne, he made a great play of her having hit his hand as she delivered the blow. He then finished the job and cracked the nut neatly in two, bent on one knee before her and offered her one half nut from which to drink the juice, keeping the other to himself. He then linked his drinking arm with hers, drew her towards him and they drank their juice, arms linked in truly romantic style.

She was now quite a star, but more was yet to come. In the final dance, the Ura Peani (the European's dance, a clever play on the words Ura, meaning dance, and European), in which the tourists are invited to dance with the experts, she was again first to be picked. But not by the alpha male this time. One of the younger boys in the dance team had his wits about him, and made a dash for her, getting in before the alpha male, much to his chagrin and everyone's amusement. After the show, Tere and some of the local boys joined us again for the general dancing, so Leanne made even more friends.

Friday night is always lively on Rarotonga. Dinner at the Flame Tree was a mouth-watering experience.

After eating, Leanne became interested in seeing the nightlife of Rarotonga, so I took her back on the motorbike to Avarua where it all happens. We stopped off first at the Cocobar to give her a glimpse of local colour. I was greeted there by several acquaintances, including Tere and the local lads. They were bound for Banana Court, so we followed a few minutes later.

And it was there that a whirlwind arrived in the shape of Junior – a big Maori rugby player (now a pro in Australia). Born in New Zealand of Cook Island parents, he was a nephew of Adrienne's, the hostel manager. I was standing talking with Leanne when I suddenly spotted his face in the crowd, thrusting people aside, making a beeline for me.

"Papa John!" he exploded – Junior doesn't do things by half – and then he smothered me in a great big hug. "Papa John, it is so good to see you again."

"Aye, good to see you too, big fella," I muttered from somewhere under his armpit. They were over from Auckland for the International Rugby Sevens Tournament in which Junior was playing. Also in his wake came cousin Nancy, Adrienne's daughter, who had recently returned home after two years working in Brussels.

I had met them all the previous year at Christmas when Junior and I had enjoyed some memorable 'bonding' moments. Having imbibed a little too much Christmas spirit on Christmas Eve, he got a wee bit out of hand – well, so much so that the term 'hyperactive' would be a gross understatement. He was all over the place, greeting everyone with cries of "Merry Christmas", wandering out on to the middle of the road to ensure that those in cars did not miss their share of his Christmas goodwill, and coming close to ensuring that it would be his last if someone didn't rein him in. Nancy had promised to get him home safely, but he was proving to be just too much of a handful, and would not do as he was told. She was now verging on tears, so wild and erratic was his behaviour. I told her to leave him to me, that I would see him home. A little assertive diplomacy was required.

Grabbing him by the shirt collar and drawing him down to my height, I growled a few caring words into his face. He simply needed a bit of firm and patient handling. It had the desired effect, and he ended up draped over my shoulder as I dragged him home – I tuck in neatly under his armpit.

He kept on muttering, "Papa John, I'll do anything you say. I respect you, Papa John. Papa John, Aunty Adrienne doesn't need to know a word of this." And when I assured him my lips were sealed if he behaved himself and got to bed, he said, "I'll be good, Papa John. I promise you. I respect you, Papa John." When I left him at his chalet he called out, "Papa John, you're one cool guy."

I smiled. "Yeah, cool." The absurdity of it all amused me.

Now, a year later, he was back among us, creating more mayhem. And so, with the rugby boys, Tere and the local lads all joining us, we had the ingredients of a really good party.

It was agreed that Saturday should be a rest day after that night out. Leanne, however, was keen to do the cross-island trek, so we decided to do that on Sunday afternoon. I was now Papa John: Jungle Guide.

It was a pleasant afternoon and we made good time to The Needle, a tall pinnacle rising from the central volcanic ridge. After a rest there, we dropped down through the rainforest canopy with its giant ferns to the waterfall at the far side of the island. I pulled off my boots and shirt and plunged into the cool refreshing waters beneath the falls. Leanne slipped off her outer layer to reveal a bikini, all in place and ready for action, and she joined me in the pool.

When we returned to the chalet, I got busy in the kitchen. Papa John: Chef, prepared dinner, with Lars assisting. Volker, another German from the next chalet, dropped in, and I issued an invitation to join us, so we had a foursome for dinner.

The conversation flowed with ease and with plenty of laughter until 11.30pm when I had to drive Leanne back home. Papa John: Chauffeur.

The following day she was leaving for a few days on Aitutaki. On the day she returned she had twelve hours to wait for her flight back to England, so again Lars and I offered her the use of our chalet to rest and have something to eat before her flight. We had shared some good times, and I felt I had executed my various duties as Papa John in a fitting manner. Leanne seemed to think so, too. We exchanged email addresses, and she came to sail with me in Scotland the following summer.

It is a demanding life being Papa John.

Chapter 40
Unexpected Outcomes

A traditional dance team from the small northern island of Rakahanga had won first place in the National Dance Competitions and were putting on a performance at Banana Court.

A good crowd had assembled, including the visiting rugby players taking part in the international sevens tournament. The show was very good and, as usual, some of the audience were invited to dance with the dance team at the end, which is all a bit of fun. After the guests had done their bit, the compere asked if there were any others in the audience who wanted to try some Cook Island dancing.

No volunteers.

He cast his eye slowly around the crowd. His gaze stopped at me. "Hey, there is a Scottish man wearing a kilt. How come you didn't get picked to dance, sir?" I shrugged my shoulders, and tilted my head sadly. "Well, let's put that right. Would you care to join us for some Cook Island dancing now, sir?"

Hungry for the sight of a kilt swinging to the primitive drumbeat of Maori music, the spectators were cheering me on. It would have been a shame to disappoint them, so I accepted the challenge and walked on to the dance floor.

"Now, first of all, greet your partner, sir, and say 'Kia Orana'," called out the compere. I knew the form. Most people shake hands with the partner and give a brief peck on the cheek. But I'd done this before. Coming from one of the most northerly islands, this was one of the few dance teams that didn't know me, and if they were going to get some entertainment at my expense then I was taking all the perks going, so instead of the usual timid tourist tickle of lips on cheek and handshake at five paces I stepped forward assertively and like a true warrior wrapped my arms around the girl, pressing her body to mine in a huge hug. Call me insatiable if you like, but at my stage in life you don't get that many chances, and I need to make the most of every opportunity. The girl played along beautifully – they just need a hint of encouragement. Her eyes flashed with a look of ecstasy/desire/passion/lust – just pick a word, any one will do. She eagerly responded to my embrace and wrapped her arms around me. I waggled my rear end and swung my kilt just to show how much I was enjoying myself, the girl giggled with delight and the crowd roared. So too did the compere.

"Hey Papa! Get your hands off! That's my wife!" The crowd erupted again with laughter. I released her, flicked up my eyebrows and smiled at her. Her eyebrows flicked up too, and she smiled back. Affirmative: she'd enjoyed it as much as I had.

Then the drums started to beat. The girl said, "Just knock your knees together like this," and gave a weak impression of the male dance. She had no idea I had rehearsed with one of the professional dance teams and had practised while watching videos back home in Scotland.

"Och, hen, I can dae better than that," I retorted and launched into a vigorous impression of Maori warrior dancing. I began to circle her, knees oscillating rapidly, enclosing her within my outstretched arms and hands, which were making all sorts of gestures, each one suggestive of something – and whatever it was, her eyes opened wide in wonder.

"Hey, that's great!" Then she really launched herself into the female part, hips going like a washing machine, hands and arms telling their story in response to mine, her gyrating body snaking within my arms in a deliciously seductive manner. The audience loved this and cheered, but I was listening intently to the drumbeats. I had to synchronise the ending, properly and creatively, just as the pros do. I once saw a professional dancer execute a marvellous ending in which he had whipped the girl off her feet and sat her on his bended knee in perfect time with the final drumbeat. That was too optimistic for me, but I was reading the drumbeats accurately, and as I recognised the final few beats I raised myself from the almost crouching warrior position, threw my arms open wide again and stepped forward one pace. The girl read the gesture correctly and stepped willingly in to my embrace, wrapping her arms around me in a flamboyant gesture. My arms closed around her and I planted a kiss on her cheek right on the final beat of the drum. The crowd erupted. It was, in Cook Island dancing, my finest hour.

I released her and she beamed at me. "That was fantastic!"

"Aye, you were no' bad either," I replied with typical Scottish understatement. The generosity of my rustic compliment quite overwhelmed her and, swept away on a tide of euphoria, she drew me to her bosom again. I savoured her embrace for a few lingering moments. The compere could shout as much as he liked. I reckon I had earned it.

Sapna, one of the backpackers at the hostel, was an Indian girl brought up in England. She had never ridden a motorcycle before, and was worried about taking the hired bike out on the road for the first time. I took her down to the market place, which was deserted as it was a public holiday, to give her some experience in handling the motorbike off road. Then we embarked on a trip round the island to build up her confidence. We stopped to have a look at the Nuku, the colourful religious pageant commemorating the arrival of Christianity to the islands. It was a big occasion, so I was wearing my kilt. Afterwards, we drove on round the island, stopping at the waterfall, a popular scenic spot. Sitting at a picnic table, a couple of middle-aged women and some young people in their early twenties were tucking into some food. The unexpected sight of a kilt attracted their attention and we were called over.

"Please, come and share in our picnic."

Sapna whispered, "Oh, we can't."

"Hospitality is part of the culture here. It would be bad-mannered not to accept," I muttered. "We don't need to take much, but it would be offensive if we didn't join them."

We sat with them and took a little of their food. Introductions over, their curiosity about us was innocent and their questions flowed freely. On hearing that I had been here before, they asked if I knew anyone on this side of the island. When I mentioned Krystina, who held the Miss Tiare title at the time, they smiled in recognition. "Krystina is my niece," said Mata, one of the women, "and these are her cousins. Her father is my brother." On this small island, everybody seems to be connected.

As we talked, the cousins went swimming in the pool below the falls. No one here seems to change into swimwear. They simply go in fully clothed and sit in the sun afterwards to dry out. I would have loved to join them, but a waterlogged kilt didn't appeal too much.

After the swimming, the picnic continued and the conversation drifted to our respective traditions in music and dancing. Sapna was asked to demonstrate traditional Indian dance, I did some Scottish Highland Dancing, and they taught us how to dance Cook Islands' style. The table became an improvised drum with Mata and her sister beating out some rhythm. The young ones all joined in, dancing in all three styles. Eventually, out of breath, we stopped for a rest. A picnic had become a party, and the party then became an event imprinted indelibly in my mind as Tara, a vivacious girl who worked as a flight attendant with Air Rarotonga, began to sing. Her dark hair was still wet from swimming, her clothes stuck wetly to her body, her smile soft and serene and she had the voice of an angel. A gentle song of love hauntingly filled the air in that lush, green, jungle amphitheatre with the waterfall whispering gently in the background. It was a moment of pure bliss. As the final notes of the song drifted away in the mellow evening air, the sun slipped slowly behind the trees, bringing a heavenly day to its close in a totally unexpected and memorable fashion.

For the prefect relaxation at the end of a day's work, a bit of snorkelling or swimming in the deliciously warm water of the lagoon is one of the delights of life on a tropical island. The quiet water of the lagoon, sheltered by the reef from the big Pacific breakers which thunder on to it, seems to deceive the eye with its unbelievable colour, an incredible pale turquoise flecked randomly by greyish-brown patches where the coral heads lie just below the surface. It is irresistibly inviting and is a favourite place to cool off after the afternoon sun has lost some of its intensity. You don't have to swim or snorkel – many of the locals prefer simply to sit there, fully clothed, in water about two feet deep, and chat with their friends and neighbours.

So it was I found myself one day after a hot afternoon, just longing for a peaceful dip in the ocean. It was quiet with hardly anyone around, and I snorkelled out across the lagoon to the reef to explore the coral and observe the brilliantly coloured fish which live there, so strikingly beautiful with their vivid colours that I never tire of watching them.

On my return, the shoreline was much busier as the mamas and children came down for a late afternoon dip. As I surfaced near the water's edge and removed my mask, a cry erupted from a few yards away.

"Papa John!" I was now recognisable, and a host of kids from the school ran towards me and threw themselves into the water beside me. "Papa John, let me try your mask," cried one – and then they all had to have a go. Some wanted me to throw them over my shoulder into the water, the young ones wanted me to put on the mask and snorkel, pretend to be a big shark and chase them through the shallows.

The idea of a quiet, reflective dip in the lagoon had evaporated. It was Playtime with Papa John now. One of the mothers who knew me came over and relaxed in the water, chatting to me as easily as though we were lounging on chairs on a veranda.

Gradually, most of them left to go home, but the one who knew me walked out on the reef now that the tide was low to gather some seafood. She had a sharp knife with her and invited me to join her. I put on my sandals and followed her out to observe. She was gathering maturori, the roe of the sea cucumber. Few things in the sea look less appetising than a sea cucumber: an elongated, snail-like lump of soft tissue, anything from a few inches to a foot or more in length, its skin has the rough texture of canvas. They are found in great profusion here, lying on the lagoon bottom or on the reef, almost immobile, sifting through the sand. Holding each sea cucumber head end up, she made a small incision with her knife on its flank and the roe spurted out of the slit she had made. It looks like fine spaghetti with a slightly pink hue, and as she squeezed the sea cucumber's sides it ail flowed out. I held a plastic box to catch the roe, and she tossed the sea cucumber into the water again. They seem to suffer no harm from this incision. They soon patch up the slit again and produce more roe, which can be harvested again and again. It is usually eaten raw, sometimes fried, and has a shrimp-like flavour.

There were plenty of sea urchins clinging to holes in the coral. She raised her eyebrows quizzically, and asked, "Ever eaten one of these before?" I shook my head. She stripped the spines off one for me, sliced her knife through it, and pulled out some gelatinous mess, leaving some light brown muscle tissue in the shape of a five pointed star exposed along the curved wall of the urchin.

"That's the bit you eat," she told me, scraping the muscle away from the shell with the knife and beginning to feed me with it – raw, straight from the shell. Well, I thought, it's the way the Polynesians have survived for centuries so it's unlikely to do me any harm. So I opened my mouth and accepted the morsels she offered me. Quite pleasant, with the fresh salty flavour of the sea, it would serve as a starter. There were also some larger black sea urchins, very striking looking, and she told me to try one of them as they taste quite different. She stripped off the spines again with her knife, slit it across. This time there was much more muscle to be had, but of a more gelatinous consistency. She scraped it all to the bottom of the shell and then told me to drink it. It had a surprisingly sweet taste; a sort of seafood dessert.

I'd had my starter and dessert, but now I was hungering for my main course, and as we made our way back along the reef to the shore, I cast my eye around. The glassy surface of the lagoon was now a burnished gold reflecting the rays of the dying sun. The coral heads, now protruding from the water were silhouetted black against the golden surface of the sea, and much of the reef was now exposed – a dark rampart against the thrusting ocean outside.

All along the reef were the huddled figures of dozens of people, silhouetted against the setting sun. Here was a picture of life being lived in timeless fashion. People out on the reef, harvesting the sea as their ancestors had done for thousands of years: doing what we had been doing – gathering food for their families.

New Year's day was quiet, but in the evening a couple of the lads came out with me to see if anything was happening in town. We drove in on our motorbikes and turned in to the Island Bar car park. I had noticed a police car parked at the roadside, and it followed us, coming to a halt between me and the boys.

"Happy New Year, Papa John!" It was Nane, one of the local female police constables. "Hey, when are you leaving?"

"Next Saturday."

"Oooooh. I'm gonna miss seeing that kilt around the island. Can I have your email address, Papa John. I'd love to keep in touch with you."

"Aye, sure. Have you a pen and some paper?"

"Tell you what, I'll give you mine and you can then email me and I'll get yours that way." She picked up a notepad and began writing her address for me. At that point, the boys came to see what was happening. Jason, noticing her scribbling on her pad, looked at me gravely.

"Are you getting booked? What have you done?"

I laughed. "She's giving me her address and telephone number." I flicked the piece of paper triumphantly at him.

Things were quiet on the crime front, and so Nane chatted with us for a while. "Okay boys, I've got to go now and look out for drunk drivers," she said, nodding in the direction of the Island Bar. "Have a good time, but be careful. If I see you coming, I'll make sure I'm looking the other way." And with a wave she drove off.

Jason stared after her in disbelief and then chuckled. "Would you believe it? What a civilised police force. I love this place."

Chapter 41
Enigmatic Easter Island

Amazing, atmospheric, enigmatic: Easter Island is so unlike any other island in the Pacific. Viewed from the air it looks more like one of the Orkney Islands off the north of Scotland: grassy hills with hardly a tree to be seen, dark, forbidding cliffs, and a rugged coastline where the big ocean swells exploded white on hideously saw-toothed, black rocks.

Known in the local language as Rapa Nui, its population of some 2,000 people live mainly in Hanga Roa, the island's only village. The rest is rolling grassland over ancient lava flows, grazed by free-roaming horses and a few cows, with couple of high hills at each end. Its rather gaunt appearance was in stark contrast to the lush tropical growth to which I had become accustomed, but this place had a unique atmosphere.

On the outer rim of the crater of Rano Raraku, an extinct volcano at the east end of the island, is the quarry where the famous Easter Island statues, the moai, were carved. These monster effigies were not cut from blocks of stone, they were painstakingly hewn out of an almost vertical rock face. The biggest of them is twenty-two metres long (over seventy feet) and its weight has been estimated at around one hundred and eighty tonnes. Using only stone tools fashioned from hard basalt (metal was unknown here until the Europeans arrived), they cut into the rock face and sculpted these enormous statues, somehow eased them out and tipped them down the slope into pits to arrest their descent. From there they were hauled upright and transported across the island, some as far as twenty five kilometres.

Various theories have been advanced to explain how this amazing feat might have been achieved. Legend tells us that they 'walked' across, and it has been demonstrated recently how this could have been done. One statue was walked back to the quarry from the other side of the island, at a speed of twenty five kilometres per *month*, using eighteen men with blocks and tackle and logs. The action was the same as you might use to ease a refrigerator out of a confined space in your kitchen, shuffling it a little to each side as you drag. Some argue that they may also have been laid flat on logs and rolled, and this method too has been demonstrated as possible. Putting the argument over the technicalities aside, it was an amazing feat of engineering.

But then just about everything about Easter Island's history is amazing. Only about twenty four kilometres long by sixteen kilometres at its widest, the fact that this tiny triangular island was ever discovered and settled by the Polynesians is remarkable, even though they were great navigators and colonised virtually all of the South Pacific islands. It is just one tiny dot in the midst of an awful lot of ocean. To the south, the next landfall is Antarctica about 5,000 kilometres away. Mexico is about 8,000 kilometres to the north. Chile, a mere 3,700 kilometres to the east, is its nearest neighbour; while Australia lies about 8,000 kilometres to the west. So the Rapa Nui people didn't meet their neighbours very often!

Thor Heyerdal, the Norwegian explorer, argued that the first settlers may have come from the east; he demonstrated in 1947 with his Kon-Tiki Expedition that it was possible to drift westwards on a balsa-wood raft from South America to Easter Island. However, there is absolutely no archaeological, linguistic or cultural evidence to support this theory, and it has been discredited. All the available evidence links the Rapa Nui people with the Polynesian culture. The language is similar to Tahitian and Maori, and the Polynesians are believed to have settled on the island around 400AD.

Deification of ancestors was an element of Polynesian culture, but the Rapa Nui people took it to extremes. They believed that building the huge moai in honour of their ancestors would bring great mana – a kind of spiritual power – to the tribe. Someone must have been very persuasive. Imagine being told: "Right boys, let's take some small pieces of stone and hack away at that rock face until we have carved out a big statue. Then we'll drag it out and hoist it upright, and then – you'll enjoy this bit – we'll walk it... yes, *walk* it... Twenty five kilometres to the other side of the island, and place it on top of the ahu, the stone platform that covers the graves of our ancestors. That will make us so powerful. And once we have it erected, we can chisel out a big circular piece of rock to put on its head to resemble the way we wear our hair tied in a topknot. We'll work out another bit of clever engineering to hoist this big rock up, swing it over and centre it nicely on the head and then it will look really good. Even better, if we do this several times and have... say... six of these monsters gazing at us, we'll be six times more powerful!"

Aye, right! Here was religious fervour gone mad.

And having convinced them that this was a worthwhile project, just think of the logistics of it all: the management of all these people, teams of sculptors, woodcutters, road makers and haulers, logs, ropes, food supplies, and cooks. They had to be kept, fed and watered, while they worked. Modern sculptors reckon it would take twenty skilled men at least six months to create just one modestly sized statue. Trees had to be cut and transported to various locations for erection and rolling purposes, roadways prepared to make the transportation possible over the rough lava flows, and then there is the actual engineering involved in transportation. How did they work out how to do it? How did they know if they could ever physically manage to move the first one? After that, they could apply their knowledge and experience and, as they learned more, they built more and even bigger statues until they reached that twenty two metre, 180 tonne monster still lying at the quarry.

There are around 800 statues on the island, of which about half have been moved to burial sites, mostly around the coast. They were erected with their backs to the sea so that they kept watch over the villages. The others still lie at the quarry.

Most of this stone carving is thought to have taken place between about the 6th and 17th century AD. By the time Captain Cook arrived in the late 18th century most of the statues had been toppled. He described the people as poor, small, lean, timid and miserable. In 1804, a Russian visitor recorded at least twenty *moai* still standing, but later disruption led to these all being pulled down. By the end of the 19th century not one of the *moai* was left standing. So what happened to bring about such a dire change in attitude? Why were those in the quarry abruptly abandoned?

What happened here was a social catastrophe: a sudden, dramatic and discontinuous change in social order brought about by an unsustainable lifestyle shaped by obsessive beliefs. It is amazing that in spite of having developed such engineering and organisational skills, they did not have the common sense to realise the significance of cutting down every single tree on the island. Having denuded their habitat entirely of trees, they had no wood left to transport any more moai. They had no more timber to build houses, light fires or make canoes, without which they could neither escape the island nor go to sea to fish offshore. The woodland habitat had been destroyed, and the wildlife with it. In short, they had emptied the larder that fed them, and left themselves without the means of replenishing it. The work had to stop.

Without the necessary logs to erect and move them, the moai had to remain at the quarry. The six tribes on the island who had competed with each other by building bigger and more powerful moai were now confronted with starvation, and warred with each other over the island's diminishing resources. The next two centuries were characterised by the complete breakdown of social order on the island. Just as they had believed great power came from erecting the statues, they also reasoned that this power could be destroyed if the statues were pulled down. So they toppled each other's moai in their bid for supremacy. With starvation an ever-present threat, cannibalism was practiced. They hadn't left themselves much choice. The population prior to the period of social disintegration has been estimated at around 15,000 people. Two hundred years later it had plummeted to about 2,000.

And that wasn't the end of their misery.

In 1862, a raid by slave traders from Peru transported a thousand islanders to the Chincha Islands to work the guano deposits there. Nine hundred of them perished, but after intense pressure from the Catholic Church the survivors were shipped back home. Tragically, this humane act by the church had devastating consequences as some of those released had contracted smallpox, and by the time the ship arrived at Easter Island, only fifteen were still alive. They took the disease ashore with them, and the island's population was decimated once more. It is claimed that only 111 people survived the smallpox epidemic.

Easter Island is a thought-provoking place. It could be a metaphor for planet Earth. We may marvel that the people who lived here were blind to the damage they were doing to their environment and could not foresee the social consequences. Their technological achievements were astonishing, but their leaders carried too much authority and the people followed blindly, thoughtlessly, until it was too late.

But wait a minute, let's not be too smug. Look at our own history. A quick glance at the history of the twentieth century and the first decade of the twenty-first, let alone all that happened before, shows that we have no right to feel superior. Two world wars and numerous other conflicts, global exploitation of human and natural resources, and the spoliation of the environment in the pursuit of commercial gain with excessive power, political and economic, concentrated in the hands of a tiny minority. And are they safe hands? Are we, too, being led along a route to self-destruction? The lessons of Easter Island and its past could be a valuable element in the education of every entrepreneur, manager and politician.

Though it came perilously close to extinction, Easter Island survived, and is becoming prosperous once more. The extension of the airfield runway as a possible emergency landing site for the US space shuttle, has given the island a viable international airport, and tourism has grown accordingly. Large cruise ships occasionally stop here now, and more prosperous times look certain for the future. It is still a relatively unspoilt island, and its remote location probably means that it will remain so, but being more accessible now than ever before offers its inhabitants the opportunity to enjoy a more secure future based on tourism, if they are careful and conserve what they now have. Had their ancestors not left them something unique, it is highly unlikely that anyone would ever come to such a remote place. The moai are finally bringing prosperity to the island's people. You get the feeling that this place deserves some good fortune.

The population is now a mix of Polynesian and Chilean, but with a sprinkling of European blood as well. Having been annexed by Chile in the late 19th century, the official language is now Spanish, even though Rapa Nui is still their native language and Polynesian influences are dominant in music, dance and art.

The tourist books will tell you three days is enough to see everything. Well, you will see the main sights, but it was not enough for me. I arrived on a Monday morning from Tahiti, left Thursday afternoon for Santiago, and it was too rushed. I would have preferred more time to do some walking, more for photography to take advantage of the early morning and evening light, and I never had time to visit the museum.

Also, Monday to Thursday is the quiet period with not much in the way of nightlife. At the weekend the place apparently is jumping, with music and dancing all night long. It was just my luck to be there mid-week, and I couldn't delay my flight out as I had other connections to make in South America.

"Oh, that's a pity," said one of the local ladies. She then flicked her eyebrows knowingly: "With that kilt you could get up to some mischief here."

Chapter 42
Misfortune in Buenos Aires

The flight from Easter Island to Santiago passed quickly, thanks to the girl seated next to me. An English graduate now living and working in Madrid for a Spanish printing company, she had been sent out to Chile to look after the company's interests there over the past few months. We talked throughout the entire journey, during which she learned that I hadn't a word of Spanish in me.

As we belted up for the landing at Santiago she told me, "Now, you do realise that you are coming in my taxi and I'll drop you off at your hostel."

Well, I can't resist an assertive woman, and so I mumbled my thanks. It was a great help, and within twenty minutes of leaving the airport I was checking into my hostel for an overnight stop.

The next morning was bright and sunny, a good day to fly over the Andes. Every mountain, valley and river could be seen with clarity, but what surprised me was how narrow the range of mountains is. We were over it in a few minutes, and the remainder of the flight was over unexciting flat country. Again, I had a good travel companion. The Argentinian in the seat next to me spoke very good English, and offered to help me by writing out some useful words and phrases. He said he would meet me in the arrivals hall after I had cleared immigration and he would help me find a taxi to get me to my hostel. He was being met by his girlfriend, but was heading in the opposite direction or he would have given me a lift.

I wandered into the arrivals hall, looking around for my Argentinian friend and almost immediately a middle-aged man approached. "Excuse me sir, you are from Scotland? I hope you don't mind if I introduce myself. My name is Duncan MacKinlay. One of my ancestors was from Scotland. It's nice to see you wearing your national dress. I wondered if there is anything I can do to help you. Do you speak Spanish?"

"Not a word. But thanks for the offer. Actually, I'm looking for an Argentinian man I met on the plane who said he'd help me find a taxi."

"Oh, well, in that case I'll leave you my business card. If there is ever any need for help, with interpreting or whatever, please do not hesitate to contact me. How long are you staying in Buenos Aires?"

"Only one night."

"Oh, what a pity. I would have liked to invite you to my home to meet the rest of my family. We are very proud of our Scottish ancestry."

At that point, the guy from the plane arrived. I explained who my new friend was and introduced them. He laughed, "Now I understand why you wear your kilt," he said, "it is a good way to meet people."

My kilt attracted more than a few glances when I dined out that night. Opposite me sat an American couple. My steak and chips arrived, and I heard him mutter to his wife, "Those French fries look real good."

"Go on, have some. There are more on the plate than I can manage." Initially embarrassed, he was soon tempted to lay his inhibitions aside in the knowledge that he would be doing me a favour by taking some. A few minutes later, another glass of beer arrived at my table. The waiter indicated with a brief flourish of his hand that this came with the compliments of my American friend. I looked over and acknowledged his hospitality.

"That's very kind of you. Thank you very much."

"Well, you were kind enough to give me some of your fries."

"Aye, but I think I got the better part of the deal," I laughed.

When they had eaten and were starting their coffee they invited me to join them. Both ornithologists, they taught in Boston and had visited Scotland a few years previously to study the bird life in the Shetland Isles. They were now on their way home from Antarctica.

Buenos Aires was proving to be much more pleasant than I had anticipated, and that view was reinforced on my way back to the hostel when I met two young men who wanted to have photographs taken with me. They were football fans and knew more about the current state of Scottish football than I did. They get it all on TV there. I was really beginning to like Buenos Aires. Its people were proving to be so friendly that I regretted my schedule only allowed me one night there.

After a leisurely breakfast and shower, I packed and called a taxi. I was at the airport more than two hours before my flight was due, but I thought I could check my luggage in first then have something to eat. I took my passport, return flight ticket for Ushuaia, and wallet out of my hand luggage and stuck them in my sporran, ready for use at the check-in desk. I was turned away: internal flights only check in one hour before the time of the flight. I found a seat and laid my rucksack on the floor in front of me and my hand luggage down by my right leg. I wasn't ready to eat just yet.

For the first time ever, wearing the kilt brought misfortune. An Englishman, currently living in Aberdeen, spotted it and sat beside me. He had just arrived from Scotland, having been delayed by hurricane force winds a few days previously. I had heard about this in an email from home. We chatted for about twenty minutes. I had half turned towards him as we talked and when I turned back, the hand luggage that had been sitting on the floor by my right leg had disappeared! In it was my laptop computer and all the photos taken in the three months I had been travelling, my expensive new digital camera, cellphone, travellers' cheques, plane tickets... All gone! The initial sickening feeling was counter-balanced by the relief that I had my wallet with some cash and credit cards, my passport and the ticket for the return flight to Ushuaia in my sporran ready for the check in.

But my good feeling about Buenos Aires had evaporated.

I then had to file a report with the police; I just managed it in time to catch my flight to Ushuaia. The police had telephoned the check-in desk and made special arrangements for me; an officer escorted me through. A really nice guy, he shook hands with me and said, "I would like to apologise on behalf of my country for this despicable incident. I hope you will find that most Argentinians are very hospitable people who are happy to welcome you to our country." They were.

I had plenty of time to reflect on my folly during the four-hour flight south to Tierra del Fuego, to Ushuaia, the city at the end of the world. However, I resolved not to let that bit of misfortune spoil what had been such a memorable trip up to that point. Weighing it all up, I had some great memories. I was still alive and well. I had my passport, cash and credit cards. I would get some financial recompense, but not all of it, from the travel insurance. I could replace the computer, camera and phone. I could arrange for new plane tickets to be issued. I could return some day to Easter Island, Tahiti and Rarotonga to replace the photographs that had been stolen. Yes, I now had a good excuse for going back to Easter Island.

Ahead of me lay a trek in the spectacular mountains of Patagonia, and what could possibly be the most memorable experience of all – visiting Antarctica. My accommodation in Ushuaia was very good, and dinner that night was excellent. There was no point in being miserable. Everything would get sorted out.

However, there were a few other obstacles to overcome first. A major telecommunications fault had developed somewhere between Ushuaia and the rest of the world. Telephone contact was impossible: not even mobile phones would work, and all the computer links were down. The shops could not use their credit card links, the banks had to close, and the airlines could not access the booking systems. I couldn't get flight tickets re-issued. I couldn't email. I couldn't telephone to contact my insurers, or anyone else by any electronic means. I reverted to good old-fashioned letter writing, but the post office was choked with people who had been forced to do the same, and I had to wait in a queue for forty five minutes just to get a stamp. Business in Ushuaia went into meltdown. Well, that's a dramatic way of saying that they shrugged their shoulders and decided there was no point in hanging around waiting, so they all had a holiday. *Que sera sera.* So I shrugged my shoulders and had a day off too.

I surprised myself at the way I had accepted the situation, refusing to let it get me down. Could I have handled this as well just a few years ago? Then, even the slightest mishap had a tendency to be blown out of proportion in my troubled mind. The ability to adapt to unforeseen circumstances is essential if you embark on extended, independent travel, and I seemed to be adapting not too badly. Next day, when the fault had been repaired and it was business as usual, I managed to replace my camera, finding exactly the same model in Ushuaia. That was all I needed at the moment.

Ushuaia has an Alpine feel to it. The most southerly city in the world, it is very much a frontier place, with Cape Horn just around the corner. To the South, beyond Cape Horn, there's a lot of emptiness. To the North there was also a lot of emptiness. We were about 2,000 miles south of Buenos Aires with very little habitation in between. The Patagonian plain to the north of Tierra del Fuego is a cool desert. Long dirt roads crossed this arid plain: seldom was there a vehicle to be seen on them. This desert continues across the Magellan Strait into Tierra del Fuego. Only at the south of the island does the landscape change, abruptly from desert plain to a ridge of dramatic, jagged, snow-capped mountains dropping steeply into the sea. And there, on the edge of the Beagle Channel, lies Ushuaia – the city at the end of the world.

Chapter 43
The Patagonian Mountains

El Calafate, an hour's flying time north from Ushuaia, is a small modern town on the edge of a national park famed for its mountains and glaciers. My Patagonian trek had been booked with GAP Adventures, the Great Adventure People. There were five of us in the group. Natasha, our courier – half English, half Peruvian – spoke fluent Spanish. She had shepherded us to the airport at Ushuaia and had a minibus organised to pick us up at El Calafate.

Driving towards El Calafate from the airport, the landscape looked like a scene from a Hollywood western: an arid, ochre terrain covered in desert scrub with an inhospitable chill wind blowing over it.

"There's always a wind in Patagonia," said Natasha, "so be prepared. Even if the day starts still and warm, a wind will blow up from somewhere."

And dust. Always dust. Road vehicles traversed this terrain like comets, a long tail of dust marking their passage across the desert.

To the east, the rolling plain stretched up to a plateau, the Patagonian steppeland, and to the west there were mountains, darkening now in the light of the setting sun. I had never been attracted by deserts, but this place had an alluring, atmospheric quality about it, particularly in the soft golden light of the setting sun. It would be a good place to explore with a camera. In the morning, we headed west into the mountains, led by a local mountain guide who told us the story of the creation of this landscape.

The Andes Mountains were thrust up from the Pacific Ocean around sixty five million years ago, and they are still rising about one centimetre per year. Some parts are as young as only twelve million years. These are geological infants compared with the gnarled, old crags of the pre-Cambrian period (formed between 1,000 million and 4,000 million years ago) where I live in the northwest highlands of Scotland.

The prevailing wind is westerly, and sweeps in unchecked from the Pacific Ocean, heavily laden with moisture. The air is forced to rise when it encounters the massive wall of rock that is the Andes. As the air chills, the moisture condenses and precipitates as rain on the mild west side, snow on the cold mountain tops and, by the time it has crossed the ice-capped summits, all the moisture has been extracted so there is nothing left to drop on the east side except cool air, hence the cold desert plain of Santa Cruz that stretches all the way to the Atlantic coast.

Covering the high ground is the Patagonian ice-cap, where compressed snow forms an enormous ice-field from which numerous large glaciers grind their way downwards, usually ending in pale turquoise coloured lakes. The characteristic colour is caused by minute mineral particles ground from the rocks by the glacier and held in suspension in the water. The Patagonian ice-cap is the third largest source of fresh water in the world, behind the two polar regions. This is also the source of the infamous Patagonian wind. As the air in the valleys warms it expands, becoming less dense, and the more dense cold air above the ice-cap comes roaring down the mountains, sometimes with astounding ferocity.

Our destination that day was the Perito Morena Glacier. A trek round the lake took us to an enormous terminal wall of ice, sixty metres high and over two kilometres wide. Shedding lumps of ice with a crack like thunder, huge blocks crashed into the lake every few minutes. Probably the fastest moving glacier in the world, it slides forward at an average of 1.7 metres per day, and the visitor is guaranteed a spectacular show of calving every few minutes as huge lumps of ice break off and crash into the lake. This spot is accessible by road, so busloads of tourists pour over the slopes to view the ice show. Inevitably, there are professional photographers taking photographs of the tourists with the glacier in the background.

That day the glacier had a competitor. My kilt. I was getting as many people wanting to pose with me as the professional photographers were with their glacier. And it was fun. I had a lot of cuddles from sexy, smiling, dark-haired Argentinian women who sidled up to me, put their arms around my waist and ordered their husbands to operate the cameras. Two of the ladies I met that day were named MacKinlay. Argentina is an enormous country, yet in only three days I had already met three MacKinlays, all descended from the same Scottish ancestor who had settled in Buenos Aires in 1804.

That evening, back at El Calafate, we just had time to change for a five-hour bumpy bus ride over the dirt roads of the desert to a wee place called El Chalten. It had a real frontier look about it. Situated on a narrow plain between mountain ranges, it consists of a random scattering of small, lapboard shacks, one or two modest hotels, a couple of shops, the ubiquitous bright red cocoa cola signs, dirt roads, no sidewalks and a mournful wind that sweeps through its only street, whipping up small tornadoes of dust. This was spaghetti western country. I wouldn't have been surprised to meet Clint Eastwood and Lee van Cleef in a shoot out. Until twenty years ago there was no town, only a sheep station. El Chalten owes its existence to the trekkers and mountaineers who come to explore this wonderland of spectacular mountains and glaciers.

In the morning, a long trek up through forests of southern beech took us to a great glacial valley and over some terminal moraine marking where the glacier had receded 150 years ago. Before us lay a scene from a fairy tale. Beyond a small glacial lake rose Los Torres, a scenic wonderland of elegant rock spires: enormous, silvery-grey pinnacles of granite with sheer walls soaring skywards, their feet swathed in winding, deep-furrowed glaciers. We sat on the shore of the lake eating our packed lunches and marvelled at the splendour before us. It was hard to believe it was real. It was the most surreal landscape I had ever encountered.

However, the nine-hour trek next day to Mount Fitzroy exceeded even that. One of the most spectacular mountains in the world, it was named in honour of the captain of HMS Beagle, the ship that took Charles Darwin on his famous voyage of discovery. The ship's boats had explored this area, rowing 200km up the Santa Cruz River. The weather was perfect and the trek outstandingly scenic. The last pitch was a scramble up 350 metres of tortuous rocks – that's about 1,150 feet in old measurements. The ascent of this enormous mound of glacial moraine required the use of hands as well as feet in places.

It was energy sapping work, but the view at the top was heavenly. Mount Fitzroy now boldly confronted us. A stupendous peak, like an elongated nipple, with sheer, slab-sided faces soared 3,400 metres (over 11,000 feet) into an azure sky. Like a scarf wrapped around its shoulders, its attendant glacier curved downwards to melt in a deep turquoise blue lake. Through the binoculars we could see two tiny figures high up on one of the rock faces, painstakingly climbing their way to the peak. That really put the magnitude of the mountain into perspective. Our guide had climbed Mt Fitzroy. It took five days. At night they had to bivouac on the precipitous slopes, lashed on to slim ledges in biting cold winds. Technically, it is a difficult enough climb, but the fickle weather is the real enemy of the mountaineer. Exposure takes on a new meaning on these icy, wind-scoured slabs.

The way up the moraine may have been energy sapping, but the way down was painful. With so much loose rock and scree it was potentially dangerous, and my knees, constantly taking the braking strain, suffered burning pain. I regretted leaving my trekking poles behind that day. A pleasant diversion on the return trek was a detour to cool off in a picturesque, but rather cold, lake before attempting the final descent down to El Chalten. The weather had been glorious again, and the scenery outstanding. The trek had been fairly tough, and the body knew it had done some work, but after a hot shower it glowed.

Sleep came easily that night.

We had to be up again at 6.00am to catch the bus to take us over the border to Chile. The Chilean customs officers were great, all smiles and, "Hey come on over here. Never mind your baggage. Let's see your kilt."

Chile matched Argentina in both the beauty and power of its landscape. The treks were strenuous, but richly rewarding with unforgettable scenery. In the Asciena Valley, a skyline of towering crags gave way to long scree slopes sprinkled with a few patches of tenacious vegetation. The scree tumbled steeply into a deep V-shaped valley with a gushing white river cascading over rocks far below. The trek took us along a narrow path, with steep drops down hundreds of feet of scree or along rock faces bordering the river. We climbed higher and higher until finally, as always it seemed, we had to face yet another scramble 370 metres (1,200 feet) up an enormous heap of glacial debris. This had to be scaled to secure the ultimate reward for our labours. Towering majestically from the far side of another glacial lake, a series of huge, glacially sculpted granite peaks, the Torres del Paine, pointed their fingers up into the sky for another 2,000 metres or more (7,000 feet). These soaring pinnacles are a magnet for climbers, and are a test of the skills of the best mountaineers in the world.

Also a magnet for photographers, the mountains charmed us that day with a striptease show. Coyly drawing swirling clouds around their peaks, they shrouded themselves in mystery, offering only an occasional, ghostly glimpse. A few moments later, the warmth of the sun drew breezes that forced them to cast aside their white drapes and they exposed themselves once more, revealing the full glory of their breathtaking beauty against a backcloth of bright blue sky. Their feet lay swathed in the icy wraps of curling glaciers, which ended on a sun-kissed shelf of rock. There, the ice melted into hundreds of streams of water, painting the rock in dark stripes where they flowed over it and down its steep face into the lake. This was a place to rest, restoring tired bodies with food and filling cameras with images, gazing in wonder at a landscape constantly changing in tone and texture as the clouds danced merrily around the peaks. It was difficult to drag ourselves away, such was the power of this ever-changing scene. The real reward would have been to spend the night up there in order to capture the glowing colours of the rocks illuminated by the red light of dawn. Our tents were already pitched at a campsite four hours walking time away, so we had to prise ourselves from this rocky paradise and descend once more.

Campsites are always sociable places, and sitting round the campfire late at night telling stories can be one of their great pleasures. Herñan, our mountain guide, a likeable wee Chilean chap who had married an English girl, sat there wide-eyed as I told some tales of Scotland's gory past, light and shadow dancing on my face by the light of the flickering flames. Before going to bed he told me, "John, I wish I had a video camera here. That's the kind of storytelling I'd love my children to see."

Next day, it was all low level walks, trekking in lashing rain and a howling wind in the morning, with a boat trip in the afternoon up the long Grey Lake to view the enormous glacier at its northern end. The Grey Glacier is very stable, so the boat could get relatively close to its towering walls, fissured deeply with crevasses and sculptured with pinnacles of pale blue ice. We disembarked at a campsite just below the glacier. A cool wind swept down from the massive ice fields above. The wind was welcome, though. Hanging up our sodden clothing at the campsite, the blustery wind had it dried before bedtime.

Having arrived the easy way – by boat – we walked back through the mountains the next day. A ferry transported us across the lake where our minibus awaited to take us back to Puerto Natales. That last trek was a joy. The sun shone though broken clouds scudding across the mountains. The rain stayed away and the fresh wind on our backs prevented us from becoming too hot. The week's trekking had hardened the feet, and the knees were no longer complaining. The lungs had been cleansed and the blood purified by the clean mountain air. The muscles were now nicely toned, and it was a joy to go pounding up and down the slopes, feeling the body working like a well-maintained machine. Such a sense of well-being and general fitness was euphoric. My youth had been restored and it was with considerable sadness that I viewed the end of our meandering trek through the unforgettable mountains of Patagonia.

Herñan, our guide, was one of these special people with whom I had felt an instant connection. We'd talked a lot together on our treks and sitting beside him in the minibus on the way back we both fell asleep. Our heads rolled sideways and our bodies collapsed against each other.

His head rested on my shoulder, tucked neatly under my cheek; my head leaned on top of his, using it as a pillow. Amused by sight of two tired amigos snoring away in affectionate harmony, the others got the cameras out to capture the moment.

Back at Puerto Natales, when we finally said goodbye, he paused briefly, threw his arms around me and gave me a big hug. "John, my amigo," he told me, "I wanna come to Scotland to hear more of your stories. That night at the camp fire was the highlight of the trip for me."

Chapter 44
Across The Drake Passage

"How many of you have brought seasickness pills?" asked Ian Shaw, the expedition leader. A forest of hands went up. "A few of you haven't, I see..."

I was one of them – well, I was an experienced sailor after all. The pause and the way he tucked his chin into his chest and looked over his non-existent spectacles expressed his silent disapproval. The typical schoolmaster pose, I'd used it often enough.

"Let me tell you about the Drake Passage..." He used the pause again to good effect. "You are about to enter the most turbulent and unpredictable sea in the world, a place where even the most experienced mariners throw up. The wind here travels all the way round the world, unhindered by any land except when it is funnelled between Cape Horn and the Graham Land peninsula on Antarctica. Because of this long fetch by the wind, the seas build up to enormous heights: waves fifty metres high are not uncommon here. Ocean currents are also deflected between South America and Antarctica, and interfere with the main stream running through from west to east to produce even more violent and very steep seas. Even the most experienced sailors take anti-seasickness medication here – so if you haven't brought any, my advice is to buy some now at the ship's reception desk. Oh, and don't make the mistake of waiting to see if you are going to feel sick first and then take the pills. It will be too late then. Seasickness pills will not cure seasickness. They are preventative, not curative, and should be taken before you start the voyage. The only way to cure seasickness is to go and sit under a tree."

He paused for a moment to let the futility of that sink in. Silence. He certainly used these pauses effectively. We were now steaming down the sheltered waters of the Beagle Channel between Tierra Del Fuego and the group of islands to the south which constitute the tail of the South American continent, ending with Cape Horn.

"And let me tell you something else," he continued. "Seasickness is ten times worse on an empty stomach, so eat plenty. We provide plenty of food all through the day for that very reason."

He'd told a good story, so I decided to play safe and get some pills. After all, this was supposed to be a trip undertaken for pleasure. Even if the sea is rough it can still be enjoyable, but not if you are bombarding the other passengers with the contents of your stomach. It's a personal thing, but I don't like to share my vomit with anyone else. Whether it was the pills or my experience as a sailor I don't know, but I had no problem. Many others were sick in spite of taking the medication.

We were having our initial briefing on board *Explorer*, a ship designed and built in Finland in 1969 for polar exploration. She was a tough little ship, with a double strengthened hull. She carried a maximum of 108 passengers with around fifty of a crew and was reputed to be the ship that would boldly go where no other ship could in these waters. She had been the first ship to carry passengers to the Antarctic, the first passenger ship to sail south of the Antarctic Circle, the first ship to take passengers through the North West Passage between Canada and the Arctic ice cap, and on her way from one end of the world to the other, she had cruised 2,000 miles up the Amazon, travelling up river as far as Iquitos in Peru. Having just had a major refit in 2004, she was now pushing the limits once more. Her small size, reinforced hull and shallow draught allowed us to force our way into narrow ice filled channels to get to some interesting landing spots. Her crew, many of whom had sailed in her for many years, regarded her with great affection – a good sign. By the end of the voyage, most of the passengers felt the same way. She had a winning way with her.

Sadly, in November 2007, she struck ice and sank. Thankfully, all the passengers and crew were rescued.

The briefing went on to describe what we were likely to do, weather permitting, where we would try to go, the safety procedures and the domestic arrangements. The captain introduced the officers on the ship. They were all Europeans, but the rest of the crew were Filipinos with four Filipinas (females) to clean the cabins and serve as waitresses. It was a pleasure to meet such cheerful people as they went about their work each day. Melody, the lovely girl who cleaned my room and served in the dining room, never failed to greet me with a delightful smile and a cheery, "Good morning, sir."

"Och, call me John," I suggested.

Next day I was greeted with, "Good morning, Sir John." I was the only person during the voyage to be elevated to a knighthood.

The other members of the expedition team introduced themselves. We had experts on birds, marine mammals, Antarctic history, geology, geography, and photography to educate us with lectures on our way southwards and help us interpret what we would see when we got there.

I looked around the assembled passengers. It was quite a mixed group. Most were in the age range forty to seventy, but the group also included some teenagers in a couple of families from the USA, some students in their early twenties and several in their thirties. To want to go to the Antarctic you have to be interested in exploring one of the most extreme environments on Earth and be moderately fit. Being over sixty, I had to have a medical certificate to testify that I was fit enough to undertake such an expedition.

Just looking at the faces and the body language, I could sense an affiliation with several already. My gut feeling once more proved correct as over the course of the trip, though we mixed randomly most of the time, loose social groupings gradually tended to form. I found myself drawn into a group which consisted mostly of those in their twenties or thirties with cries of, "C'mon John, you're coming with us," when the boats were being loaded to go ashore. They were the people most likely to gather round me at the dinner table. When I remarked on the thirty to forty year age gap between me and most the rest of this young group, I was told, "Ah, but this is not the young group, it is the young-at-heart-group. So you qualify."

The weather was kind to us on the way south with no more than a moderate breeze and a gentle rolling swell to contend with. Sleep came easily in such conditions. So did regurgitated food. On my way to the dining room next morning someone's breakfast had already made a hasty exit and was being cleaned off the carpet by a smiling Filipino steward. The next two days passed quickly with a series of interesting lectures interspersed with opportunities to photograph the wonderful mastery of flight of the albatrosses following the ship.

Swooping low, well behind our stern, with motionless wings they glided swiftly alongside, soared upwards, flipped over and circled round behind us once more in an elegant aerial ballet performed with effortless grace. It is difficult to judge just how big these beautiful birds are in such a spacious environment, but the largest of the species, the wandering albatross, has a wingspan of more than three metres (ten feet). Capturing their flight on camera presented some challenges, but the digital camera proved its worth here. So many images could be shot and downloaded onto the computer on the ship, so you could edit and get at least a few that were worth keeping. If you failed to get any good pictures you just went out and tried again. Having witnessed such advantages, several people were converted to digital photography during the trip. The ship carried some digital cameras for hiring out.

This was also a period during which people got to know one another. We had a group of twenty seven Portuguese on board, three of whom were journalists, one from radio, and one from a TV company – resplendent with camera crew. Wearing my kilt at dinner on the first night, I got to know them all very quickly. I was called over to their tables for introductions, photographs and the usual admiring looks. A lively bunch, very enthusiastic and determined to enjoy every experience the voyage had to offer, they were always the last to go to bed. They all wore red jackets emblazoned with The Expedition To The End Of The World on their backs.

It was one of the Portuguese who was first to spot an iceberg on the evening of the second day at sea. Dinner that night was punctuated by cries of delight as yet another iceberg was spotted and the ship would list to one side as people left their tables to rush over to see the latest lump of ice. Twenty-four hours later icebergs had become such a familiar part of the scene they were hardly noticed.

That night, as the ship slowly pushed her way through the grinding ice flows in the Gerlache Strait, most people were on deck taking pictures. Mountains clothed in deep snow rose steeply from the sea on both sides of the channel. Whales lay motionless on the surface of the water, seals languished on ice flows. It was a windless night, the ice gently tinted by the warm glow of the sunset at around 11.00pm. Even after the sun had slipped below the horizon, we were in such low latitudes that the afterglow continued throughout the night. It was the kind of night when you simply did not want to go to bed.

We had been told in the briefing that a visit to Antarctica could prove to be a life changing experience. So many people who have come to this most forbidding of continents find it addictive: like a drug, it compels then to return. In this land of extremes, nothing inhabits the realm of ordinariness. It is the coldest, windiest, driest place on earth. It is the world's largest desert and has on average less than two inches of snowfall per year over the entire continent. Deep in the interior it may not snow for many years at a time, but the wind blows it about a bit. Its sheer isolation can induce 'Polar madness', a condition first identified by a scientist who travelled with Scott and Shackleton.

This can have serious consequences. Some years back during a game of chess, a soviet scientist was killed by his opponent wielding an ice-axe. Quite clearly something had to be done about that, so the Soviet authorities banned playing chess. An American expedition led by Admiral Byrd, the first man to fly over the South Pole, recognised the risks and had two coffins and twelve straightjackets listed in its inventory. I looked around the faces in the lecture room, wondering. Strange things could happen in this place. A few days later they did.

Despite its forbidding nature it has such an alluring beauty and sense of peace. Five weeks after our return, Geraldine, a 23 year old French girl, wrote to me:

'I have never felt better in my life than when I was there. It's difficult to explain. The best description I can use is that it was a spiritual experience. It's an ideal setting to think about the meaning of life and all those related philosophical thoughts. There was no daily hassle, no time. Day and night were meaningless as it never got dark. It was all stress free, experiencing and feeling life in a new light. You just let yourself get absorbed by nature. Hearing or seeing glaciers break apart, watching penguins swimming, feeding, running after one another, making sounds to recognize their mate, swapping space over the nest to keep their eggs warm. Watching leopard seals relaxing on icebergs; smelling the fishy odour of the whales' breath. Looking out from the bridge windows on the ship, taking millions of photos. These memories have left deep marks on me.'

My first image of Antarctica was gained as a boy, when I was one of thousands of British schoolchildren to troop through the doors of their local cinemas to watch the film *Scott of the Antarctic*. Made in 1948 and starring John Mills, it was considered to be of educational value. The heroic, though some might argue stupid and ill prepared, attempt by Captain Robert Falcon Scott to be first to reach the South Pole, had captured the imagination of the British establishment. Here was a hero who gallantly died in the attempt, a glorious failure in the best traditions of the British Empire. The visual images of that film stuck in my mind. The icebergs, the striking contrast between the blue of the sea and the white of the snowfields and glaciers, the terrifying crevasses, the blizzards and the flimsy tents, flapping ferociously in the howling wind that tormented Scott's party on their return from the Pole and prevented them from reaching the food at a supply depot only eleven miles away.

I had harboured a desire to see this for myself, but always it seemed so remote, so unreachable.

My dream was now being realised.

Chapter 45
Revealing Secrets

We had hoped to make it as far south as the Ukranian operated Vernadsky Base. Formerly a British research station called Faraday, it was handed over to the Ukranians several years ago. It had a unique claim to fame: it boasted the only pub in Antarctica.

Back in the 1950s, two British carpenters had been hired to construct a hardwood extension to the pier, but with the weather conditions being against them they passed the time lovingly building a classic English pub instead. The wharf was never completed and the men were dismissed. Their immortality has been assured, however, in the magnificent polished woodwork of the bar – a facility now treasured by the Ukranians. I was looking forward to wandering into the most southerly pub in the world wearing my kilt, but although the ship could force its way through, the ice floes were too much for the zodiacs, the rigid inflatable boast we used for landings, so we couldn't make a landing.

Instead, *Explorer* thrust her way though to Petermann Island, home to a colony of Adelie penguins and some blue eyed shags. We dropped anchor close to the site of a British research camp comprising of a wooden hut and a scattering of yellow tents secured somehow to a few patches of unyielding granite rock. The first of several research bases we encountered along the peninsula, the scientists there were monitoring the impact of human interaction with the penguins.

Despite its barren appearance and inhospitable reputation, Antarctica is a bustling global laboratory and museum. For here, written in the rocks, is much of the story of planet Earth: the origins of its life, the movement of continents, and the ever-changing climate are all archived in its rock and ice strata. That so much life can survive here in such extreme conditions is astonishing, ranging from the tiny microscopic mites living under frost shattered rocks which have developed their own antifreeze, a glycerol type of compound, to the giant humpback whales which daily filter tons of krill, the small shrimp-like crustacean which is the core of the food chain here.

It was the ancient Greeks who theorised that, in order to maintain the balance of a spherical world, the land mass of the northern hemisphere must be counterbalanced by a significant mass of land somewhere in the south. Described later on maps in Latin as *Terra Australis Nondum Cognita* (the southern land as yet unknown), it remained so until its discovery in the early 19th century. Captain Cook had been sent to try to find this continent – if indeed it was a continent, for it could have been just a collection of islands – and was the first navigator known to have crossed the Antarctic circle.

His first attempt was blocked by the pack ice, but he retreated to Polynesia and returned the following summer reaching 71 degrees south, a good ten degrees further than anyone had ever gone before. Unfortunately, Cook had gone to the wrong places, probing deep into the continent's broad bays. Had he explored just a bit to the east he would have been where we were now at the Graham Land Peninsula, the long arm reaching up towards South America. Blocked again by ice, he wrote in his journal: "Ambition leads me not only further than any other man has been before me, but as far as I think it possible for man to go."

Time proved him wrong, and the continent was discovered in the early 19th century. There was a gradual growth of interest in Antarctica until the 1890s when a mixture of imperial ambition, scientific curiosity and a thirst for good adventure stories by the media inspired an eruption of enthusiasm for polar exploration, culminating in the rush to be first to reach both the North and South Poles in the early 20th century. While it was the expeditions of Scott and Shackleton, both good publicists, that gained all the credits, other expeditions had proved to be much more valuable from a scientific point of view. Today the research goes on by scientists from all over the world. Camping in tiny yellow tents while they do their fieldwork, or analysing data in laboratories in centrally heated buildings at the major bases, they are slowly revealing much of the natural history of this planet.

Research on the rocks has proved that these frozen wastes once supported tropical forests. This suggests not that there has been such a dramatic change in climate, but that this continent was once located much further north as part of a landmass in the tropics. As the world's continents drifted apart, it has been the fate of this particular continent to drift southwards and endure the frozen eternity that is Antarctica.

Antarctica forces you to re-think many of your concepts. To the human mind, rock is hard, impermeable, permanent. Not so, for here is contained the evidence of rocky continents fragmenting, floating around the world, colliding, crushing, coalescing over thousand of millions of years.

Studies of glacial activity show how ice sheets can alter the climate of the planet. Global warming is an issue of major concern, and rightly so, but is it a natural phenomenon or the result of our pollution of the atmosphere? The issue is a complex one: 18,500 years ago, when Scotland lay under ice a mile deep, South Georgia was deglaciating. In the so-called Mini Ice Age of 1,500AD to 1,900AD many glaciers advanced beyond their normal limits. Recession from those limits represented the end of that cold period. The present warming may be a natural phenomenon – or it may not.

Research on glacier margins and ice cores reveals evidence that the Earth's climate is far from being stable. It has been likened to a flickering switch. The short period of time over which meteorological records have been kept is miniscule on the scale of the earth's climate history so that the warming we have now may be a minor blip, which could be followed by a rapid descent into another cold period. The truth is, no one knows for sure. The research continues. Whatever the truth may be, Antarctica appears to have many of the world's secrets locked away in the fastness of its ice.

Though still a relatively inaccessible place, it is not as remote as it once was. Polar tourism has expanded rapidly in the last twenty years, and now around 25,000 visitors arrive each year. But don't expect to see the Antarctic Hilton standing proud on these ice-girt shores. On the way down, one passenger from the US asked, "What are the restaurants like? What kind of food do they eat there?" It has surprised me to discover that many people do not know that there are no indigenous people on Antarctica, imagining it is home to tribes of southern Inuits, living in igloos, hunting polar bears – but there are none of them either. There are no land-based mammals. This continent has only marine mammals, such as seals and whales. There are no towns, only a few temporary residents in the scientific bases. It is the emptiest place on earth.

In this highly sensitive environment, all tour operators subscribe to a strict code of practice. Prior to every excursion off the ship we were thoroughly briefed on environmental issues. Footbaths were set out for us when we returned to the ship to minimise the risk of carrying infection from one site to another. Nothing must be left behind. Body waste management was therefore important – you don't pee in the snow here. The taking of souvenirs was absolutely forbidden. Throwing stuff overboard was forbidden. No one disagreed with this, but it took more than a few rules to alter the mindset of the slovenly cigarette smoker among us who thoughtlessly cast a fag end into the sea when he had finished. If only he could see the number of discarded cigarette ends swallowed by birds, fish and turtles in their legitimate quest for food.

Stepping ashore on that first day, the childhood memories came flooding back to me. Here I was at last, on the most desolate, most inhospitable, yet still remarkably beautiful continent on earth. Now I could meet the inhabitants – a colony of Gentoo penguins. The first thing that hits you when you land at a penguin rookery is the noise, and then as you get closer, the smell – a pungent fishy aroma which you soon become accustomed to. Their lavatorial habits are primitive. They simply squirt a jet of foul smelling waste from their rear ends with scant regard for the environment or any passing neighbour. Very tolerant of humans, we were often regarded with much curiosity by the penguins.

The two main rules when approaching wildlife were: stay at least five metres away from any wildlife; and do not stand on a penguin highway. They have their own highways from nest to shoreline, and they are not too pleased to find them blocked. If you inadvertently stand in their paths they will look at you very directly, with a silent gaze that says: 'when are you going to get out of my way?' They are delightful to observe, displaying a wide range of behaviours on the nest and as they travel to and from the sea; both parents take turns on the nest and at the fishing.

A couple of immature elephant seals were also found lying on the rocks. They lay side by side, indolent, blubbery masses with cute facial expressions as they raised their heads to watch us, then deciding we were behaving ourselves, they settled down to sleep once more.

Overhead, a few skuas swept low over the rookery, always on the lookout for an unguarded egg or penguin chick for dinner. Wherever there were penguins nesting there were skuas, always menacing from above or even on land, one bird taunting a parent penguin to get it to move off the nest while another skua sneaks in from behind to steal the egg. Scattered around the nesting Gentoo penguins were several broken eggshells, evidence of skua predation.

An evening excursion took us to Dorian Bay, where the subtle evening light created dramatic effects on the surrounding mountains. The zodiacs transported us from the ship to another penguin rookery at Damoy Point. On the way in, I could have sworn I heard the sound of distant bagpipes. Was this the first sign of polar madness? No, it surely must be a recording being played on the steelhulled yacht *Gambo*, which lay at anchor close to the shore. Wrong again. As we drew closer, I could see a bearded Scot on her deck playing the bagpipes to welcome the expedition team from *Explorer* to Damoy Point. *Gambo*'s flag proudly bore the Welsh dragon, but she had a mixed crew: a Welshman, an

Englishman, an Irishman, an American and a Scot were all on board. Adventurous young men, they were combining cold climate sailing with some mountaineering. Two whole lamb carcasses were strung from the rigging to keep them chilled – the refrigerator was for the beer.

Once again, it was the kind of night when few people felt like sleeping. And as the ship moved on, a Portuguese guitarist, an American pianist, and myself on harmonica and spoons, provided some musical entertainment. The Portuguese radio journalist dashed below to get her recorder and microphone. That was another first for me: I was recorded playing spoons for Portuguese radio! It was 2.30am before I got to bed.

A sunny morning found us anchored off the Orne Islands. This was the first time the ship had been here, and the expedition team had no idea what to expect. They got more than they bargained for. The aim of our exploration of the island was to record the different species of bird and any other life we might find, but the sun shone brightly so this was definitely a day for wearing the kilt ashore. I was greeted with incredulous stares as I waited to embark on the zodiac, but with the temperature soaring to a sweltering five degrees above zero it would have been regarded as a fine day in Scotland, even in summer. The island had a good covering of snow, but on several rocky outcrops, small colonies of Chinstrap penguins and skuas nested among the ice-shattered stones. While the penguins were tolerant of our presence, the nesting skuas were certainly not and mounted diving attacks on the head of anyone who inadvertently ventured too close to their nesting sites.

However, the wildlife in the kilt attracted as much camera attention as the penguins. Here, the mountain scenery in the background was very striking, with saw-toothed ridges, precipitous slopes and deep snow fields contrasting with a blue sky flecked cheerily with white clouds. Large icebergs graciously courted each other as they floated past in stately fashion. With such a backcloth, it was the prefect location for an interview with the TV crew. I began to feel like a celebrity: recording for Portuguese radio the night before, and now I would be seen wearing the kilt in Antarctica on their TV screens as well. Even better, every one of the Portuguese ladies insisted on having a photograph taken snuggled up close to the man in the kilt.

Our next anchorage was Neko harbour. A natural haven sheltered by high mountains around which enormous glaciers swirled and eased their cracking and crashing way into the sea. The site of a former whaling station and one of the few places with a beach, the only sign of human activity now was a hut occasionally used by scientists. The scale of the glacier here can best be seen when viewed from a vantage point high on the hill above. Plodding through knee-deep snow on the climb up to a rocky bluff was not easy, but it was well worth the effort, offering an aerial view of the front of the glacier which was deeply fissured with crevasses.

Coming down was much easier and quicker: the slope here is so steep all you have to do is lie on your back and slide down. I had left the kilt aboard the ship this time, and had dressed in conventional polar gear. There are limits to what I will do, and lying flat on my back tobogganing downhill, sans toboggan, while wearing a kilt, would have been polar madness. It would certainly have brought a flush to my cheeks – and the shrinking effect elsewhere doesn't bear thinking about. And the cameras would all have been working overtime. No, I know where to draw the line. Or so I thought.

Having made a rapid descent to the beach, glowing with exhilaration over this childlike pleasure, I caught up with Wendy, a young Australian student teacher. She had impressed me greatly, and we had spent some time discussing education the day before, an event she had described as 'inspirational'.

"H'y'gan Wendy," I called out in true Australian fashion, "enjoying the expedition?"

"Hi, John! Yes, I am. Hey, you've established quite a reputation. I was talking to an American couple today who asked me if I'd met 'that Scotsman who wears a kilt'. They'd been talking with you at lunch and several other people have mentioned you. Yeah, you've become a bit of a character. Even the Filipinos in the crew are talking about you."

"Oh?" I shrugged my shoulders modestly. But what had I done? I began to understand what she was talking about later that night.

Chapter 46
As Others See Us

It was over two hundred years ago that Scotland's national poet, Robert Burns, in his poem *To A Louse* expressed the desire to be able to see ourselves as others see us. Well, sometimes it does happen – and it can be a shocking experience. When I embarked on *Explorer* I found the ship sufficiently cosy to be able to walk about in only a light cotton shirt, tropical shorts and bare feet, as I had done in the Cook Islands where I had spent most of the previous three months. The other passengers came on board well prepared for the chill winds of Antarctica: thick socks, boots, thick trousers, woollen sweaters, parkas and woolly hats, even scarves – and this was what they wore *inside* the ship. My bare legs and feet attracted the most incredulous stares.

"Oh, you Scotsmen must be so tough," exclaimed more than one of several admiring women whose gaze always longingly followed my athletic, sun-bronzed legs.

"Och aye," I replied, smiling modestly. "It's the porridge we eat that keeps us warm." Then, when I went ashore and trudged through the snow wearing my kilt, my reputation was assured. I was not only tough, but decidedly eccentric as well.

There aren't many beaches in Antarctica, and at our briefing session that evening Wendy had asked Ian, the expedition leader, if there would be an opportunity to have a swim anywhere. Yes... a swim! In the Antarctic Ocean, among the icebergs! During the time we had been there, the daily sea temperature had never soared above one degree Celsius, and that had been in the midday sun. I shook my head in amusement. Wendy must have had a wee touch of polar madness. Well, maybe not, students often tend to be a little deranged.

Of course, I hadn't been a student for a long time, so I had been un-deranged – or so I thought. I hadn't even been daft enough to swim in the sea in Scotland since 1976. The memory of the agonising, throat-constricting shock of icy cold water hitting my chest had remained with me – and that was in summer. I knew what really cold water felt like. Those mad enough to be interested in going swimming were invited to meet with Ian after the briefing. I smiled the superior smile of the cognoscenti, and sensibly wrapped myself up for an evening excursion into the next bay to observe the wildlife and the glacial scenery.

We were transported in the zodiacs to a surreal world of spectacular glaciers with caves carved into the pale blue ice walls by wind and sea action, great tower blocks leaning drunkenly against each other and elegant, cathedral-like spires soaring heavenwards. And on an ice floe, quite unimpressed by it all, a large leopard seal lay sleeping. Normally we think of seals as having cuddly, puppy-like faces with big lovable eyes. The leopard seal does not match this image. These guys look mean. That's because they *are* mean. Weighing in at around 500kg (over 1,000 pounds), they have big jaws and a vicious set of teeth. One of the great predators of the seas, they prey on other seals and penguins and have been known to attack humans. A British scientist diving among them was attacked and killed not long ago. One of Sir Ernest Shackleton's crew was chased across an ice floe by a leopard seal during the epic voyage in 1916 after their ship Endurance had been crushed by ice. As he could run faster, it dived into the sea, swam under the floe and came up again at the other side to confront him once more. He was saved by the prompt action of one of the crew with a rifle. This was another good argument against going swimming.

We approached this one closely, but carefully, for photographs. He raised his head once and showed us his teeth. With such a fearsome reputation we had no desire to upset him. We backed off and observed from a safe distance, silently.

Suddenly, an enormous report like a gunshot echoed around the bays. Followed by a lengthy thunderous roar – it was a glacier calving. We switched our attention to the glacier behind us. It remained unaltered. The calving had occurred just around the corner, in the bay where the ship lay at anchor. An enormous wall of ice had crashed into the sea, filling the entire bay with glacial debris. The initial momentum, having scattered the ice well out into the bay, had now dissipated, but *Explorer* was now completely hemmed in. The bay was packed with brash ice, floes and small icebergs and the zodiacs simply could not force their way through the mess. We were stuck outside it all, unable to get back. It was 10.30pm, and we were now cold and hungry. The ship's captain called us on the radio. He had ordered the bow thruster into operation and the sideways wash from it slowly propelled the ice floes away from the side of the ship. A gap opened up, and after about thirty minutes the zodiacs were finally able to drive through to the ship. Those who had been back aboard early that night had seen it all happening. A wall of ice several hundred metres wide had tumbled into the sea in a domino effect. No one had ever seen anything quite like it before, not even among the crew or the expedition team; not even Ian, our expedition leader, an Antarctic junkie on his 79th visit.

The last zodiac arrived – the one with all the swimmers. As they climbed back aboard, I was met with howls of disbelief. "John! Where were you? Why did you not come for a swim? You're always up for a bit of fun."

Did I look that stupid? This sentiment was echoed among the other passengers in the lounge. They were incredulous, the Portuguese in particular. They would have bet good money that I would be leading the charge into the icy waters of the Antarctic. What had happened to me? Had I gone soft? I was amazed at the reaction. And it wasn't just the passengers – it was the crew too. All my delightful Filipino friends, the boatmen, stewards and the cleaners looked at me with the same disappointment written all over their normally smiling faces. The expedition team, hardened veterans of many Antarctic explorations, also looked stunned: "Oh, you've let us down, John. We thought you would have been the first to volunteer for a dip among the icebergs. We thought you were a hard-as-nails kind of guy who would try anything." Gunther, the German head chef, shook his head in disbelief, and sadly turned away to sup his beer, too embarrassed to say anything.

I cringed. I was actually beginning to feel ashamed. Burns's words came back to haunt me: "To see ourselves as others see us." It was happening to me now. Here I was among people, none of whom I had known a week ago, who saw me as some sort of swashbuckling adventurer, noted for my youthful spirit and hardiness – and now, it seemed, also for foolhardiness! To them, I was game-for-anything, young-at-heart, John. I thought of all the other things I had done fearlessly: sailing single-handed in turbulent seas, jungle trekking, kayaking in crocodile infested waters, sky diving, scuba diving, feeding sharks, kissing sting rays (as you do!), swimming in the dark, subterranean lakes of limestone caves on remote islands, climbing coconut trees, eating raw sea urchins and the roe of the sea cucumber out on the reef at Rarotonga, trekking kilted through the snowfields of Antarctica... I had kept myself open to new experiences and been enriched by them.

But what had I done now? I had failed to buckle my swash and heartily lead my followers into the shivering seas. I had constrained myself, denied myself that wonderful euphoria that comes from doing something so utterly ridiculous. All these people on the ship had admired me, respected me, looked to me for inspiration and leadership.

And I had let them down! I crawled off to my cabin and wallowed in black, burning shame throughout a sleepless night.

But before I had arisen next morning I had already resolved to salvage my reputation. Today, I would swim in the icy seas of Antarctica. I sought out Ian, our expedition leader, and put it to him. In the sober light of day he looked at me, sat back and folded his arms. His head tilted to one side, quizzically.

"How old are you, John?"

"Sixty three."

He gazed at me silently; another of his famous pregnant pauses, a sure sign of disapproval. I did not flinch. He saw the thrawn look in my eye and shrunk before it. "Okay. Tonight." And as I smiled and walked off I heard him mutter, "You're bloody mad."

Maybe. But I was happy to be mad.

And so it came to pass that at around 10.15pm on the night of January 25, the anniversary of the birth of Robert Burns, I saw myself as others see me – the bold, fear-nothing adventurer once more. A full boat load of spectators from the ship came to see me, as they saw me: to record the event on cameras, both still and video, to show to their incredulous friends back home in the USA, Japan, Korea, Portugal, Norway or wherever they came from. And I plunged headlong into the Antarctic Ocean, among the icebergs and brash-ice, from a rock in Cierva Cove, thereby adding to the diversity of life studied by the scientists at the Argentinian research station there, for that night they witnessed another divergent life form, *Homo sapiens non compos mentis* – which, for those of you who did not have the privilege of studying Latin at school, may be loosely translated as 'some guy out of his mind'. We'd had to get their permission to land, and they were out, all snug in their thermal long drawers, balaclavas, parkas and mittens, looking on in disbelief.

Three others had accompanied me. They just jumped in and straight back out again, like one of those film clips when they play it backwards. But I had a reputation to live up to – I went *swimming*.

I hadn't wasted the sleepless, shame-filled hours of the night before. I had done some thinking, applied a bit of science to the problem. Thermal shock is caused when the nerve sensors in the body experience a sudden and substantial difference in temperature. I reasoned that if I were able to reduce the temperature differential between my skin and the sea I would experience little shock. In fact, the sea temperature might even be just above the air temperature – at that time of night it would be around zero or maybe below, so it might even feel warmer in the water.

Encouraged by that thought, I stripped down to my swimming shorts on the rock. That brought the body temperature down considerably. I immediately began to splash seawater all over my body, spreading it everywhere, into the warm, tender parts. I wanted my skin acclimatised, every blood vessel contracted, every pore tightly closed, every goose pimple standing proud. That done, and without a moment's hesitation, I dived from the rock, headfirst, straight into the icy sea. My first reaction was one of satisfaction. It wasn't nearly as cold as I had expected. The temperature differential theory was sound. Isn't education a great thing? Exulted, I surged through the water in a gentle upwards sweep and, as my head broke the surface, those on the boat gave a resounding cheer. Cameras clicked and whirred and someone called, "What's it like?"

"Boiling!" I retorted. Well, I reckon I'd earned the right to a bit of hyperbole. I swam a few more strokes, smiling, posing for the cameras. Then it hit me. Not a sudden shock like hitting a brick wall, but more of an overpoweringly chilling sensation. The intense cold had penetrated right into my body and I could feel everything contracting, stiffening. I imagined my lungs going solid, my heart being frozen stiff, my blood crystallising. Somewhere in the recesses of my mind I seemed to recall reading that those poor mariners who fell into polar seas had only a few minutes to live, if they were fully clothed. I only had bare skin. My time was running out. Maybe I only had seconds to live. I won't say I panicked, but I was overcome by a sense of urgency unique in my lifetime. I swam my fastest-ever front crawl back to that rock. Now, have you ever seen film footage of penguins flying out of the sea and landing feet first on the rocks? Well, that was me that night!

I grabbed my towel and dried the droplets of water before they froze on me, gasping as I did so, dancing furiously to get the feeling back into my numbed feet. Then there was the most wondrous sensation. Free of the chilling effect of the sea, the blood vessels in my skin opened up once more. The taps were all turned on again, and my body positively glowed with hot blood surging through my arteries, warming my skin. Every atom of my being seemed to exult in this relief. I felt great.

The boatload of spectators was still there, with cameras focused on us as we were getting dressed. Voyeurs! Right, I thought, I'll give the paparazzi something to crow about. I turned my back to them began to slip my shorts down, not right down of course, just enough to reveal a hint of posterior cleavage, no more than you can see on any building site when a beer-bellied bricklayer bends over. That got another cheer from the crowd and cries of, "More! More!" So I began to dance, a sensuous swaying reminiscent of the Polynesian hula. With my towel wrapped around my waist, I let my shorts slip to my ankles as I writhed to the rhythm of the tune *The Stripper*, the slit in my towel occasionally revealing a tantalizing glimpse of upper thigh and maybe just a hint of lower left buttock just to keep them interested. Once at my feet, I flicked my shorts up into the air with my right foot and caught them with my forefinger, twirling them round and round in the best striptease fashion, hips swaying seductively all the while. I then flicked the wet shorts off my finger and into the crowd who cheered every move. At that point Ian, our leader, was getting cold waiting for us and called for a halt to this tomfoolery, shaking his head in disbelief. Swimming *and* a striptease among the icebergs! What next?

Back on shore, the Argentinian scientists applauded. Well, they don't get much entertainment down here. I gave them a departing wave. The boat's engine roared into life and we were off. My reputation had been salvaged. I had seen myself as others saw me. Yes, the real me!

Or was it just a bout of polar madness?

Chapter 47
Round The Horn

Wilhelmina Bay basked in warm sunshine. Its high mountains soared out of the sea, their ridges edged with crisp snow cornices. It had a reputation as a good place to see whales, and we were not disappointed. Some orcas and a couple of minkes had been spotted on our way north, but humpbacks were much more in evidence here. Humpback whales, which can grow to lengths of sixteen metres (fifty feet), are seen in the tropical waters of the Pacific during the breeding season, but migrate south to the nutrient rich waters of Antarctica in the Austral summer.

Cruising up close to a mother and her calf we cut the zodiac's engine and drifted slowly towards them. We got close. Real close. No one spoke. The mother was a mere five metres away, and both whales seemed quite relaxed about our presence. They rested calmly on the surface, looking at us. We looked at them. Mother and calf breathed alternately, blowing fine mists into the air, the ripples emanating from the rhythmic swelling of their giant bodies gently ruffling the silky surface of the sea. We sat, motionless, spellbound, inhaling the fishy odour of their breath as it drifted languorously towards us on a windless afternoon, the sun warm on our backs. We were totally enthralled, hushed, hardly daring to breath lest anything we do might disturb the exquisite serenity of the moment. It was more than a moment – we were privileged to commune with the two leviathans for a good twenty minutes.

One of the other zodiacs then drew near, but drifted too close. They started to paddle back and suddenly the spell was broken. The mother's back reared up out of the water, showing the classic hump, a sure prelude to a dive, and like a huge wheel rotating, her body rolled silently into the sea. The massive tail flukes surfaced. The tail rose majestically, cascading droplets of water glowing like diamonds in the sun, and a final flick revealed its scarred underside, the distinctive marks by which, like a fingerprint, each individual whale can be identified. The tail flukes then slipped quietly beneath the surface and she was gone. That was one of life's most memorable experiences.

On our way back to the ship the icebergs attracted our attention. The bay had a scattering of large icebergs, some tabular, others angular, pyramidal, or in such abstract forms as to defy description. The oblique light of the early evening sun illuminated them beautifully, offering a haunting perspective, highlighting contours, defining areas of light and shadow against the magnificent backcloth of an awe-inspiring landscape of windswept snow and ice.

The ship repositioned overnight. We were now among the South Shetland Islands, an impressive archipelago of volcanic origin. These islands lie about seventy miles off the north west coast of the Antarctic peninsula, their more northerly, and maritime, location ensuring a milder climate with only a few patches of snow. We dropped anchor within a stone's throw of Hannah Point on Livingston Island. This bay is an ancient volcanic crater with some impressive cliff scenery, and in this milder climate some patches of greenery, mostly moss. The fragility of the environment was again emphasised during our briefing. On no account should we step on the moss as it could take up to a hundred years to recover from the damage caused by one human footprint.

In terms of wildlife it was the most diverse spot we had yet visited, with lots of relatively mature gentoo penguin chicks wandering about, some very noisy chinstrap penguin colonies, kelp gulls, southern sheathbills, skuas and giant petrels. Another highlight was the impressive elephant seal wallow, a great pile – there is no more appropriate word to describe it – of young males wallowing on the beach. A few clownish macaroni penguins, easily spotted with their bright yellow, hair-like head feathers, pottered about amongst the chinstraps. Macaronis are primarily a sub-Antarctic species with only a very few making it as far south as the peninsula. The almost fully-fledged penguin chicks, a consequence of the milder climate, contrasted sharply with those we had seen further south where there were still some un-hatched eggs.

The latitude was similar to that of the Shetland Islands to the north of Scotland, yet the climate here was so much colder. Our midday temperatures here in high summer were in the range 1 to 6 degrees Celsius, which is comparable to winter in the northern Shetlands. The difference in climate is due to the benign effect of the Gulf Stream, that warm ocean current flowing from the Gulf of Mexico over to northern Europe. The warm sea temperature keeps the ice at bay in the northern latitudes, and the warm moist air it brings maintains a much milder climate all year round. The importance of this natural phenomenon was really brought home to me as I surveyed the barren, almost lunar, landscape before me here in the South Shetlands. Apart from a few tufts of some sort of tough grass in sheltered spots, only mosses and lichens grow here. In the absence of any depth of soil, there can be no cultivation, no crops, no pasture. The resultant lack of vegetation ensures that no grazing animal could survive here. The only food source is the sea. And it occurred to me that if one day, by some whim of nature, the Gulf Stream ceased to flow across the Atlantic Ocean, Scotland would become uninhabitable.

That afternoon, we moved on to the Aitcho Islands, another scenic archipelago with conspicuous spires of rock soaring out of the sea. The peculiar name Aitcho derives from the British Hydrographic Office initials ('H.O.'), which once had a base there. The delicate moss beds on Aitcho are among the biggest in the Antarctic, and the predominantly green appearance of the island was a welcome relief after the harshness of rock and ice to which we had become accustomed. Here again we found a diverse range of birds and seals, our arrival at the beach being greeted noisily by a fur seal and a small group of elephant seals. The penguin colonies were by far the largest we had encountered, but were less densely populated in what was a very spacious and easily accessible arena. Over on the west side a huge leopard seal lay sleeping at the water's edge close to a penguin colony, the penguins showing no fear of him while on land. His cumbersome bulk is not conducive to hunting ashore, but in the sea it is a different matter. Then, sleek as a torpedo, he is just as deadly.

Only a few metres from our landing site a southern giant petrel and some skuas were scavenging a recently dead gentoo penguin chick, ripping it apart and gorging themselves on its innards. One forlorn looking penguin, probably the mother, hovered around a couple of metres away, making a couple of inept rushes at the scavengers as the chick was ripped apart. No one had seen the kill, but I suspect the chick had become too adventurous and wandered away from its mother's protection. One blow from the feet of a diving skua or giant petrel would easily break its neck. This was nature in the raw. Survival here was a daily struggle.

That evening we were again ploughing our way across the Drake Passage heading northwards to South America, and this time it did it live up to its reputation. The wind freshened, and by bedtime we were plunging headlong into a full gale. The view from the bridge windows was thrilling. As the night wore on, the sea became wilder; the ship shuddered as she smashed her bows into each wave, sending a wall of spray lashing over the ship. Cape Horn lay ahead. The captain took us to the west of the cape and then ran eastwards past it. Unfortunately, this was at 5.00am in poor visibility, so there was only a dark mass of rock in the murky, grey light of a dismal morning, but I suppose that is how Cape Horn appears to most people who have sailed these waters. I crawled back into my bunk again with my thoughts.

I had been 'Round the Horn' in a gale, and I am happy to be included in the select band of people who have done that. I had been to Antarctica, the most remote place on earth, the only continent on Earth whose permanent human population is 0, whose temporary inhabitants number just a few hundred scientists and a few summer tourists on a continent about one and a half times the size of the United States. It has been estimated that in just under two hundred years since Antarctica was discovered, no more than 250,000 people have ever set foot on it.

Whether it will be a life changing experience for me remains to be seen. It is perhaps best considered as one among many influences. My son once wrote in response to an email account of some of my adventures in the Cook Islands: 'Who is this guy? Or maybe I should be asking, who is the person we see here in Scotland? Which one is the real you?'

Was I really so different? Maybe. Behaviour is a function of environment, and while the physical environment may stimulate, challenge, induce a sense of relaxation or give cause for thought, the interaction with people creates an even more profound effect. Behaviour can largely be influenced by the expectations of others, how they perceive you. And that is often determined by their preconceptions and the power of stereotypes. Watch people when a dog comes into their presence. If the dog approaches wagging its tail people are more likely to react in a positive manner towards it, yet some may still recoil in fear, a response to their own prejudices. How the dog is received, whether it is accepted or rejected, will determine its behaviour thereafter. In my home community, I am defined as father, grandfather and retired headmaster – all roles with attendant stereotypical expectations. Perhaps it is difficult to shake off the burden of expectation in the local environment – but while travelling, these constraints don't apply.

It would be difficult to identify any one place or any single aspect of all my travels as having changed me, although perhaps my first visit to the Cook Islands was a particularly formative experience. That was my real initiation into the backpacking community: a sort of loose brotherhood, in which people are generally very ready to help each other, where there are few barriers, few stereotypes and age doesn't matter. Maybe one day I will actually believe that. Maybe one day I will have 'found myself'. At present, I am still only 'seeing through a glass darkly', but through the eyes of other people that has been an illuminating and curative experience.

My naivety and innocence have been partially washed away, so I am perhaps no longer a 'virgin' backpacker.

The ship arrived early at Ushuaia, and we spent the last night tied up in harbour. When some of the Filipino crew came off watch that night they insisted that I join them for a run ashore: "You always talk with us, Sir John, so we want to buy you a drink before you leave."

I felt honoured.

They were interested in knowing where else I had been on my world travels, and one of the stewards asked me, "Why don't you come to the Philippines?" I told him I was now thinking about a visit, having been impressed by the friendliness of the boys in the crew and the girls who tended the cabins.

He beamed. "Come and stay, John. You would have a nice warm climate, the scuba diving is very good, it is a cheap place to live, and on your pension, with the strength of the British currency, you could live like a millionaire. Marry a nice Filipina girl and she will take good care of you."

"Och, but no Filipina would want an old guy like me."

"No, no, John. I see you talking with the Filipina girls on the ship. They like you. I'm sure you would have no problem finding a nice Filipina girl who would want to marry you. You would be a very attractive prospect as a husband. Age doesn't matter. *You are never too old!*"

Mmm? Tropical islands... cheap living... affordable diving... warm seas... friendly, caring, sun-tanned maidens...

What more could a man want?

Next trip, I must go to the Philippines!

The End...

Of the beginning.